THE COMPLETE GUIDE TO

Consulting Success

THE COMPLETE GUIDE TO

Consulting Success

Howard Shenson
Ted Nicholas

Enterprise · Dearborn
a division of Dearborn Publishing Group, Inc.

While a great deal of care has been taken to provide accurate and current information, the ideas, suggestions, general principles and conclusions presented in this text are subject to local, state and federal laws and regulations, court cases and any revisions of same. The reader is thus urged to consult legal counsel regarding any points of law—this publication should not be used as a substitute for competent legal advice.

© 1993 by Dearborn Financial Publishing, Inc.
© 1987, 1991 by Howard L. Shenson, CMC

Published by Enterprise • Dearborn
a division of Dearborn Publishing Group, Inc.

Printed in the United States of America

95 10 9 8 7 6 5

Library of Congress Cataloging-in-Publication Data

Shenson, Howard L.
    The complete guide to consulting success: a step-by-step handbook to build a successful consulting practice complete with agreements and forms/Howard L. Shenson, Ted Nicholas.
        p.   cm.
    Includes bibliographical references and index.
    ISBN 0-79310-492-0
    1. Business consultants. 2. New business enterprises—Management.
HD69.C6S516 1993   92-36901
001'.068—dc20   CIP

Contents

Figures

Appendix

Preface

Looking to the Future

As a consultant you are part of the fundamental and pervasive changes affecting the American free enterprise system, and yours is one of the most challenging businesses in the American economy. This is a book about the future of consulting in the American economy and about the future of your business in consulting.

While addressed primarily to consultants who are developing and building a practice, this book can be extremely valuable to those who are just starting a consulting business or are already well established.

Most new consultants have plenty of experience in their specialization, but they are generally new to being in business for themselves when they start out. Suddenly, they have to handle all the details of a business. As that business grows, the consultant faces the challenges of change and increased management responsibilities. Chapter 1 will look at some of the basics of the consulting business. It will be of greatest interest to the beginning consultant, and it may contain some valuable points of information for the developing or established consultant.

Building your practice demands a solid understanding of the special financial arrangements and billing procedures used in consulting. Those who leap into consulting without planning soon find themselves bankrupt and out of business. Many beginning consultants fail to take overhead, expenses and profits into account. Like any business, a successful practice requires financial planning and sound accounting procedures. Special accounting techniques for consulting practices will be reviewed in Chapter 9 on fees and finances.

However, there is more to running a consulting practice than balancing the books and allocating resources. As a consultant, you have to look to the future, anticipating changes in your market and areas of specialization and predicting new trends. If you don't, you become part of the past. Chapters 4 and 5 on finding and using opportunities demonstrate how to assess future directions and take advantage of them.

As a consultant you also look to the future by marketing. Just getting a contract, no matter how big, will not guarantee continued success. You win by building and managing your practice. Chapter 6 on marketing will show you how to avoid the periodic famines that result from inconsistent or ineffective sales efforts.

Another reality of business life is competition. Consultants who fail to update their practice and evaluate their market position end up wondering why they aren't getting new contracts. You need an edge in competition, and you need to keep that edge sharp. Chapter 3 on skills inventory shows you how to stay ahead of your competitors.

A successful consultant is professional. When a professional consultant is retained by a client, the relationship that follows is handled as a business contract. A flamboyant nod and a handshake are not enough. Chapter 10 on contracts and client relationships covers the subtleties of this important area.

Success in consulting calls for more than just expertise in your chosen field. To be successful, you must be able to build a strong reputation, publicize your abilities, have prospective clients see the need for your service and handle contracts. Besides being a good technician you need to be a marketer, manager and planner. Most of all, you have to be willing to work for your fee by rendering a valued service. The simple truth is that a consulting practice is a business like any other, and its success depends on your ability to manage it.

We owe an enormous debt of gratitude to Paul Franklin, editor of *The Professional Consultant,* for his invaluable advice and contribution to this revised edition.

1

The Business of Consulting

Small business, the backbone of the American economy, is still alive and well. The entrepreneur's spirit of adventure and risk is a compelling idea to many Americans. In *How To Buy a Business* (see the bibliography), the authors show that small business is indeed big business: "Taken in aggregate, small privately held businesses make up a major portion of our economy.... Since 1982 the U.S. has been creating new businesses at the rate of 600,000 to 700,000 per year." Our country and economy have made fundamental shifts from the stable military-industrial complex that flourished following World War II. Because of these shifts, "corporations are downsizing, people are retiring earlier, and college graduates are increasingly disenchanted with the career opportunities available to them.... People are beginning to realize that they must create a place for themselves in the more competitive global economy that has emerged with the 1990s."

Consultants are an important part of this growth in small enterprises. Most consultants start out as sole practitioners, and many stay that way throughout their careers. Only 69 percent of all consultants work in firms of three or more professionals.

In *The Best Jobs for the 1990s and Beyond* (see the bibliography), Carol Kleiman looks ahead to the changing demographics of America in the next century: "Because of the influx of foreign workers and the need to upgrade the skills of all workers, employment opportunities for management and training consultants will increase. The need for a better-educated, more technically trained work force will be apparent at every level." In fact, Kleiman cites management consulting services as one of the fastest-growing industries whose biggest responsibility is "training a diverse work force and helping firms meet employee's work and family needs."

1

Although the double-digit growth rate of the past five years has slowed considerably, many consulting firms still say they're growing faster than ever (*The Wall Street Journal*, Sept. 1990). In fact, the number of people pursuing business management/consulting careers has increased more than 45 percent in the past ten years.

Consultants have experienced gains in both daily billing rates and income, enjoying significant gains in times of economic recovery. At the same time, there has been a decline in overhead and an increase in backlog. The latest figures on fees show that during the past 12 months almost all consultants increased their fees:

Change in Fees	% of Consultants
Increased by 25.1% or more	2.3%
Increased by 20.1 to 25%	1.1%
Increased by 15.1 to 20%	3.0%
Increased by 10 to 15%	16.3%
Increased by 6 to 9%	20.3%
Increased by less than 6%	13.2%
Unchanged	38.3%
Decreased	5.5%

Source: *Economics of the Consulting, Training & Advisory Professions, Consulting Fees, Incomes, Operating Ratios, Marketing Strategies*, May 1991. Reprinted by permission of National Training Center.

This healthy growth rate in fees demonstrates the value that clients place on the services that these consultants are delivering.

The median daily billing rate and income of consultants provides another measure of how healthy the field is. Figure 1.1 shows a breakdown of information gathered from more than 7,000 consultants. The table shows only a few of the multitude of consulting specialties, but they are representative of the range of fees and incomes.

The income figures represent income after business expenses and before taxes. You can see that consultants are well paid for their services. And as we examine how the consulting business works, you will learn how the top ten percent of consultants make the most of their business.

The Demand for Consultants

The increasing complexity and sophistication of business call for the expertise and special skills that a consultant can deliver. Increased competition means that an organization needs more skills and knowledge than it can either find or afford to hire full time. Consultants give companies the talent and flexibility needed to win. The old image of the consultant as an ivory tower expert no longer applies. Consultants offer a wide range of services that has become an integral part of the American economic system.

Consultants also offer valuable services to government agencies and nonprofit organizations. These groups, which cannot afford to employ all the skills they need, are turning to consultants in increasing numbers to buy these services. New legislation, the need for operating capital and proposal writing are only some of the sources of opportunity for enterprising consultants in the public and nonprofit sectors of the economy.

Consulting is no longer a part-time diversion from golf for restless retirees. It is a rapidly growing, even trendy business enterprise that is having a major impact on the American economy. New consulting firms are on the cutting edge of innovation. Consultants work in every area of the economy, from planning for government agencies to developing new products for the latest high-tech companies.

Consulting Is Unique

Several qualities set the consulting practice apart from other businesses. First, consultants tend to work in rather small entrepreneurial environments. They often worked for large companies prior to entering business for themselves, which requires a withdrawal from the corporate welfare system. Now that they are in business for themselves, they have to go out and find work. One of the purposes of this book is to help you master marketing strategies, which should generate 70 to 90 percent of your opportunities through referrals and reputation. And, of course, even though many professionals seem to sit in their offices awaiting the stream of walk-in business, they and most others know that full waiting rooms usually result from carefully structured marketing plans. In short, success—theirs or yours—doesn't happen by accident.

Second, consultants have to love problem solving and creative challenges. They are frequently asked to look at a complex situation, define it, isolate its most relevant parameters and develop practical approaches or solutions.

Third, consultants are loners. They work in a vacuum. In most cases they do not have a big staff to implement their solutions or assess their strategies. Almost three-fourths of the consulting practices consist of one or two professionals with limited clerical support. Unlike people working for large organizations, they don't have colleagues to consult with. Most of their interaction is with their clients. Because of the client/professional relationship, they usually can't just float an idea to their clients and hash it out as they could with their peers.

Finally, consultants are self-starters. No one tells them to get up in the morning—they do that themselves. They get to work on time because they decide to. They set their own schedules, decide on their goals and create their own businesses. These factors make consulting unique in the free enterprise system.

Figure 1.1   Median Daily Billing Rate and Average Annual Income of
Consultants by Selected Specialties

Field of Consulting	All	Top 10%	Average Income Before Taxes
All Consultants	$1,102	$1,994	$104,188
Advertising	1,113	2,513	105,482
Aerospace	1,116	1,490	110,375
Banking	1,119	1,756	100,026
Broadcasting	993	1,595	99,902
Business Acquisition/Sales	1,022	1,891	103,348
Chemical	1,069	1,955	97,454
Data Processing	1,087	1,715	92,290
Dental/Medical	1,202	1,993	111,098
Education	821	1,306	66,023
Engineering	1,277	1,723	109,343
Export/Import	1,182	1,678	103,285
Finance	1,148	2,231	110,772
Fund Raising	877	1,456	75,311
Graphics/Printing	781	1,451	79,660
Health Care	1,230	2,142	113,458
International Business	1,147	1,974	105,440
Marketing	1,109	2,034	104,920
Personnel/HRD	901	1,986	78,997
Psychological Services	761	1,446	88,778
Public Relations	883	1,552	80,048
Purchasing	1,102	1,629	93,383
Quality Control	1,107	2,088	103,885
Research & Development	1,261	2,211	121,349
Scientific	1,299	2,256	125,092
Security	881	1,486	93,860
Training	914	1,652	84,818

Source: *Economics of the Consulting, Training & Advisory Professions, Consulting Fees, Incomes, Operating Ratios, Marketing Strategies*, May 1991. Reprinted by permission of National Training Center.

The Successful Consultant

What sets successful consultants apart from those who are struggling to stay afloat? One outstanding characteristic of successful consultants is their ability to market their skills. They are good at getting out and selling themselves. This isn't the hard sell we often associate with the classical used-car salesman. Successful consultants know how to "sell without selling," a concept that will be dealt with in detail in Chapters 6 and 7.

Successful consultants understand the purpose and goals of a consulting practice. They serve the interests of their clients. No interest comes before that of the client—not even the consultant's self-interest. Successful consultants avoid any conflict of interest. They are attentive to clients; they pay attention to clients and hear them; they don't offer pat answers or give the impression that they know it all.

Prosperous consultants are architects of reality. Often their solutions are not the optimal solutions that could be found with unlimited time and funds. However, their solutions are workable and effective; they get the job done for the client and in a timely fashion.

Successful consultants are disciplined. They keep their business in order and set aside time for marketing and management as well as actual consulting. Those who can develop the habits and approaches of a successful consultant stand a good chance of becoming one—given that they have a marketable skill, are competent in their field, and have the desire and motivation to succeed.

The Importance of Motivation

Motivation and desire drive every successful consultant. The need to succeed and get the job done makes consulting worthwhile. One consultant started with the cushion of a year's severance pay that he used to cover living expenses while he got his practice off the ground. He spent the first month picking a name. He devoted the next month to designing a logo and a letterhead. The third month he looked for office space. The fourth month he undertook a thorough search for a good secretary. The next month he sent out promotional materials. This slow start led to failure. The necessary hunger to succeed was missing. It was not until his fifteenth month, when he was out of funds, that he began to get serious and started along the road to his eventual success.

Getting off to a good start in consulting doesn't require large amounts of capital. If anything, too much capital can be detrimental. Successful consultants are those who must succeed. Another consultant lost his job unexpectedly on a Friday afternoon. He vowed that he would never again work for a corporation and put his fate in the hands of other people. He decided to go into business for himself as a consultant.

He woke up on Monday morning and said to himself: I cannot go to bed tonight until I have made $600 in personal income. He went to bed at 4 A.M.—after he made that $600. When he got up at 9 A.M. on Tuesday, he repeated his goal. He was a bit more successful because he got to bed at 2 A.M. after making another $600. On Wednesday he repeated his goal and was even more successful because he got to bed that night at 11 o'clock. Within a week's time, he figured out how to make $600 each day in personal income and get to bed at a reasonable hour. He met his objective because he had to—he was motivated.

The Three Big Myths

Consultants are as much the victims of stereotyping as other professionals. In the world of romantic dreams, consultants render sophisticated and desired services at very high fees. They live a life of abundance, working a few days a week and spending much of their time enjoying the fruits of their labors. While their clients vie with one another for their services, these consultants become fully self-sufficient, perfectly self-confident and completely self-actualized.

The reality is that most consultants are working hard, some are struggling to get by, and the successful ones are in such great demand that they have little time for a life of leisure.

This dream world is founded on the Expert Myth, which is one of the three myths that cause most of the confusion about consulting and keep people from seeing the profession as it really is. The other two myths are the No Security Myth and the Big Competitor Myth.

The Expert Myth

Believers of this myth think that being an established expert is all you need to start and succeed in consulting. They assume that an expert just has to open his doors for business and the clients will flock to him. The fact is that clients don't come to you simply because you're good at what you do. Even when potential clients are aware of your talents and skills, they do not necessarily see how you can be of service to them.

A successful consulting practice requires all the skills and talents that any other business needs. Technical expertise is just one of the requirements for success. The experience of countless successful consultants confirms this finding: Successful consultants sell clients *results*, not expertise, because results are what hold meaning for clients.

The top experts in most fields are usually too specialized to handle the demands of a real business. The nitty-gritty fact is that you may spend most of your time doing the necessary research to be an expert, which will not leave much time for starting a business and making it succeed.

As a result very few consultants are the world's leading authorities in their specialty. Instead, they are active, practical, energetic people who put the theory to work and make it pay. You should not feel unqualified just because you do not rank as number one in your field. Clients want results, not theory.

The No Security Myth

Every consultant—even a highly successful one—can expect to be told that there is no security in independent consulting. Again and again you will hear that the only real security is in getting a regular salary.

Poor business practices and ineffective marketing can make this prediction come true. If potential clients don't see your services as valuable, then your consulting practice is certainly less secure than a salaried position. However, if you can make yourself indispensable to clients who see the need for your services and can pay for them, you have a far more secure position than the typical employee. An employee has only one "client," and the loss of this "client" can be catastrophic. The typical consultant has about seven clients simultaneously, so the loss of one or two is far less devastating.

The Big Competitor Myth

This myth insists that an individual consultant is bound to lose when competing with large consulting firms. The truth is that if you are competing with the large firms in their own fields, you won't automatically lose, but you may be in for a good fight. Their size and vast experience often work very much in their favor.

On the other hand, big competitors are usually slow and ponderous. Because their overhead is higher, they are often more expensive. The expense of thicker carpets on the higher floors of expensive office buildings, sabbatical leave for top personnel, libraries, internal staff managers and other embellishments are passed on to the client.

Because of high overhead, a large firm has to offer more generalized services to generate enough business, giving the smaller consulting practice an opportunity to offer specialized services at a competitive fee. Clients often see the specialist as offering quality work that they can't get from a larger consulting firm. And they prefer the special attention afforded their "account" by the principals of the smaller firms.

It is also difficult for large firms to enter new areas. It may take a large firm a year or more to discover that you are in competition with them, and 18 months or so before they plan any response to your challenge. By that time you will have established yourself firmly in your area and be in control. The big firms may even want to subcontract to you when their clients need assistance in your specialty.

The fact that you are small and flexible gives you an added advantage. You can anticipate changes in technology and economic conditions and respond rapidly, whereas a large corporation, beset by bureaucratic inertia, is slow to respond to change.

A Successful Transition

Lloyd attended a seminar on building a consulting practice. During a break he shared his personal goals and fears. Because of bad business fortunes, he had been suddenly and involuntarily laid off by the firm where he had served as personnel director for eight years. He enjoyed being a personnel director but was having difficulty finding another job. He wasn't sure he wanted to be a consultant. He asked for advice.

It was clear that Lloyd was worried about the possible lack of security in consulting. He was used to receiving a regular salary and wasn't sure he could compete with large firms. He also had doubts about his expertise. He had been a good personnel director, but he wasn't a noted authority on the subject.

We suggested that he start a consulting practice that would allow him to have the security and income of consulting while continuing to do what he loved best—being a personnel director. We told him that he could compete effectively if he "set up shop" as a personnel department for several small businesses that could use his service but couldn't afford a $65,000-a-year personnel director. By contracting with several companies, he could have security in numbers. If he lost one or two contracts, he had others to fall back on. Six months later Lloyd called to let us know that he had followed our advice. He had eight clients paying between $1,000 and $1,500 for an average of $1,250 a month to be "the outside personnel director." He had overcome the three big myths that prevent consultants from being successful and was reaping the benefits.

The Consultant's Orientation: Task or Process?

Many consultants limit their opportunities for success by being task-oriented rather than process-oriented. Task-oriented consultants seek out consulting opportunities that are almost identical to the tasks they carried out for their last employer. For example, a consultant who has worked successfully with lasers may decide to establish a practice limited to laser applications. The practice concentrates on what tasks the consultant can perform, instead of looking at the marketplace to find out what is needed that matches the consultant's wide range of talents. Because we all have many potential and realized talents, concentrating on a limited range of tasks can severely limit our opportunities for growth and financial success.

Process-oriented consultants take a much broader view of the marketplace. Instead of looking at their past organizational achievements, they consider all their skills in determining how they can best meet their clients' needs. They seek opportunities to apply their skills in ways that are valuable to their clients. This added flexibility greatly enhances their chances of success.

Being process-oriented rather than task-oriented requires looking beyond the knowledge and skills learned in a class or from a book. The skills that make a difference in consulting often come easily and naturally and may have been evident even in childhood. Successful process-oriented consultants offer the ability to negotiate, build a consensus, analyze a problem and handle many variables simultaneously, as well as various other skills that may have nothing to do with formal book learning or training. Process-oriented consultants are not unreasonably concerned with the specific nature of the task or with the working environment. They are comfortable in a factory, a laboratory or an office, depending on what the job calls for. Process-oriented consultants are not limited by their past experience. Indeed, their past experiences serve as a springboard for new opportunities. Although they may seem to be different specialists to their various clients, they are actually generalists who are applying a wide variety of skills in meeting each client's needs.

Suppose Tom Phillips is in charge of planning for a hospital's critical-care unit and decides to become a consultant. If he is task-oriented, he will seek consulting opportunities related only to planning for critical care units at hospitals. Whereas, process-oriented consultants will realize that there are numerous areas in hospitals where their skills are valuable. They will also see that their skills are applicable in organizations besides hospitals. By emphasizing their *process* skill, which is planning, they will find a larger market.

Obviously, your market is broader and your prospects will be brighter if you take a process-oriented approach.

Competing

Competition is what makes the free enterprise system work. Consultants who don't face the need to compete are failing themselves and their clients. You need to develop your abilities just as an athlete does. Winning athletes are aware of what they can do and what they can't. They know their abilities and work hard to develop them. In basketball it is an advantage to be tall, but plenty of basketball players aren't. In Chapter 3 we will go through a skills inventory. The first part of the inventory deals with business skills, and the second part covers consulting skills. Getting away from concentrating on just one or two tasks that you are good at enables you to see the larger picture and become process-oriented. By becoming familiar with the consulting *process*, you will no longer be limited by what you have done in the past, and you will be able to explore your potential to its fullest.

The sport of handball is a good example of how concentration on the process gives an edge in competition. The best players don't have unbeatable serves; they aren't the hardest volleyers. The best players know strategy: They are in the right place so they don't have to run to make a shot; they make their opponent do the running. Older players are often the best because they have integrated their skills and have the experience to make the best moves.

Protecting Your Turf

After you have developed your skills, both in business and consulting, and acquired some clients, you want to make sure that you keep those clients and continue to build your practice. An inventor is allowed to patent a new product, and a writer can copyright a novel. Whereas the law grants writers and inventors a legal monopoly on the product of their minds for a certain time period, consultants have no such protection. Anyone can imitate your work. The only recourse you have is to protect yourself by identifying your unique skills and matching them to what a given market needs. That means you can't be complacent. You have to update your approaches and stay in touch with your client's needs so that you have a jump on the competition. And you can be certain that if you are successful, plenty of competition will materialize.

Protecting your market position involves two basic steps: First, you must choose an area where you can achieve quick recognition. Second, you must thoroughly and quickly channel your resources toward being identified as the consultant with the unique skills needed in that area. Your purpose is to offer a service that few or no other consultants can provide so that you are seen as the one who can best meet your prospective clients' needs.

Successful consultants are perceived by their clients as uniquely qualified individuals who are accessible and informed authorities. Perhaps it is the consultant's ability to meet clients' needs in a rare or unique way. Maybe the consultant was the first to establish himself or herself as the authority. Or the consultant may have deliberately chosen and perfected a service that clients cannot get elsewhere. You should not feel squeamish about planning to protect your market position—such planning is not only important, it is essential.

If you plan for exclusivity, you have every reason to expect success. If you do not, you can expect failure or mere survival. The profitability of your business hangs directly on the degree to which your clients see you as the exclusive provider of an essential service. If you offer a service that they can get anywhere, your fee is subject to negotiation and compromise—even if you have a large market. As your talent gets closer to being unique—or to being perceived as unique—your fee becomes less of a consideration in the decision to retain your services. Then your *supply* of services becomes scarce in comparison to the *demand* for them. The price of your services can naturally rise, and success is certainly within reach.

Look at defining and defending your market position as a way of getting a *patent* or *copyright* on your skills and ideas. Just remember that whatever you call it, *defending your turf is the key to your success in consulting*.

Tips

The word *consultant* often conjures up the image of a life-style that bears little relationship to reality. Consulting is like any other business. Make sure that you want to be a business owner and manager before you decide to become a consultant.

Any number of books on the market can help you analyze your readiness for the entrepreneurial venture in general. Unfortunately, some consultants are like inventors who work out of a garage. They may have discovered a good idea, but because they don't know how to sell it, they just barely survive. Chapter 6 on marketing will help you avoid that pitfall.

All consultants, at some point, have to decide whether they are running a real business or simply being an inventor working out of a garage. Do they remain the same in size and scope or expand and grow?

This decision seems to be more difficult for consultants than for owners of other types of business. Consultants probably enjoy the "doingness" of the consulting business more than the management and marketing of their practices—that is just the nature of the beast. Most consultants would rather spend time and energies on client projects. They view efforts toward expansion and growth as diverting precious time and energy from doing what they enjoy most. A larger and more complex *operation* is viewed as needing an inordinate amount of maintenance.

Yet failure to expand limits income and opportunity. The ability to handle larger, more complex assignments and clients is reduced; there is less economic insulation in the event of illness or disability. This situation can create unhealthy stress.

It is not the work itself that creates the stress but the consultant's attempts to take on more responsibilities without a corresponding expansion in operations. The practice becomes more difficult, more complex, and lacks the necessary support systems.

By being aware of these issues as you enter the profession, you can prepare yourself to handle the challenges and changes that come your way. On the basis of your abilities and interests, you can decide what kind of practice is right for you. If you take a businesslike approach from the start, you will develop the skills you need for a long, successful career.

2

Starting Your Practice

This chapter is devoted to the basics of getting a consulting practice off to a businesslike start. Those who have been in consulting for a while may want to skim this chapter and go on to the next one on Personal Skills Inventory. However, even those who have been practicing for several years may find a useful pointer or two, particularly in the section on writing a capabilities statement.

Reviewing Your Business Skills

This section is aimed at the entry-level consultant. As you undertake the challenge of beginning a practice, you can benefit greatly from a review of your business skills. You already have extensive skills in business, but you may not associate them with the enterprise of consulting. Some of those who have been successful at consulting have learned from painful experience that no practice succeeds without the application of basic, practical business skills.

Business Skills Inventory

To succeed as a consultant you need *practical* business skills. In reviewing your business skills, keep in mind that you already have plenty of business experience. You are really looking to relate what you already know to your consulting practice. To assess your level of ability in each area, list related tasks that you have handled, then draw up a second list of the skills that you used in carrying out the task. For example, some of us are better at handling money than others. With an accurate estimate of your ability in this and other areas, you can plan your business to use your strongest skills and supplement the areas where you are weak.

The following six areas are of prime importance in building and maintaining a consulting practice:

1. Basic business knowledge

2. Financial management

3. Marketing

4. Sales

5. Predicting trends

6. Human resource management

As you review each kind of business skill, use the worksheet on business skills provided in Figure 2.1. Write down your experiences in the left-hand column and your skills in the right-hand column. Be absolutely honest with yourself, as you need an accurate picture of your business ability to be a success in consulting.

Don't confuse the skills you use in consulting with business experience. If you are an engineer, you will be selling your skills in engineering—that is your product. Selling that product is a business skill. You may well learn more about business by managing a hamburger stand for three months than you could in four years of college.

Basic Business Knowledge

You need information about business licenses, taxes, drawing up an operating plan, forecasting profits and losses, and so on. The skill involved in this area is knowing where to go to get the information you need. You have a number of resources at your disposal: books, periodicals, seminars, business courses, other businesspeople and government agencies such as the Small Business Administration.

Financial Management

List your experience in handling monetary forecasting and planning. You are looking for skills and for areas where you have difficulty. In business it is just as important to know what you can't do as to know what you can do.

Marketing

You will be marketing yourself. Have you had experience in setting up marketing plans? Are you skilled at making contacts? You may have worked for a volunteer agency and helped put together a publicity campaign. Pay particular attention to your networking ability, since making and using contacts is the most important avenue to getting requests for your services.

Sales

If your self-marketing is successful, you will have the opportunity to make sales. Making a sale in consulting is a matter of being credible and persuasive. Usually, the hard sell doesn't work. List your experiences in sales and in *persuasion*. Skills you want to look for are your ability to gain the confidence of others and to get them excited about a project.

Predicting Trends

Consultants need to predict trends in their fields of specialization as well as for business and society in general. If you are doing just one kind of work and the market changes, you may be out of business. Think of times when you have successfully anticipated future trends in your specialty and in other areas.

Human Resources Management

Most consultants start out in business by themselves or with one or two other people. This involves skill at managing yourself and your clerical support. With time you will face the choice of expanding your business or staying small. Expanding involves working with partners and/or hiring workers. This means coordinating efforts, motivating workers, scheduling activities and managing time.

Carefully assess your ability to handle time. Is your schedule smooth or messy? Can you work comfortably and effectively with others? Can you get yourself and others motivated and interested? Knowing your strengths and weaknesses in these areas is important when starting up and later when you face the choice of expanding.

Reviewing Your List

Don't be discouraged if you find some areas where you lack ability. In some areas like basic business knowledge, you can learn what you need. In other areas you may need to supplement your skills. Those who succeed in business either have the necessary skills, hire someone who does or acquire those skills on their own. If you regularly mess up your checkbook, get an accountant who will take charge and organize your finances. If you aren't a good manager, hire one or work with a partner who is. With experience you will learn more about scheduling and time management. Chapters 6, 7 and 8 will show you how to set up a marketing plan and handle sales.

An honest appraisal of your business skills is a guide to planning your career. By relying on your strengths you can increase your effectiveness.

Beginnings

There are certain down-to-earth business realities to consider when opening a consulting practice. One of the first things to decide on is the appropriate form of business: sole proprietorship, partnership or corporation. You may also decide to:

Figure 2.1   Business Skill Worksheet

Activities	Skills
Business Knowledge	
Business Knowledge	
Business Knowledge	

Figure 2.1   Business Skill Worksheet (Continued)

Activities	*Skills*
Sales	
Price Trends	
Human Resources Management	

- Choose a lawyer.
- Contract with an accountant.
- Establish a working relationship with a banker.
- Become a member of one or more professional associations.

Once you have established an ongoing practice, you will want to periodically reevaluate your arrangements and make changes.

The Form of Business

You can establish one of three business forms for your consulting practice:

1. Proprietorship
2. Partnership
3. Corporation

Your choice depends on whether you are working alone or with others, the size of your business and the anticipated risks. For example, if you have considerable personal assets to protect, you may be less interested in entering a proprietorship or partnership in which you may be responsible for all liabilities.

Law and current business practices influence your choice. You may start out in one form, then change as conditions and legal requirements change. One of the important considerations in choosing a form for your business is the tax rate you will pay. Changes in tax laws should be taken into consideration, as they may affect the relative advantages of each form. For example, many people who found it advantageous to incorporate converted back to a proprietorship in response to changes in federal tax laws.

Proprietorship

This type of business is owned outright by one person. Typically, the success of the business depends completely on the skill and active involvement of the owner, or proprietor.

The proprietorship has two drawbacks: (1) The business usually folds if the owner is knocked out of the picture by sickness or death, and (2) the proprietor is personally and wholly responsible for any liability of the business. You can protect yourself with insurance against some types of business-related legal claims, but insurance does not cover bad debts or business losses.

Some consultants operate as sole proprietors when the prospect of incurring a large liability is either very remote or easily covered by insurance. Nevertheless, proprietorships can entail a high degree of risk relative to business forms.

Partnership

In a partnership two or more parties contribute assets to the business and share in the profits. In a general partnership the partners may be responsible for the liabilities of the business to the extent of their assets. In a limited partnership the partners are personally liable for all business debts to the extent of their participation in the business. The extent of responsibility for general and limited partnerships vary from state to state; a lawyer's advice may be needed on this point.

Partnerships assume several different forms. If a partnership interests you, first discuss the possibility with your accountant and lawyer.

A partnership is much like a marriage. You can spend as much time with a partner as you do with a spouse. So, like marriages, when partnerships work well, they are beautiful. When they don't work well, they can be hell on earth.

While contingent liability is the biggest problem for all partnerships, consultants who go into partnership face an even greater danger. In most businesses, if the partners disagree strongly, they do not destroy the assets. If two partners in a shoe store have an argument and decide to break up, they have not destroyed the assets, which are the stock and equipment. One partner can continue to sell the shoes.

However, in the case of a consulting practice, the consultants *are* the assets. Their synergy and ability to work together—the major assets of the business—are destroyed if they are fighting and undercutting each other. The business may be unable to survive with only one of the partners.

Most people enter partnerships for the wrong reasons. A partnership works because of the absolute dependency of the two people on each other to run the business. However, many partnerships are entered into because people want someone to commiserate with; they need someone to talk to. You can get conversation from your friends for a great deal less trouble and risk than by entering a partnership.

Consultants can work together, which is valuable and beneficial, in other ways. Consultants can associate with each other and work on projects while each has an independent business. They can share offices, split the rent, go 50-50 on a coffeemaker, hire a secretary, subcontract with each other and discuss matters—without entering into a partnership.

Corporation

In law a corporation is defined as a legal person. Although a business may be your creation, it becomes a separate legal entity. You may be an officer in the corporation, become its employee, or even consult with your own company, but you are not legally the company itself as in the case of a proprietorship.

Incorporating offers several advantages. The foremost benefit is that the business is liable for its own debts. Creditors may empty the firm's treasure chest, but they cannot take your home away. There are exceptions—for example, if you are found guilty of fraud or, as corporate treasurer, of neglect in withholding taxes.

The tax advantages of a corporation may or may not pertain to your financial situation. The essential question is: At what point do corporate tax rates help me more than individual tax rates? Your accountant can advise you on this point.

Perhaps the chief drawback of incorporating is the increased reporting requirements. A corporation's tax obligations and its legal requirements are more complex than those of other forms of business. As a result there is more of a need for accounting and legal assistance. Also, you can't always control a corporation as easily as a proprietorship or a partnership.

Give serious thought as to whether or not you want to incorporate. If you want to protect your personal assets from being attached as a result of a lawsuit, talk to a lawyer about the option of placing your assets in a trust and operating your consulting practice as a proprietor.

If you decide to incorporate, you have two options: profit and nonprofit. A nonprofit corporation has several advantages. First, the cost of doing business is less than it is for profit-making firms. Suppose Roberta Riggs, a consultant who is incorporated in California, wants to give a seminar in Texas. If she has set up a profit corporation, she would pay a fee each year for the privilege of doing business in Texas. A nonprofit corporation based in California would pay a one-time flat fee to the State of Texas and continue to give the seminar the rest of its corporate life. Nonprofit corporations are often eligible for a significant number of government and foundation grants, whereas profit-making corporations rarely are.

Incorporating as a nonprofit organization does not necessarily mean that you cannot make any profit. Under the law in many states, nonprofit corporations are permitted to engage in incidental profit-making activities. However, most state laws are not very specific about what is meant by incidental. You can make some profits, but you are not usually allowed to withdraw them through dividends. Most members of a profit-making corporation don't withdraw profits as dividends anyway. They simply retain profits in the corporation, with outlays going for salary and various fringe benefits. If you are not planning to distribute dividends, you should consider establishing a nonprofit corporation. Consult a lawyer who worked with nonprofit corporation proceedings before. Those who have not tend to avoid recommending nonprofit corporations (perhaps because they aren't familiar with the procedures).

The chief disadvantage of the nonprofit corporation is that in most states the board of directors must consist of three or more people. The board members of a profit-making corporation don't affect your control because you hold the stock, thus have the final say on everything. But a nonprofit organization does not issue stock, thus each board member has a say that could affect your control of the business. Unless you can fill the board positions with people you trust, you may want to avoid the nonprofit corporation. For more information, see the book on incorporating by Ted Nicholas referenced in the bibliography.

Reviewing Your Choice

As your business grows and changes, you will want to evaluate the form you have chosen. After starting out as a sole proprietor, you may decide to enter into partnership with other consultants to offer a broader range of services. If you find that your risks of liability have increased, you may choose to incorporate to protect your personal assets.

Depending on circumstances you may want to switch your corporate status from profit to nonprofit. If there are rapid changes in your business, you should set aside time at least once a year to review the status of your business and the arrangements you have made. If the form of your business doesn't match the realities of your operation, you may be losing money or running unnecessary risks. An annual checkup will protect you.

Your Support System

In establishing and maintaining your business, you will require the help of competent professionals. Your lawyer, accountant and banker make up your business support system. How do you find the professional help you need? One way is to ask for referrals from other consultants who are not your competitors. Alternatively, you can buy an hour of time with the senior partner of a leading law or accounting firm. You will get a referral either to a junior staff member who bills out at a lower rate or to someone outside the firm. This approach works better for finding a lawyer than an accountant.

Make your selection of professionals with some deliberation. Some points to consider are:

- Does the professional have expertise that suits your needs?

- Can you establish a harmonious working relationship with the professional?

- Are your personalities compatible? When you don't like dealing with a person, you cannot reap the full benefits of his or her assistance.

- Is an independent practitioner more or less appropriate for your practice than a large firm? Larger firms often cost more, but one staff member is generally ready and willing to turn you over to another as necessary and appropriate. Even though solo practitioners tend to cost less, they might be hesitant about turning you over to another professional outside the firm.

Choosing a Lawyer

In addition to helping you select the business form that best suits your needs, your attorney can advise you on two other areas that require legal expertise.

Unauthorized Practice of Law   The work of many consultants involves what amounts to practicing law. For example, a financial planner may be asked about a point of tax law. If the question is simple and straightforward, the consultant can respond without being concerned about practicing law. But consider a more complex question, such as whether a client might be considered a tax evader because of a certain tactic. The planner who advises action of any kind is likely practicing law without authorization.

This is not to say that a consultant cannot perform any legal functions. You may, for instance, act in behalf of others when you have formal power of attorney. Or you may prepare a contract that you and your client both agree to sign. Perhaps the best rule to follow is to consult your attorney when you find yourself performing services normally provided by an attorney. In this way you are protected at minimal cost to yourself and your client.

Malpractice   Theoretically, malpractice means neglect. Professional people cannot be held responsible for failing to cure patients, losing a legal case or failing in a consultation if they did everything that could be reasonably expected. However, there is a fine line between what constitutes your best effort and what comprises neglect.

In general, consultants do not guarantee that their advice will solve the problems for which their services are retained. The law normally requires that they give the best advice possible under the *prudent man doctrine*. That is, if your client can demonstrate that you have been fraudulent or grossly negligent, you could be held liable for damages. Errors in decision making are not usually sufficient to constitute neglect.

Some consultants face a greater liability because they work in a profession licensed or regulated by the state. This kind of liability, known as *professional* or *personal* liability, is similar to a medical doctor's liability. Those with a professional liability are normally required to *warrant* their work in compliance with a set of standards established by law or their profession.

Malpractice or professional liability insurance is usually available for consultants with a professional liability requirement. If you feel that you may be professionally liable, you should check with a lawyer and the appropriate state or federal agency that regulates your profession. With regard to contractual limitations of liability, note that limitations exist in all states as to the rights of individuals that may be removed by contract. In this case, as in all legal questions, competent legal advice is a good investment.

Choosing the Right Accountant

In selecting an accountant, consider retaining a certified public accountant. CPAs generally have a higher level of training and are considered to be better prepared than accountants without the CPA degree. Their analyses may, therefore, be considered of greater worth. In addition, under certain circumstances, your books may have to be reviewed by a CPA anyway. Having one do the work originally saves you the time and expense of getting another accountant. Excellent non-CPAs are available, but this option should be approached with caution.

The working relationship you establish with your accountant is especially important during the beginning phase of your practice. To obtain guidance and information about financial matters, you should be comfortable talking with your accountant. If you feel intimidated about asking questions or don't understand what you are being told, the problem may be with your accountant.

When your practice is larger or you are working with several consultants, you may need the services of a larger accounting firm. Because you will have acquired knowledge of accounting practices, you can afford to have a more distant relationship with your CPA.

Selecting a Banker

A bank is more than a place to keep your money and apply for loans—it is also a source of information and guidance. A good bank is interested in helping its business depositors and ensuring that any business to which it loans money succeeds.

The banking system in this country developed somewhat haphazardly. As a result there are federal banks, state banks, commercial banks, savings banks, and savings and loan institutions. During the 1980s and 1990s, the banking system has been undergoing a transition leading to a more unified system. One result is that banks are striving to be more competitive and are offering more services, particularly to business customers.

In most communities the commercial bank is still the primary institution for financing business. A larger and established bank often suggests to those you do business with that you are solid. On the other hand, many fine smaller commercial banks specialize in different approaches to business financing. Many consultants, feeling that smaller banks give better, more personalized service than the giants, opt for this choice.

You should select your bank, whether large or small, on the basis of an interview with the officer in charge. Find out how your personalities and attitudes mesh. Try to create a personal relationship. Get to know one another and keep your banker informed as to what you are doing and how your business is going.

Professional Associations

Professional associations related to consulting are worth consideration. At meetings you can mingle with prospective clients in an informal setting. Joining a local organization for consultants also offers you the opportunity to size up the competition as well as keep up with the latest developments.

The professional organizations to which you belong can impress prospective clients. Some organizations, such as certain national engineering societies, are open only to members who meet certain requirements. Others accept anyone who has the entry fee and can pay the dues. A few savvy clients know which organizations have stiff standards, but most simply glance at the list of societies to which you belong.

Joining civic organizations, such as the Chamber of Commerce, provides access to business people and presents you as a business owner in your own right. The benefits of joining other, more socially oriented organizations, such as country clubs, depend on the kind of clientele you will be working with and the cost of joining, which can be considerable.

Below is a list of some of the major societies and organizations for management consultants. These and other organizations for almost any specialty are listed in *The Encyclopedia of Associations* or *The National Trade and Professional Associations of the United States*. See the bibliography for more information on these sources.

ACME-The Association of Management Consulting Firms
521 Fifth Ave.
New York, NY 10175
(212) 697-9693

Founded in 1929, ACME is the grandfather of management consulting groups. Originally limited to larger firms, it is now more representative but still maintains strict entry requirements. ACME reaches beyond its membership, however, conducting surveys and maintaining an information center covering a wide segment of the profession. The 50 member firms, 15 percent of which are foreign-based, have offices in 100 countries worldwide. ACME also maintains an office in Brussels for international representation.

Member firms employ more than 45,000 management consultants, have annual billings in excess of $5 billion and list more than 130 separate areas of practice.

Applicants must normally have been in business for approximately five years, have a permanent staff of at least five full-time consultants and derive more than 50 percent of total revenue from management consulting services. Other considerations include experience, reference and evidence of professional and ethical conduct. All members adhere to a strict code of professional responsibility.

Dues are based on billings. The minimum is $4,950, and the maximum is $49,500. In addition to meetings, the association offers professional growth and development training sessions, representation in Washington, D.C., research reports, referral service, resume file, management surveys, library facilities, public relations, newsletters and international representation.

In addition to its directory of members, the association also offers *How To Get the Best Results from Management Consultants*. A price list of other publications is available.

Institute of Management Consultants (IMC)
[Includes the former Association of Managing Consultants (AMC) and Society of Professional Management Consultants (SPMC)]
521 Fifth Ave., 35th Fl.
New York, NY 10175
(212) 697-8262

A certifying body for individual management consultants, IMC grants the designation CMC (Certified Management Consultant) to those who qualify. It was founded in 1968 and represents a major, well-regulated commitment to professionalism. Approximately one-third of the more than 2,200 members are consultants in the larger independent management consulting firms. Another one-third are Management Advisory Service (MAS) practitioners in the major CPA firms, and the rest are also practitioners and consultants in smaller firms.

Membership is restricted to individuals who spend well over one-half of their working time in the public practice of management consulting (by serving a number of different clients on a fee basis). Candidates for certified membership must have at least five years of management consulting experience, including a year of project responsibility, with three of the five years immediately prior to application. A college degree or the equivalent is required. Applicants must fill out a detailed form ($100 fee) and pass a written examination and oral review. Candidates for membership must be practicing full-time in the management consulting field and be sponsored by a CMC.

Certified member dues are $300 per year with a one-time $150 entrance fee paid after election to certification. Member dues are $120 per year. The institute offers opportunities for professional development and networking via chapter, regional and national activities. Other membership benefits include a monthly newsletter, a directory and numerous discount programs and services. The directory is available to nonmembers for $50. The Institute provides free membership information including a copy of its *Code of Ethics*. Also available to members and nonmembers for $16 per year is *Update II*, a quarterly newsletter that offers practical advice for consultants by consultants.

Council of Consulting Organizations (CCO)
521 Fifth Ave.
New York, NY 10175
(212) 647-9693

Formed in 1989 by the consolidation of ACME and IMC, the Council of Consulting Organizations (CCO) is an umbrella organization of associations in the field of consulting to management. It functions as an information exchange for the various societies, associations, institutes, organizations and groups representing the management consulting profession in the United States. The council also has an affiliate, the Foundation for Excellence in Consulting and Management.

The CCO holds meetings and offers information exchange and inter-association representation. There is no directory. Entry requirements are not applicable, and there are no dues.

Management Consulting Services (MCS) Division
American Institute of Certified Public Accountants (AICPA)
Harborside Financial Center
201 Plaza III
Jersey City, NJ 07311

The American Institute of Certified Public Accountants (AICPA) is the professional society for CPAs who provide accounting, audit, tax and management consulting services in public practice for clients, as well as CPAs in industry, government and universities. The MCS Division of the AOCPA focuses on the consulting services provided by CPAs and issues practice standards for those services and practice aids, which may be purchased by nonmembers.

The MCS Division also administers the MCS Membership Section of the AICPA, which has more than 5,000 CPA members who pay an additional fee to receive the division's quarterly newsletter, *The CA Management Consultant*, and other MCS Section membership benefits. Institute members may join the MCS Section and qualified non-CPA consulting personnel in CPA firms may be sponsored as MCA Section Associates.

There are more than 20,000 full-time consultants in CPA firms, mostly in the six largest firms, but most of the 130,000 plus Institute members in public practice provide some management consulting services to their clients.

Academy of Management (AM)
PO Box 39
Ada, OH 45810
(419) 722-1953

Since its inception in 1936, the academy, with 8,700 members made up largely of business school professors, has been furthering scholarly research of management. The Division of Managerial Consultation became a special interest group (there are more than 20 others) in 1970. While its primary thrust is theoretical, it also monitors management research and provides a window on the extensive world of academic consulting.

AM is open to all who feel they can contribute to its objectives. Dues are $65 annually, allowing selection to two divisions. The annual meeting is $70.

The academy publishes three magazines (*AM Review*, *AM Executive* and *AM Journal*) and a newsletter for each division. Registrants at the annual meeting receive a copy of the proceedings. There are also regional meetings and a placement service. The directory is free to members only for Academy and Management Consulting Divisions.

Association of Internal Management Consultants (AIMC)
Margaret M. Custer, Executive Secretary
PO Box 304
East Bloomfield, NY 14443
(716) 657-7878

AIMC is an association of individuals founded in 1971 to provide a forum for the exchange of information, give formal recognition to the internal management consultant's role in modern business, raise standards of the professionals so engaged, represent the profession in matters of common interest, and promote the development of techniques and methods to improve the practice and management of internal management consulting.

There are 280 members—34 percent of these in service industries, 30 percent in banking, finance and insurance, 15 percent in manufacturing, 14 percent in utilities and 5 percent in public administration. Many members have responsibility for external consultants and monitoring their work. Membership requires current engagement as an internal consultant at senior or project-leader level, plus at least five years experience. Associates are admitted without experience or management requirements. Dues are $175 a year for professional members; $125 a year for associate members. No application or entrance fee is required.

The association offers regional roundtables, an annual meeting, a journal (*AIMC Forum*), a newsletter (*AIMC Newsletter*) and educational programs. A directory is available to members only.

American Consultants League (ACL)
1290 Palm Ave.
Sarasota, FL 34236
(813) 952-9290

Founded in 1983, the American Consultants League is an interdisciplinary national association embracing 220 disciplines with approximately 1,000 members. The league has two divisions—The Consultant's Library (the publishing arm) and the Consultants Institute (an educational division). A complete list of titles for the former is available. The latter offers individual consultant courses and a Certified Professional Consultant (CPC) certificate on successful completion of six courses.

Membership dues in the organization are $96 per year, which entitle members to a bimonthly newsletter *Consulting Intelligence*, the *ACL Directory* and other benefits. ACL also offers its members a consultant's hot line with expert advice on consulting practice.

There are many other professional and trade organizations that might be beneficial for you to join. Two such groups are:

American Society for Training and Development (ASTD)
PO Box 1443
1640 King St.
Alexandria, VA 22313
(703) 683-8100
55,000 members

International Association of Business Communicators (IABC)
One Hallidie Plaza, Ste. 600
San Francisco, CA 94102
(415) 433-3400
11,500 members

ASTD is composed mainly of trainers and those engaged in organizational development. Many consultants and industry representatives are members. IABC is for individuals engaged in organizational communication and information management either in-house or as consultant.

These and similar organizations can provide contact with potential clients and give an overview of what is happening in your area. The value of belonging to such organizations depends on your needs and whether the organization offers services to meet these needs. Membership composition and activities vary considerably from city to city, but attending one or two meetings will give you a good idea of whether association with a particular group is of potential value. The reference materials listed in the bibliography, such as the *Encyclopedia of Associations*, will guide you to several potentially useful societies in your field of specialization and geographic area.

Specialty Business Consulting Associations

The following specialty consulting associations related to business are listed in the *Encyclopedia of Associations* (see the bibliography). Consult this source for detailed information on each and for specialty associations in other fields such as health care, engineering and education.

American Association of Insurance Management Consultants (AAIMCo)
c/o Ken Pollack
RWP Group, Inc.
PO Box CS1880
Westbury, NY 11590
(516) 683-3000
Founded in 1978; 35 members.

American Association of Professional Consultants (AAPC)
9140 Ward Pkwy.
Kansas City, MO 64114
(816) 444-3500
Founded in 1983; 250 members.

Association of Outplacement Consulting Firms (AOCF)
364 Parsippany Rd.
Parsippany, NJ 07054
(201) 887-6667
Founded in 1982; 54 member firms.

Association of Professional Writing Consultants (APWC)
3924 S. Troost
Tulsa, OK 74105
(918) 743-4793
Founded in 1982; 200 members.

Consultants' Network (CN)
57 W. 89th St.
New York, NY 10024
(212) 799-5239
Founded in 1972.

Franchise Consultants International Association (FCIA)
5147 S. Angela Rd.
Memphis, TN 38117
(901) 761-3085
Founded in 1986; 2,860 members.

Independent Computer Consultants Association (ICCA)
933 Gardenview Office Pkwy.
St. Louis, MO 63141
(314) 997-4633
Founded in 1976; 1,900 members.

Institute of Certified Professional Business Consultants (ICPBC)
600 S. Federal St., Ste. 400
Chicago, IL 60605
(312) 922-6222
Founded in 1975; 270 members.

Institute of Tax Consultants (ITC)
7500 212th SW, Ste. 205
Edmonds, WA 98020
(206) 774-3521
Founded in 1981.

International Association of Merger and Acquisition Consultants
(INTERMAC)
200 S. Frontage Rd., Ste. 103
Burr Ridge, IL 60521
(708) 323-0233
Founded in 1973; 40 members.

Investment Management Consultants Association (IMCA)
10200 E. Girard Ave., Ste. 340C
Denver, CO 80231
(303) 337-2424
Founded in 1985; 400 members.

National Association of Career Development Consultants (NACDC)
1707 L St., N.W., Ste. 333
Washington, DC 20036
(202) 452-9102
Founded in 1987; 35 member firms.

National Association of Computer Consultant Businesses (NACCB)
1250 Connecticut Ave., N.W., Ste. 700
Washington, DC 20036
(202) 637-6483
Founded in 1987; 80 members.

National Association of Management Consultants (NAMC)
3101 Euclid Office Plaza, Ste. 701
Cleveland, OH 44115
(216) 431-0101
Founded in 1985; 50 members.

National Association of Personnel Consultants (NAPC)
3133 Mt. Vernon Ave.
Alexandria, VA 22305
(703) 684-0180
Founded in 1960; 2,300 member agencies.

Professional and Technical Consultants Association (PATCA)
1330 S. Bascom Ave., Ste. D
San Jose, CA 95128
(408) 287-8703
Founded in 1975; 400 members.

Qualitative Research Consultants Association (QRCA)
PO Box 6767, FDR Station
New York, NY 10021
(212) 315-0632
Founded in 1983; 312 members.

Society of Professional Business Consultants (SPBC)
612 Plainfield Rd., No. 308
Willow Brook, IL 60521
(800) 344-8129
Founded in 1956; 200 members.

Society of Risk Management Consultants (SRMC)
c/o John J. Crout
Blades & Macaulay
2444 Morris Ave.
Union, NJ 07083
(201) 687-3735
Founded in 1984; 124 members.

Naming Your Consulting Practice

What's in a name? Marketing experts take the naming of a product or service seriously. To make your company's name sell itself, consider three possibilities:

1. Should the name of the practice contain your name?

2. Should the name of the practice precisely and immediately communicate the services that you provide?

3. Should the company name cause others to view your practice as being a public-interest, nonprofit organization?

Using your name in your practice's name has a distinct advantage. Clients like the personal touch. If your practice consists of your individual services, your marketing efforts may well be helped by having clients and prospects identify you as an individual.

Some marketing authorities say that specifying your services in the name of your business or practice makes your marketing more efficient. The name helps sell the service. A few examples of such names are:

- Solar Energy Systems Advisory Group

- Telephone Marketing Consultants

- Medical Automation Services, Inc.

Naming your business so precisely has one disadvantage—it locks you into a predetermined market and service. If you later decide to expand your services, the name may be a hindrance. Some marketing authorities argue that for maximum impact the name of a consulting organization should imply a public service of a not-for-profit nature. If you accept this argument, then the name of your firm should make the company sound like a public interest organization instead of a commercial one. Public interest groups usually have names with such phrases as:

- The Center for _____

- The _____ Resources Center

- The Institute for the Study of _____

- The Alliance to _____

The marketing advantages of such a name are worth considering. Most consultants using this approach believe that the advantages have to do with prestige. They feel that just being introduced as the director of an institute lends credibility to their image. The fact that their field is important enough to warrant the founding of an institute or center is also a plus.

One question that arises in connection with prestige is the use of titles after your name. If you have a PhD or other prestigious title, your name will obviously have a favorable impact on some clients. However, others may feel that you are another impractical "egghead." Client attitude is the determining factor. In general a PhD is regarded as a significant achievement that demonstrates important, useful attributes. On balance having one is still likely to be of benefit.

You may want to consider the use of a fictitious name other than your business name. This is also called an assumed name or *doing business as* (DBA). The advantage to such an arrangement is that you keep your operating name distinct from the corporate name.

If you want to retire or just withdraw from the business, you can sell your operating name but keep your corporation. Fictitious names are also useful for trial efforts. If they flop, no harm is done. When they succeed, you simply have your corporation take the credit. Requirements for establishing a fictitious name or DBA vary from state to state and, in some cases, within states. In some cities you simply go to the office of any newspaper of general record, fill out a fictitious name statement and submit it to the newspaper. The newspaper sends a copy to the county recorder and publishes the notice three times. The charge is usually nominal. The rules will vary from state to state and even from city to city. The advice of a lawyer and perhaps of an accountant is helpful.

Whatever name you choose for your business, it must contribute effectively to your marketing approach. At the very least it should not undermine your marketing. So consider your company's name long and wisely. It will effect you now and in the future.

Developing a Brochure

Most consultants include a brochure as part of their marketing plan. (See Figure 2.2.) A good brochure describes what you have accomplished and outlines what you can do for the client. But its main aim is to get the potential client interested in you.

Generally, clients are more interested in what you have accomplished than in what you have learned. Concentrate on past successes, not on your education. Those successes don't even have to come from your consulting practice. They only need to stimulate the prospect's interest in buying your services.

Don't let your ego dictate which accomplishments to include in the brochure. Make your selections based on what you think the client wants to hear. One consulting firm included the following vignette in its brochure as an example of its past accomplishments as an incentive to buy their services:

> The management of a major trunk airline wanted to change its advertising campaign to reclaim its market share on its major (and highly competitive) routes. In the past they had changed advertising emphasis from personnel to timeliness to food service to quality of ground service, and so on. The philosophy had been to keep the name of the carrier in front of the public and to stimulate awareness by changing ad content.

> Unsatisfied with the modest results they were getting, the airline and its advertising agency retained the market division of our agency to find out what the ads should say. In less than 60 days, with an expenditure of less than one week's budget, we undertook a comprehensive consumer study to determine the factors that caused an air traveler to choose a given air carrier in those competitive markets.

> The results of this study were used by the carrier's agency to develop a totally revolutionary emphasis to the carrier's advertising program. Today, that airline is a leader in five of its seven competitive trunk lines.

> The techniques applied in this important consumer research are applicable to a number of industries. We think you, too, will be amazed by these findings and our agency will be pleased to share the findings with qualified inquirers.

In a few brief paragraphs, this vignette has explained a substantial success. It has also extended an opportunity for the reader to learn more.

Aside from vignettes, you may include some other information in your brochure:

A list of previous clients or references   In general don't link names of clients with specific accomplishments described in your vignettes; clients may prefer to be treated with confidentiality. However, a list of references or clients served is acceptable. Many consultants feel that it is not appropriate to place the names of previous clients or references in the capabilities statement. You should be prepared, however, to supply a list of individuals who can attest to your credibility, competence and character.

Your credentials or capabilities   Only a select few interest your readers. Don't underestimate the importance of practical, hands-on, on-the-job experience. For many clients it is the determining buying factor.

A statement of your operating philosophy and practice   Describe how you run your practice, how fees are charged or determined, your ethics and other points. Ask yourself: Is this information critical to the reader's buying decision?

The obvious but sometimes forgotten   Remember to include your address, phone number and other *obvious* information that is sometimes left out.

Testing the Message

Often we are our own poorest critics. Once you have drafted your message, ask some uninvolved people to tell you what your message communicates to them. There are two ways to get this feedback. One is to ask others to tell you what they understand your message to mean. This is a test of face validity, like the test undertaken by a questionnaire designer to make sure that the words communicate what the writer intended.

More important is the "test of image." You want to find out what assumptions or feelings others have about you as a result of what you have said. One inexpensive and useful way to run such a test is to contact the marketing department chairperson at the local university. Explain that you would like to work with one of the upper division or graduate marketing classes to conduct some marketing research.

You will likely be referred to a faculty member or to the student marketing association. Before long you will have a captured group to assist you. The group reviews your message or a mock-up of your completed brochure and writes a pencil-and-paper description of the consultant who would mail it out.

After obtaining the group's written reactions, which provide a kind of psychological profile, you can conduct a verbal discussion with the group to get additional findings as a result of group interaction. You will probably be surprised as you learn about yourself and your image. Use this information to modify your brochure and make it more effective. Your changes serve as a case example for the class and allow the teacher to explain the theory behind your research. It might be a nice touch to contribute to the scholarship fund or student marketing organization in exchange for the valuable input you have received.

Figure 2.2   Sample Brochure

The Twenty Questions

Most Often Asked about Consulting with Somers White and Their Answers

Q. We have heard about consulting with Somers White. Why should we consult with Somers White?

A. Maybe you should not. It is a question of dollars expended versus results.

Q. Don't consultants try to stay on forever?

A. Most consultants have as a major objective the enlargement of an engagement. What we do is get in, solve the problem and get out in one day.

Q. What is the major part of the work?

A. It is usually people who have problems with negotiating—such as negotiating with a bank, raising capital or some similar situation. It may be negotiating a deal.

Q. What other kinds of consulting do you do?

A. We also do work in management, motivation, marketing, strategy, increasing pride, professionalism, productivity and profits.

Q. Tell me more.

A. The most important part of our work is assisting individual clients in dealing more effectively with lenders and investors. Most businesspeople rank as amateurs when it comes to negotiating the best possible financial deal with a financial institution.

It is the weakest area for most business executives. Additionally, a financial institution's officer negotiates similar loans day after day and is more experienced.

Q. Doesn't negotiating for money take different forms?

A. Negotiating for money takes many different forms, including: Not being turned down, getting more money, secured to unsecured basis, borrowing for a longer time, easing terms, personal guarantee removed, lowering interest rate, lowering compensating balance requirements and improving cash flow.

Q. How long does it take?

A. I usually find that it takes less than five hours to show the client how to get the presentation into proper shape.

Q. How does it work?

A. I start out by having the client give me background information. I listen for clues of strength for which the client does not really have full appreciation. I also listen for items that turn off lenders or investors or cause them to be suspicious, and I develop the best possible answers for those negatives.

Q. What else?

A. I analyze the situation and give the client my evaluation, help the client develop the appropriate strategy and tactics, then work to determine who the client should see. I then assist the client with the written and oral presentation.

Q. I have heard about the tape recording.

A. I make a tape recording of the most important comments and of the specific plan of action. These tapes are given to the client at the end of the meeting. The client is free to record the entire consultation if desired.

Q. Can I bring someone with me?

A. Yes.

Source: Adopted with permission by Somers White, CMC. (602) 952-9292. 4736 N. 44th St., Phoenix, AZ 85018.

Figure 2.2 Sample Brochure (Continued)

Q. What about private money?

A. I do a good deal of work with those who want to seek money from private sources. As a result of my expertise in this area, I have been named as an Advisory Director for The Center for Entrepreneurial Management.

Q. What does it cost?

A. When I meet with clients in Phoenix, the charge is $1,950 for the day. I work on an advance retainer basis, and the charge is payable prior to the consultation. I work a five-hour day, starting with luncheon.

Q. What other charges are there?

A. There are no additional charges. This includes when and if the financing is obtained.

Q. What promises do you make?

A. I make no promises of success.

Q. Sometimes a consultant impresses the client, but the client ends up with a junior consultant.

A. I do the entire consultation myself.

Q. What about meeting outside Phoenix?

A. I literally go all over the world. For example, I recently negotiated for different clients in both Africa and Asia. Because I have only my time to sell, it is more expensive when I travel from Phoenix to consult with a client.

Q. If I want to hire you to negotiate in person with the lender, will you do this?

A. Yes. I usually do the negotiating for the clients right in front of them.

Q. When you meet with the client, is there a common theme or comment?

A. Yes, I hear again and again: "I should not have waited." "I should have consulted with you a year ago." "I wish I had met with you ten years ago."

Q. What do I do if I want to inquire about consulting with Somers White?

A. Pick up the telephone and call Somers White at (602) 952-9292.

Somers White, CMC, CPAE, was born in Kansas and grew up in Wisconsin. He holds a Bachelors Degree from Amherst College and a Masters Degree from Harvard Business School. He served with the 17th Infantry Regiment in the Orient and started his business career on Wall Street with the Executive Training Program of the Chase Manhattan Bank.

While he was in charge of Marketing for a new bank, deposits went from zero to $33 million in just eighteen months. At one time he held the title "Youngest Bank President in America" for any bank located in a major metropolitan center.

Since 1966 he has served as President of the Somers White Company, Management Consultants, which he founded. Somers is a former Arizona State Senator and has served as President of the Phoenix Society of Financial Analysts. He has been a member of the Arizona State University faculty, teaching courses in Management and Finance. His firm specializes in assisting organizations to present themselves properly to secure financing. Somers is an internationally known lecturer, having spoken in every state in the United States and on six continents.

Producing the Brochure

Now you have your words. What about the medium? If you opt for the written word, you should consider seeking the professional help of a graphics consultant or graphics house. One good way to select a graphics consultant is to find the individuals who have done brochures that struck you as particularly effective or attractive. The extra money you invest in graphic design, typesetting, quality paper (stock) and high-quality printing more than pays for itself.

Suppose you want 2,000 copies of a one-page, 8-1/2 x 11, two-sided brochure. The cost differential between doing a so-so job and a quality job may be only two or three cents per brochure. The small additional expenditure is well worth the payoff in results.

Distributing the Completed Brochures

You should plan how you will distribute your brochures long before they arrive from the printer. Generally, unsolicited mass mailing of a brochure does not work, even though it costs dearly. For the most part, your brochure is something you might leave with a prospective client after a face-to-face meeting. Or you might mail it out after an initial written or phone communication when the prospective client has asked to know more about you.

Brochures are also excellent to hand out following verbal presentations to a civic or professional group. They also may be mailed out the next day to those attending as a follow-up communication. Give thought to mailing a brochure along with a summary or a transcription of your remarks about a week after your talk. An accompanying letter might indicate: There were so many requests for a text of the talk, we decided to send them to everyone.

Brochures can be mailed out in response to ads. When your market is broad and likely to fully understand the nature of your consulting services—bookkeeping, computer programming, interior design, advertising, market research—give thought to small space ads in professional or business publications. These ads should encourage readers to contact you to obtain a copy of your brochure.

Tips _____

Getting off to a solid businesslike start is one of the best ways of ensuring that you will be a success as a consultant. Struggling along in an unsatisfactory partnership instead of being in business for yourself or failing to keep proper financial records can sabotage your chances of success, even though you are writing and completing plenty of contracts. A strong beginning means selecting the right form for your business, having a solid support system, choosing a good name and creating an effective brochure to distribute to prospective clients.

You may not need to have a lawyer on tap if your practice doesn't involve legal questions. You may be able to take care of your own financial records if you have an aptitude for it. You may not need a brochure if you can sell yourself effectively in other ways. (And a brochure alone is not a marketing strategy. You need to do a lot more than hand out a piece of paper to market your skills, as we will see in Chapters 6 and 7 on marketing and advertising.) But you do need to be able to take care of each of these areas—legal, financial, banking, selling, selecting a name—if you are going to succeed.

Over and above the demands of most businesses, consulting calls for a special kind of self-confidence. Remember that you can develop this self-confidence by taking stock of what you can bring to the profession.

Taking stock begins with an inventory of your personal resources. In the next chapter we will guide you in reviewing what you can do as a business manager and as a consultant. You will discover some skills you may not have known you possess. This review can benefit those consultants who are just beginning a practice and those who are already well-established.

The next step is learning how to turn those skills into business opportunities. We will explore how to find opportunities and how to turn them into money-making business enterprises. The extent to which you take your skills, apply them to opportunities and manage your business determines your level of success.

3

Developing Your Skills Inventory

You are a consultant, or wish to be one, because you have the self-confidence to explore new areas and to accept new challenges. As a consultant your stock in trade is the skills and talents you have to offer. In any given field many employees and researchers have expertise to spare. Yet they are not consultants because they do not feel sufficiently self-confident to promote their expertise and to carry it over into unfamiliar territory. While knowledge is a vital part of consulting, confidence in your ability to apply your knowledge to the problems of a client is more important.

That may sound like a pep talk, but the essential truth is that self-confidence is a key trait for consulting. Your reputation as a consultant almost invariably arises from the confidence you demonstrate to others. Their trust then feeds your own self-confidence. Without confidence in yourself and your abilities, all your expertise won't help you a bit.

Most people—even some who wish to enter consulting—simply do not have a high enough opinion of themselves to merit a lot of self-confidence. They are too modest to recognize their special abilities and accomplishments. As a result they do not know the value those abilities and accomplishments have in the marketplace. Some people have an imperfect recall of their past successes. Others function so effectively, yet so effortlessly, that they are unaware of their talents.

A review of the resources you bring to consulting will encourage that self-confidence. Nothing boosts your self-image more than remembering and recording past achievements and strengths. There's no better way to boost your confidence as a consultant than to make up a comprehensive inventory of all the abilities you bring to your consulting specialty.

Even if you have been a consultant for years, you probably have many abilities and talents that you don't recognize. The *old hand* at consulting may benefit more from a skills inventory than a newcomer. With plenty of experience under your belt, you have more opportunity to discover your skills and talents. Our most valuable abilities are hidden, and they are discovered by looking at our experiences in a new light.

A quick rise to success in consulting springs from a grouping or pattern of abilities peculiar to an individual's background. In this search for skills, you will look for unique combinations of strengths and abilities. However, to use these skills, you must learn about them in detail.

Paradoxically, the skills and strengths that are likely to be of the greatest use are also likely to be *invisible*. If you do something a lot more easily than most people do, you probably have a special ability but don't realize it. Taking a systematic inventory of your skills will reveal those talents.

The Skills Inventory

This inventory emphasizes specific skills and accomplishments. Just listing some abstract words like *creative, energetic* and *dependable* won't do much good. By listing specific accomplishments and examining them for the skills that you displayed, you will learn what you *do*. Then you can construct an *action* list of your skills.

The inventory is taken in three steps:

1. A comprehensive listing of all your past achievements.

2. A search for skills by expanding and rephrasing the items in your listing.

3. A search for talents by sifting through your skills. (Use the worksheet in Figure 3.1 for your skills inventory. List your achievements in the left-hand column and the skills you used in the right-hand column.)

Listing Your Past Achievements

Start by relaxing and just thinking about the challenges that you have handled in the past. Simply let your mind wander and review some situations at work or in life where you succeeded. What are some of the problems at work that you solved? Did you work out a particularly tricky production schedule, make an important sale or find a new application for an old technology? Use the lists that follow this section as a thought stimulator.

The focus of this skills inventory is best placed on problem solving. Normally, people are not highly paid for doing routine, predictable work. The people who are well paid are those who can deal with and prevent problems. This rule is especially applicable to consulting. As clients come to see you as a problem solver, they are more likely to pay for your services. However, first you must see yourself as someone who can tackle and solve a difficult problem. And you need the self-confidence to present yourself that way.

Figure 3.1 Skills Inventory Worksheet

Activities	*Skills*

For some people listing accomplishments is difficult. They either feel uncomfortable *tooting their own horn*, or they *just can't seem to remember anything*. Don't let this initial difficulty put you off. If you skip this important step, you can cripple all your other efforts in consulting. A skills inventory is of paramount importance because you need a single unifying theme for your consulting practice. Also you can never be comfortable with your role as a problem solver until you recast your past experience in terms of that role.

So don't give up on your list of personal accomplishments. After a while you will start seeing everything you've done as either a solution to a problem or a way of preventing one. Then you are forming the mind-set that is crucial to being a successful consultant.

Skills Inventory Aid

As you review your achievements, use the following lists to help you form your inventory of skills. Your abilities are demonstrated in five areas of achievement:

1. Past work positions
2. Previous projects
3. Education
4. Formal credentials
5. Free-time activities

Working backward in time, list your achievements in each of these five areas on the left side of the form, then ask the following questions:

1. What was the problem?
2. What was my diagnosis?
3. What skills did I use in my diagnosis?
4. How did I prevent or solve the problem?
5. What skills did I use in preventing or solving the problem?

As you think over your answers, keep these points in mind:

- *Bizarre or dubious achievements are good.* The worksheets are designed to stimulate your memory, not inhibit it. Gems may be hidden among these unusual feats.

- *Minor achievements are good.* Don't ignore seemingly unimportant accomplishments, and don't be ashamed to list them. Special skills are often hiding here.

- *"Merely" dealing with human beings is good.* In consulting, human relations skills are both prized in their own right and useful adjuncts to technical skills.

In writing down your list, avoid:

- *Elegant phrasing* Your purpose is to open the floodgates of your memory and imagination. You will have plenty of opportunity for polishing later. At this stage you want only the rough, raw material. This is almost like brainstorming.

- *Professional jargon*   You are looking for abilities that are transferable. Jargon tends to restrict your thinking to the situation in which you happened to demonstrate a skill.

After you have listed your accomplishments, write down on the right side of the form a second list of the skills you used in solving or preventing each problem. Suppose one of your problems was finding a new supervisor to replace one who was promoted. You solved the problem by realizing that one of your employees had leadership potential that others had failed to see. Your skill was *recognizing* another person's abilities. For each achievement write down one or more skills that you used, and underline the action word in that skill.

Evaluating Your Skills

Once you have drawn up your list, write down your comments about the problem situations you solved using the worksheet on evaluating skills in Figure 3.2. To help you evaluate your skills, ask these questions:

- How successful was I at solving or preventing the problem?
- How did human relations skills (or lack of them) affect me in—
    a. diagnosing the problem?
    b. devising a way to solve or prevent the problem?
    c. implementing the solution or prevention?
- Would I do anything differently if I confronted the same situation today?

One consultant selected three accomplishments from his list to concentrate on: In college his fraternity was close to dissolving; he was elected president and cleaned up the mess. On one job he solved a tricky problem with computer programming even though he was not trained as a programmer. He had also shown one of his coworkers, who was on the verge of being discharged, how to assess her likes and dislikes so she could find another, much more satisfying job.

Each of these situations was seen as a problem that he solved. Note that you do not have to restrict your list to problems that you handled on the job. Any problem-solving ability can be applied in business.

Next, he wrote down his skills. With the mess at the fraternity he was able to *analyze* a complex problem and *organize* people. With the computer problem he *simplified* the problem to find a solution. With his coworker he *elicited* the reasons for her dissatisfaction.

He applied the three evaluation questions to each situation, rating his level of success in solving each problem. Finding that each of the problems had been handled very successfully, he then applied the second test. His understanding of people helped him diagnose the problems with the fraternity and gave him insight into his coworker's job difficulties. The computer problem didn't require human relations skills to diagnose or solve.

In reviewing the outcome of the fraternity presidency, he realized that he had solved the problem, but the way he did it cost him the friendship of his fraternity brothers. He resolved to handle similar situations less autocratically, giving others more room to provide input. He had implemented the solution to his coworker's problem skillfully by leading her to find her own answers, and she was very grateful for his help.

Figure 3.2   Evaluating Skills Worksheet

_____

1. Successful in solving problem?
2. Human relation skills involved?
3. Different approach to problem?

He came to realize that, although the computer programming problem was solved without human relations skills, implementing the solution involved using tact to get the technicians to try his approach. He came away from this exercise with an understanding of the importance of human relations skills in resolving any organizational problem.

In analyzing the situation at the fraternity, he realized that he may not have been a good president in all respects, but he had acted like a good consultant. A consultant comes in and takes charge of a problem without getting involved in the organization's politics. If there are bad feelings associated with changes, the consultant leaves and takes them with him. As chapter president our consultant wasn't able to leave gracefully when the job was done. This underscores the importance of taking a close look at seeming failures or dubious achievements because special skills that are important to a *consultant* may be hidden in them.

Go through your list with the same detail. Take a long, hard look at your accomplishments, aiming toward a thorough understanding of your ability at problem solving.

Search for Skills

Skills are abilities that are acquired by experience. Very often we pick up skills without even knowing what we are doing. As a result many skills may lie hidden among our achievements. To crystallize your skills, you must go back over your inventory, expanding and rephrasing each item. Use the Expanded Skills Inventory in Figure 3.3 to do this.

You expand an item by breaking it down into the skills that you used in solving it. Let's say you listed *handling a labor-management dispute* as one of your solved problems and an *ability to find the real cause of the conflict* as your skill. Based on the steps you *actually* took to solve the problem, this skill might be expanded to several steps:

1. *Suspected* that neither side was voicing its real concerns.

2. *Won* confidence of each side's leader.

3. *Listened* to leaders' recitals of demands.

4. *Elicited* reasons behind demands.

5. *Analyzed* motivations behind demands.

6. *Inferred* plausible hidden causes for dispute.

Your objective is to isolate a matrix of unique skills that will enable you to establish a working "patent" on your business. The original skill may be too broad to protect your turf in consulting, but one or more of the subskills you discovered by analyzing the original skill might fit your plans.

One more step is required to ensure that your skills are listed in a form that reveals your unique abilities: You need to *rephrase* your skills to make the description of your skills as independent as possible from the particular environment in which you used them. Look at each skill description and ask yourself: Could this ability be useful in other environments and, if so, what is the general description of the ability involved?

46   The Complete Guide to Consulting Success

Figure 3.3   Expanded Skills Inventory

Skills	*Subskills*

As an illustration, let's take the six subskills in the previous example and rephrase them so that their general usefulness is more obvious:

1. *Suspected* could be rephrased as *an ability to recognize when communications are confused by hidden factors.*

2. *Won confidence/listened/elicited* can be combined to form *can interview leaders for sensitive information in stressful situations.*

3. *Analyzed/inferred* can be combined to form *can discern hidden motives in conflict situations.*

These skills are now beginning to form a cluster related to handling difficult situations involving negotiations. If you look at the situation only as a problem in labor negotiations, you might be limited to that kind of negotiating. But negotiations take place in a great many situations, and many organizations experience political conflicts.

Given this skills matrix, you might be very good at consulting with organizations that are experiencing difficulties related to internal politics. Figure 3.4 is a list of consulting-related skills to help in analyzing your list of subskills. This is only a fragment of what consultants do, so don't feel limited by it.

Search for Talent

Talents, unlike skills, are not acquired. Instead, they seem to be with a person from birth. Talents are natural endowments and involve special abilities or creativity.

If you emphasize your talents, your chances for achieving a great advantage in the consulting marketplace are far greater than they would be if you relied on skills alone. Others can learn your skills and can acquire your knowledge, but unless they also have your talents, they cannot compete with you effectively in the marketplace. Recognizing and exploiting your talents can be an extremely profitable exercise.

Ironically, talents are likely to be even more invisible than your skills. Your talents are far more natural for you than your skills, and you exercise them less consciously. Therefore, you should be especially thorough with this step of the exercise. By failing to detect a talent, you could be giving up a gold mine of consulting advantage. Figure 3.4 shows a good way to proceed.

- Examine your list of achievements, and note any that came easily.

- Look over your problem-solving history, and note where you exhibited the special vision needed to prevent problems.

- Evaluate your skills as listed. Talents will reveal themselves if you ask yourself these questions:
    - Are there any groups of skills that have something in common?
    - Which skills did people especially value?
    - Where was I the obvious choice?
    - Which skills did I particularly enjoy using?

Figure 3.4   Consultants' Activities

Research

identify suppliers
identify target markets for ideas or products
identify talent
identify experts
identify commercial possibilities for ideas or concepts
assess the public mood
examine political realities
trace problems, ideas, etc. to their source

Invent

create commercial possibilities for abstract ideas or concepts
design events
improve on others' ideas
update others' ideas
adapt others' ideas

Communicate

arbitrate disputes
negotiate agreements
terminate people/projects/processes
translate jargon
help others express views
help others clarify goals and values
handle difficult people
interview

Motivate

sell an idea, program, or course of action to decision makers
raise capital for nonprofit institutions
raise capital for business ventures
recruit leadership
direct creative talent

Analyze

classify data
perceive and define cause-and-effect relationships

Figure 3.4   Consultants' Activities (Continued)

Synthesize

summarize
assess people's needs
extract the essence from large quantities of data

Evaluate

assess monetary value

judge people's effectiveness

identify and assess others' potential

analyze communication situations

Recommend

suggest experts

suggest suppliers

allocate scarce resources

Forecast

plan financial matters

predict obsolescence

Adapted from *What Color Is Your Parachute?* Richard N. Bolles (Ten Speed Press)

Talents that are not revealed through self-examination may turn up in other people's comments about you. Don't hesitate to solicit these comments for the purpose of this step. You may also recall people's comments from formal or informal work evaluations or from other situations. You can get an idea of the kinds of talents that can be important in consulting from Figure 3.5.

Having completed this self-assessment, you have done something that most people never do. You have methodically produced a thorough, exhaustive listing of what you have to offer. Your special skills and unique talents provide a basis for entering the consulting profession or rejuvenating your existing practice. Periodic changes in the scope and thrust of your consulting services in response to changing market conditions are part of the normal cycle of practice development. But even more important is a regular reassessment of your skills and talents. This reevaluation, reflecting an increased awareness of the full breadth and applicability of your talents, may suggest changes in direction or emphasis that will make you more effective and efficient in providing your services.

Figure 3.5   Talents in Consulting

General

separating the "wheat from the chaff"
perceiving and defining cause-and-effect relationships
creating order out of masses of information

Data Handling

ordered, systematic manipulation of data
classification of data
mathematical ability

Management

attracting talent or leadership to yourself
getting diverse groups to work together
directing creative talent
building teams

Human Relations

alertness in observing human behavior
developing rapport/trust
bargaining
diplomacy
confronting others with touchy or difficult personal matters
judging people's effectiveness and/or potential
bringing out the creativity in others

Communication

public speaking
writing ability
thinking quickly on your feet
explaining difficult concepts
inventing illustrations for principles or ideas
hearing and answering questions perceptively

Tips

The list of consulting services that you offer is your inventory. Your services are analogous to products in that they require strong management and selling skills. In developing your inventory of consulting services, you will be looking for creative ways of applying your skills and talents to specific situations.

Figure 3.6 covers some of the services consultants offer. Use the consulting inventory worksheet in Figure 3.7 to list your skills and talents in the left-hand column and potential consulting offerings in the right-hand column.

Suppose you work in security. You can give management seminars on security. You can offer consulting on such topics as employee theft prevention, shoplifting, industrial espionage, computer security. You might further specialize in certain industries, such as construction or retail clothing outlets.

Even in a fairly limited area, you can produce an extensive list of consulting services. But a big inventory isn't necessarily good. By offering too many services, you may be spread too thin, and you will have trouble targeting markets. You may be able to do all those things on your list, but can you sell them all at once?

On the other hand, you want enough services so that you have the flexibility to respond to changes in the marketplace. In other words, you want to be process-oriented rather than task-oriented. Of course, if you do one thing well, and there is a steady demand for it, you can be quite successful. However, if the market changes, you need to be prepared to change, too.

In drawing up a potential inventory, go over your list of skills and talents. How can they be exercised in your chosen area to produce particular offerings? Suppose you have a talent for anticipating future trends and you specialize in inventory. You may want to offer warehouse space planning or setting up inventory procedures for new plants. Or you may decide to apply your talent in other areas, such as market analysis. Based on your skills and talents, draw up a list of four or five potential consulting offerings.

In the next two chapters, we will learn how to find and exploit opportunities. The work you have done in this chapter will enable you to match your skills and talents with opportunities to produce an inventory of consulting offerings. If you are clear about what you are marketing, you have a better chance to make a sale—and that leads to success.

Figure 3.6   Some Consulting Specialties

Management

planning
organizational structure
strategic business planning
feasibility studies
management audits
public relations
business surveys
customer satisfaction improvement

Administration

office design and planning
office management
office procedures
scheduling
data management

Marketing

market strategy
product research
sales forecasting
sales training
direct mail
advertising
marketing audits
pricing
consumer survey

Human Relations

labor relations
wage and salary structure
management development
personnel
attitude surveys
training programs
company communications
health and safety

Figure 3.6   Some Consulting Specialties (Continued)

Plant Operation

plant management
plant location
plant design
warehouse utilization
inventory management
production planning
quality control
shipping and distribution
automation and robotics

Finance and Purchasing

accounting
cost control
financial planning
capital investment
taxes
collection
purchasing
capital expenditures
cost accounting

Figure 3.7   Consulting Inventory Worksheet

Skills and Talents	*Consulting Application*

4

Finding Consulting Opportunities

Identifying consulting opportunities is largely an intuitive process that cannot be taught and should not be thought of as scientific. Experienced consultants usually develop a sensitivity for promising new areas for the application of their skills. This chapter shows how to uncover new sources of consulting opportunity by applying your experience and intuition to an organized review of possibilities. You may end up with more ways of increasing consulting opportunities than you even wished for.

Even in as nebulous an area as matching opportunities to your talents, you needn't resign yourself to good luck. You can actively seek out opportunities and evaluate their suitability to your goals as a consultant. Most opportunities do not come to you. You have to find them and, in some cases, help to produce them. The secret is learning to orient yourself toward filling the needs of clients as opposed to looking for clients who meet your requirements. And you can actively pursue add-on opportunities with current clients in addition to taking on new accounts.

Many consultants make the mistake of searching for opportunities only in a specific industry or organization. While that approach can be productive, it significantly limits the consultant's eligibility for greater success. Why limit yourself to one industry or business? Consulting opportunities arise in all industries and in any organization. If you know the earmarks of a consulting opportunity, you can recognize it in any situation. If you don't limit your consulting specialty, you can take advantage of an opportunity wherever you find it.

To ensure that you seek out a broad spectrum of opportunities, it is useful to approach the market with an understanding of the ten situations or circumstances that give rise to the use of a consultant:

Ten Situations That Create a Need for Consulting Services

1. The Need for Technical Assistance
2. The Need for Specialized Skills
3. Cash Flow and Business Problems
4. The Need for Capital
5. Resource Acquisition
6. Compliance Legislation
7. Political Situations
8. The Hotfoot Situation
9. Training
10. Need for an Unbiased Opinion

The Need for Technical Assistance

In the United States the single largest market for consulting work comes from the need for temporary technical assistance. This opportunity arises both in the public and private sectors whenever an organization must increase its capacity and personnel. Rather than searching for new or unusual skills, clients merely seek more of the skills they already have. Many large firms regularly fill a significant percentage of their positions with temporary technical assistance consultants. Firms in the high-technology industries—aerospace, electronics, computers, education, health care—are particularly likely to follow this practice.

Despite the fact that temporary technical assistance consulting is widespread and pervasive, it is not very romantic. You don't ride in on a white horse, do mysterious things with spectacular results and then gallop off into the sunset with a big check in hand. Instead, you often find yourself commuting to a place of business and putting in a work day with fellow consultants and employees. Technically, you are a consultant. But on a day-to-day basis, you may find that you function more like an employee. The crucial distinction between temporary technical assistance consulting and the other nine opportunities, which will be discussed on the following pages, is the issue of *supervision*.

In most consulting situations, you are viewed as the authority or expert. You may be managed, but you are unlikely to be supervised. In providing temporary technical assistance, however, you are viewed not as the sole expert, but as a temporary employee—much like clerical help from an agency. These consultants often find their work less rewarding psychologically (and financially) than that in other fields of consulting, where fees are higher and responsibility is broader. The advantages of temporary technical assistance consulting are: (1) There are plenty of opportunities, and (2) the job frequently produces other more rewarding consulting possibilities.

An organization has two basic reasons to seek out temporary technical assistance consultants: (1) Such assistance is often more economical than hiring permanent personnel, and (2) by using consultants, the organization remains more flexible than it could be with permanent help.

Hiring costs an organization a lot of money. Firing can cost even more. Much of this expense is the result of complex government regulations. It can take a team of well-paid personnel officers to interview and evaluate potential employees to make sure federal and state regulations are followed. Reliable statistics indicate that a large organization typically takes between five and seven months to locate, hire, train and orient employees for managerial, technical or professional positions. That estimate may sound high, but consider the severe shortages in this country of personnel who are available and trained to be installed in the right position. Consider also the complexity of the personnel process: advertising, prescreening, resume reviews, interviews, testing, follow-up interviews, medical examinations, orientation, break-in periods, and so on.

By the time a person is hired, trained and oriented, most large employers can expect to expend from 70 to 90 percent of the employee's first-year salary. For someone hired at, say, $50,000 a year, that dollar amount would be $35,000 to $45,000! For an organization to hire someone on a permanent basis, it must be very certain not only that the individual can do the job and will do it but also that the employee's talents will be needed for as long as he or she is with the company.

The organization's expense does not end when the employee is hired. Besides salary and benefits, an employer has overhead expenses with each employee, such as providing a place to work and support personnel. Changes in circumstances can cost money. Perhaps technology passes the company by, or the large government contract expires. In that case the organization must either arrive at a termination settlement with the affected employees, find them other jobs to do or simply "carry" them.

In the worst case, if the employee does not work out at all, the employing firm may encounter further difficulties. The firm cannot arbitrarily let an employee go. It must show just cause, such as inability to perform the work, unwillingness to do so, criminal activity or some other good reason. Employees who respond with legal action can cost the firm incalculably long after they no longer produce any benefit for the employer.

An organization does not incur the same cost or liability when it takes on a temporary technical consultant. Consultants pay part or most of their own *hiring* expenses. They often make themselves known and available through their promotional and advertising efforts, thus reducing the firm's cost of searching for them. Once on the job, they normally do not participate in the benefits enjoyed by permanent personnel. And the management knows that if a consultant does not become a contributing member of the team within a reasonable period, the most the firm is liable for is payment over the short-term contract.

Because they are easy to discharge, consultants are obliged to become effective contributors sooner than employees. The role expectations for consultants are different from those for employees. Permanent personnel are expected to take a long time to become oriented and adjusted, whereas consultants are expected to start contributing on short notice. A temporary technical consultant must be noticeably effective almost from the start, contributing at least as much as a permanent employee.

The Need for Specialized Skills

In rare instances a person has a skill or expertise that few others have. Even rarer, an individual can offer a service that no one else offers. That person has something unique to sell.

Classically, consultants are considered to possess specialized expertise—the command of special or unique talents, skills and capabilities that make a person rare or unique in the marketplace. Traditionally, when we think of consultants we imagine the Red Adair's of the world. However, the success of such specialists arises from our *perception* of their uniqueness, rather than its reality. In most cases specialists are not unique; they have merely found a niche in the marketplace in which the application of their skills creates the appearance of uniqueness.

One direct response specialist has skills that are commonly available and uses techniques that are not unique. Yet this person is perceived as an accomplished specialist because he has taken general knowledge and applied it in a unique fashion to a specialized industry.

True uniqueness, then, is not a requirement. Fewer than five percent of the consultants in the market have a truly unique set of skills, but many have found a way of being seen as special and different in their clients' eyes.

Cash Flow and Business Problems

There are many opportunities in both the private and public sectors for consultants who wish to serve organizations that are experiencing business or cash-flow problems. Previously confined to the private sector, these problems now extend to the once cash-flush public sector, which at one time could raise funds by going to the voters or donors but now finds itself on hard times. In the last three years, the use of consultants to assist public organizations has increased fivefold.

Another source of consulting opportunities arises when an organization runs into a cash shortage. A company experiencing a *cash-flow crisis* typically reduces its expenses by laying off personnel and curtailing other costs. This situation gives rise to two types of consulting opportunities. The first is for temporary technical assistance to help the firm avoid the cost of hiring and maintaining permanent personnel. Temporary technical assistance consultants can come into the organization and perform the work, then cease being a financial obligation to the organization.

The second opportunity is the greater of the two. Whenever you see a firm trying to solve its cash flow problem by cutting costs, you have reason to suspect that the organization has a deeper, more pervasive problem of which the cash-flow crisis is merely a symptom. Management soon realizes that reducing expenses is not enough to solve the larger problem.

With this realization, management usually recognizes the need for turnaround consultants. Two types of consultants are generally needed. The first type specializes in creativity. Perhaps the firm needs more adaptive marketing, more ingenious engineering talent, more flexible personnel management, and so on. The creative consultant, in solving this part of the problem, typically becomes preoccupied with day-to-day matters. The other type of consultant is concerned with control and management. This is the hard-nosed, common-sense, bean-counter type of manager who ensures that the firm's creative energies are focused on turning a profit. Finding opportunity of this sort depends largely on keeping your ear to the ground. By the time a firm's problems become news in the trade, industrial or professional publications, the time has come for the embalming committee, and the need for a turnaround consultant has long since passed.

For much more reliable referral to dying-but-not-dead businesses, you can turn to local bankers, accountants and attorneys who are intimate with the financial standing of the community's businesses. Although you should not expect bank officers and professionals to give you any information on their customers and clients, you can make your services known to them. In turn they can refer their clientele to you at their discretion.

You'll find that referrals by bank officers do not come just from the goodness of their hearts. If a bank customer is in trouble, a bankruptcy could mean a loan gone sour. You can actually help the bank by saving the business. Everyone is happy—the business is saved, the bank's loan is repaid and you earn your fee. (See *The Turnaround Survival Guide* by A. David Silver in the bibliography.)

A number of consulting firms specialize in wresting businesses from the brink. One firm relies on only two banks for referrals of terminal businesses. With an hourly rate often exceeding $200 and more than 80 percent of their business from bank referrals, they have enjoyed a growth rate of more than 30 percent a year for the last five years.

The Need for Capital

Needing capital is different from needing cash. Even organizations that are cash-flush have to go into the money market to raise long-term and short-term capital. Large organizations have people on staff to meet their capital needs, which means that few consulting opportunities are available there. But smaller firms, which don't need to raise capital as often as larger companies do, don't usually need to keep such talent around on the payroll full-time. When the smaller firm needs to raise capital, it creates a consulting opportunity for you.

You should have many more such opportunities in the future. Economists predict dramatic capital shortages in this country at least until the year 2010 and perhaps beyond. Due to the present severe shortage of capital, the capital acquisition area is the fastest growing sub-market of consulting opportunity in the United States.

A major factor in its growth is the competition for funds from the public sector, which must now vie for the same capital that once flowed only into the private sector. The need for capital naturally affects public as well as private organizations. With their growing resistance to bonded indebtedness, increasing taxes and tax overrides, taxpayers are forcing public agencies to turn to what was once the sole preserve of private firms to raise capital—institutional lenders. As public agencies draw upon funds normally reserved for the private sector, the capital shortage grows more acute, increasing opportunities for consultants.

Surprisingly, you don't have to be a financial specialist to benefit from this abounding opportunity. Much more is involved in raising capital than running down to the corner bank with a fistful of financial statements. Today, the process of obtaining capital requires that the client be packaged carefully for the close scrutiny that accompanies applications for capital. They must often demonstrate that:

- They are in compliance with federal laws, such as equal employment opportunity, affirmative action, occupational safety and health.
- Their personnel policies and practices will produce a steady stream of qualified, capable personnel into the organization in the future.
- Their marketing is sufficiently large and well-developed to ensure long-term sales.
- Their production capability is appropriate and suitable to the market demand that they are likely to encounter.

So you may well possess nonfinancial skills that are valued in the capital acquisition area, provided you take the time to market them effectively.

Firms needing capital also have to spruce up their images. So if your specialty is in public relations, marketing, forecasting, product development or any field that can help a firm look its best, you may have a consulting opportunity.

Not only are the opportunities for consulting great in this submarket, but the fees earned are among the highest. Capital-seeking organizations are quite willing to pay a substantial amount to raise capital. Because they operate on the assumption that the consultant's fee (cost of capital acquisition) will be repaid from the proceeds, they tend not to scrutinize the size or reasonableness of the fee quite as closely as they would in other kinds of consulting. If a firm is setting out to raise $600,000 in capital, it usually won't mind investing $40,000 to $50,000 to get it.

Even if you cannot get the primary contract for this type of work, you may be able to market your services to other consultants. Perhaps a team of consultants has to be formed to meet the needs of a client. Or maybe the firm's financial consultant identifies a number of areas that need attention—personnel, marketing, production, and so on. Since the first consultant is unlikely to be expert in all fields, the services of other consultants will be required.

If you have the appropriate skills, look for firms that are about to raise capital. Follow the business press for trends. See which industries are developing and which are getting a lot of business—these organizations will need capital. Look also for public agencies, which are reported in the newspaper all the time. Simply follow their budgetary procedure.

Resource Acquisition

Resources can take the form of the physical plant, inventory and personnel. Specialized consultants can make a good income by finding the resources a company needs. It is often much cheaper to buy a factory and refurbish it than to invest in new facilities. Consultants with knowledge of who needs what and where to find it can charge hefty fees for overseeing the transfer. Part of the job is finding what is needed; part is consummating the transfer. Some plant brokers also oversee the remaking of the old facilities and even installing the work force. However, significant parts of such a project often are handled by subcontracting.

Scarcity of resources creates special opportunities. For a while the spot oil market was the hottest thing going. But shortages in any area can create opportunities. If you know how to find what is in demand, you can get contracts as a consultant.

Professional headhunters are also looking for a scarce resource. As a consultant your opportunity comes from your broad contacts in management. You may work finding particular executives or employees, or you may specialize in putting teams of consultants together for demanding contracts. Even as companies provide executive searches as part of their services, many executive search consultants offer related services in response to market needs. Resource acquisition, one of the fastest-growing areas of consulting, is wide open to the freewheeling entrepreneur who knows how to find and exploit opportunities.

Compliance Legislation

Every time Congress convenes, every time the state legislature meets, and every time the county supervisors or city councils gather, they pass a law to make someone comply with something. Compliance legislation leads to the *sudden availability of funds*. Because of the new laws, organizations have to respond rapidly and effectively to avoid sanctions and injunctions.

Consider the Environmental Impact legislation. When this was signed into law, the compliance requirement jumped dramatically, pulling consulting opportunities along in a more gradual curve, as seen in Figure 4.1. Right after the effective date, the compliance requirements were minimal. But no one had much experience in writing such reports, so many firms turned to consultants. At that time you didn't need a technical doctorate to write an EI report—all you needed were an understanding of the process and good writing skills. For a while the demand for good report writers was great. Consultants in this field were enjoying top fees, plenty of work and a lot of independence.

Eventually the demand is bound to taper off for a number of reasons:

1. People who are smart at procuring consulting services often use the consultant as a trainer rather than as a consultant. In this way they get their own staff trained and don't need the consultant any more.

2. Many consultants are wooed away to become the captive of the client corporation at high salaries. They take over a part of the market that would ordinarily go to consultants.

3. Eventually universities and business school programs see the need for such specialists and start to offer suitable courses. Some years later those schools are turning out people who will be full-time personnel, trained in areas that used to belong solely to consultants.

Where do you find out about new compliance requirements? Browse through *The Congressional Record* on a regular basis. Don't read all of it—just by scanning, you can identify important legislative trends. If you read major metropolitan newspapers, such as *The New York Times* or *The Wall Street Journal*, you will keep abreast of new legislation. On a local level, watch what is going on at the supervisor's meeting or at any meeting of the local government agencies. When you see compliance requirements coming up, be ready. Find out the nature of the legislation. Determine what compliance is going to take. Keeping your eye on compliance legislation may lead to a number of business opportunities.

Figure 4.1   Impact of Compliance Requirements on Consulting Opportunities

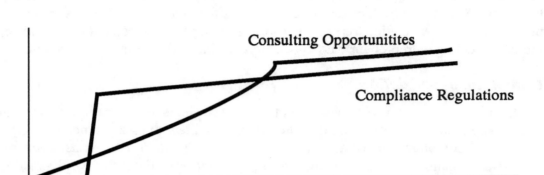

Political Situations

Both private and public organizations frequently engage in activities that they deem essential for their survival but that are likely to provoke attacks from others. The news is peppered with stories about actions taken against organizations by activist groups, the general public, the government, competitors and even the organization's own employees.

When a firm or an agency is under fire of this sort, this is a *political problem*. The company needs to shield or buffer itself from the adverse or unpleasant efforts of its opponents. In such situations the organization often retains the services of a consultant to become the fall guy, to *take the rap*. Obviously, this type of consulting calls for a very thick skin.

Perhaps the nature of this work is best demonstrated with a case example. The office of education in a major metropolitan county was supposed to start a regional high school and post-high school vocational training program. The office's management decided that such a program would be financially advantageous for the county as well as educationally desirable for students.

But the plan met some opposition. Most of the dozens of operating school districts in the county felt that the county office of education should not operate school programs, especially in competition with them. Moreover, the state, which paid out a sizable dollar amount for every hour of student instruction, feared that the anticipated program was large enough to bankrupt it. The issue became very hot politically. With all this opposition, the county office was expected to drop the program since it had deferred to local pressure in the past. But this time the county office decided to press for its planned program, despite the possible loss of voter support.

Rather than take the brunt of possible negative publicity and face the anger of the local school districts, the county office decided to retain a consultant. As *Project Director* of a feasibility study, the consultant was highly visible and the target of much acrimonious criticism. The county office hid behind its *hired gun*, smiling benignly and protesting its innocence.

The county office did not have to place itself in opposition to local school districts or to the state board of education. It buffered itself so that it could redirect any attack on the program or its feasibility toward the consultant. If the feasibility study had gone against the program, the consultant could have made a very convenient scapegoat. Fortunately for the consultant, the regional occupational program was found to be feasible in every way—educationally, politically and economically. With the approval of the state board of education, the program became a reality. In fact, it is operating now.

In the case of a political problem, consulting work is always booby trapped with the possibility of an ethical or moral dilemma. From the outset of the vocational program case, the unspoken dictum was that the study prove the program to be feasible. The consultant was not really supposed to be concerned about what the data actually showed. In this case the study did show what the client wanted it to show. The consultant did not have to face the moral issue of having to tell the county office management that they were wrong about the program. But what would have happened if the study had indicated that the program was not feasible?

Sooner or later every consultant must face the problem of presenting clients with results that they do not want to hear. This is particularly true for political situations. As a consultant, what do you do? Do you hide behind your professional standards? Do you shade your results toward your client's desires? In most cases the answers are not simple, not clear-cut.

Perhaps the best protection against this type of moral dilemma is to obtain a clear understanding from the start with your client as to your ethical responsibilities. If circumstances seem to warrant bluntness, tell the client that your work must remain unbiased and that you cannot allow it to be influenced by any outside political factors. You would be advised to have the contract structured to ensure that you are compensated for your services, even if the results are not what the client wants. By keeping the understanding clear from the start, verbally and in writing, you can avoid the dilemma that sometimes crops up in the political situation.

The Hotfoot Situation

Occasionally, valuable and highly placed employees encounter particularly troublesome problems. As they struggle to get out of the trap, they merely become more entangled. Although such a person is otherwise a valued contributor to the firm, someone higher up in the organization wants to dump the employee with the problem. Perhaps the corporate officers are also looking for some cuts in division management, or maybe a parent company wants to replace the subsidiary company's leadership little by little. In effect, the employee's feet are put in the fire and held there until the situation changes or the employee quits.

Consultants are often contracted in situations like these to put out the fire or at least to save the victim. This kind of consulting is becoming more popular since employment is becoming more and more a person's principal economic asset. To the employee the job is what tools were to the tenant farmer. When the job and the employee's professional stature are threatened, steps have to be taken to ensure protection.

A case in point involved a company that had its regional headquarters in northern California and its national headquarters in New York. During a product development market test, the assistant branch manager in California was reporting to the corporate headquarters in New York. The three-year program was seriously in trouble. Running a year and a half behind schedule, it could not be regarded as working out well, even in the most optimistic opinion. A consultant was brought in, not by the New York office or the assistant branch manager, but by the branch manager in California. He knew that his assistant, while not performing adequately in the eyes of the New York office, was otherwise important to the operation of the branch. But New York was holding the poor man's feet to the fire.

The branch manager—aware that if the assistant failed on this particular job, there would be no opportunity for him to grow with the company—called in a consultant to help on the marketing study. The assistant branch manager's job was saved, though the product's fate was less certain. That much success was at least helpful to the assistant branch manager—and obviously useful to the consultant.

In another case a major bank in a California county went through an extensive personnel shake-up. The changes were so unusual for the banking industry that many observers wondered how the bank got away with them. Although the bank management made the decision internally, they knew they would be in for a scorching. Their solution was to have a consulting firm justify the decision, announce it and take the heat.

Obviously, you don't market this kind of consulting work as such. No organization runs an ad saying: *The division manager is in big trouble at XYZ Co. Consultants, please apply at side door.* In the course of marketing your services as a managerial or technical consultant, communicate to prospective clients your availability for other assignments. You might express that you have the sensitivity, discretion and judgment to successfully negotiate in difficult circumstances.

In the course of your consulting activities, be alert to the following circumstances that might lead to consulting work of this nature:

- People in high enough positions in an organization can bring in their own consultants when they get into trouble.

- Supervisors sometimes retain consultants to help their subordinates. In this way the subordinates cannot blame their poor performance on their superior's lack of ability in delegating tasks. Consultants act as third-party arbitrators in such situations.

- In a few rare instances, subordinates get together to retain a consultant for their superior.

- Consultants most commonly enter into hotfoot contracts laterally at the request of a peer to the person in trouble. For example, the manager of Division X will retain a consultant on behalf of the manager of Division Y.

The hotfoot situation calls for sensitivity and tact. You need a real understanding of the realities of corporate politics and management strategies to pull this one off. Besides earning your fee, you have the satisfaction of knowing that you have kept a good employee working for a company and may have saved the employee's career.

Training

Previously, I pointed out that some companies have consultants train employees as part of their contract, eliminating the need for having to recontract for the same services periodically. Some consultants use this need as the main source of their practice.

New legislation can create a training opportunity. For example, a western city recently experienced an outbreak of hepatitis due to the poor hygiene of restaurant employees. The city council passed a law requiring training for restaurant employees. Two consultants, recognizing that restaurants were not prepared to give such training, put together a program that met the city's requirements and was within the restaurants' budgets. For several months after the legislation went into effect, they were in high demand. There has also been a slower but consistent demand for their services after the original rush.

Training seminars are a special area that is constantly changing. They present excellent opportunities to the consultant who can put a good program together and market it.

Need for an Unbiased Opinion, Evaluation or Critique

Many executives realize that management has a tendency toward tunnel vision. The company creates a corporate culture that encourages every employee to look at problems and business in the same way. A consultant can bring in fresh, new perspectives and opinions.

There may be trouble on the horizon that company members don't see or are afraid to discuss. The consultant is under no compulsion to make the boss happy. Employees can confide in consultants and share concerns and perceptions that they usually hide—if the consultant can communicate a sense of reliability and confidentiality.

Companies often fail to see opportunities that a consultant can perceive as a result of wide experience in several different areas of free enterprise. Working with several different firms in one year can give a consultant special perspective and understanding of the directions that an industry is taking. This knowledge is worth money to executives who recognize its value.

These ten sources of consulting opportunity work because of the immediacy of need or benefits. Pressure in the form of cash shortage, legislation, deadlines or the hotfoot situation creates an awareness of need, even a sense of urgency. As a consultant you are in the position of being able to step in and save the day. As a temporary technical consultant or an expert with a special skill, you can generate income for a company. If you can make the advantages of retaining you as their consultant apparent, these opportunities will turn into employment and profits for you.

Opportunities with the Government

Because of the special conditions surrounding government contracts, consulting work with the federal government deserves its own section. The federal bureaucracy is vast and extremely complex, and it generates a multitude of consulting opportunities.

Measured in terms of the dollars it spends, the federal government is the free world's largest consumer. When its spending is combined with that of state and local governments, the total 1992 estimated budget of the U.S. government is $1,445.9 billion dollars, according to the Executive Office of the President and Office of Management and Budget. Even with cutbacks in spending, the government in Washington represents one of the largest markets in the world for consultants. As one area is cut back, another opens to create even more opportunities.

This market is especially suitable for temporary technical consulting. Because of bureaucratic timetables and delays, the contract recipient usually has to do a lot of work in a short period. As there is no time for normal employment procedures, the contractor needs effective assistance fast.

Most government contracts run for one year, even though they often involve work that requires 13 or 14 months to complete. In addition, the government bureaucracy being what it is, a contract might not be signed for two, three or more months after the start of the fiscal year. So contractors typically have only nine or ten months to do more than a year's worth of work.

In the past when government contracts were relatively predictable, the recipients of these contracts, aware of the time constraints, started work before the contract was signed and physically delivered. In the mid 1970s, however, the awarding of government contracts became less automatic. Funds could be impounded or the need for outside services eliminated by changes in legislation or administrative policy.

With these changes, contractors who traditionally hired personnel, paid salaries and incurred other expenses were occasionally notified that they had no contract. Left holding a bag of expenses and liabilities, they naturally became reluctant to pay high-level technical people to sit around waiting for a signed contract to come in the mail. Also, an increasingly budget-conscious government is unwilling to accept the additional high overhead that results from keeping a full-time staff waiting around for the next round of government largess.

By the time signed agreements are executed, contractors cannot afford to waste five to seven months finding and breaking in the necessary personnel. They need expert help right away—and those with larger contracts need a lot of it right away—hence the need for the temporary technical consultant.

Information on Government Contracts

Information on the contracts awarded in the public sector is plentiful and accessible. All government agencies are required to make public:

- The names of available contracts.
- The dollar amounts they involve.
- The nature of the contracted work.

The federal government publishes this information in a regular format that is readily available to the public. Also, you may request it from government procurement agencies on the state and local levels if it is not readily available.

Relevant information on federal contracts of significant size is listed in *The Commerce Business Daily*, the federal government's procurement or purchasing newspaper. Published every business day, it is available in all major libraries. You can also purchase a subscription from the Department of Commerce. This newspaper contains the contracts awarded by the federal government both to private firms and public agencies, naming the awarding agencies and the contract recipients. It also contains notices of the government's intent to contract, requests for proposals (RFPs) and requests for quotation (RFQs). You may or may not land a contract of your own with the information in this publication, but you can contact the contract recipients to advise them of your availability, capability and interest in working with them as a consultant. You should be able to find a great many opportunities, since you are likely to be precisely the kind of talent they need.

Government and Foundation Grants

Billions of dollars are given out every year in this country in the form of grants, the bulk of it by the federal government. Roughly 32 percent of your tax dollars are allocated in the form of grants to states and localities and to private and public agencies for national defense (1992 Estimated Budget of the U.S. government). In addition, many foundations give out money as grants. Where do you find those billions of dollars?

Sources of Information

There are two main sources of information on grants—one for government funding and the other for foundations.

Government-issued grants are listed in the *Catalog of Federal Domestic Assistance*, which is published and sold by the Government Printing Office (see the bibliography). This publication contains information on:

- Federal domestic aid programs that the government supports (the bulk of those programs release their funds through grants).
- The name of the funding program.
- The enabling legislation.
- The agency that administers the program.
- How much money it gave away last year, is giving this year and expects to give next year.
- The eligibility requirements.
- Examples of funded projects.
- The official to contact to apply for the grant.
- The criteria for selecting proposals.

This book, which can be ordered from a federal government bookstore, is a subscription service that is updated quarterly. It is also available in any federal depository library or in any library with a significant research collection.

In the private sector the *Foundation Directory* lists the largest foundations in this country (see the bibliography). This directory, published by the Foundation Center, is available in almost every library with a research collection, and it contains information on:

- The foundation officers and directors.
- Purpose and activities of the foundation.
- Types of support offered.
- How much they gave last year (total dollars and number of grants).
- Total assets.
- Application information.
- Number of staff members.

This book lists only the largest foundations. Other books, such as the *Directory of Research Grants* and the *Annual Register of Grant Support*, list some of the smaller foundations (see the bibliography). Interested readers should consult a major research library for additional information on government and foundation grants.

The Grant Process

As a consultant your role consists essentially of putting two parties together. One is the funding source, which is either the government agency or the foundation that has the money. The second is the fiscal agent, sometimes endearingly called *the money drop*. As an independent consultant you find the funding source, develop the grant application, bring the money into the fiscal agent organization and take a subcontract back to do the work.

Many fiscal agents—a public agency or a private nonprofit organization—receive grant funds on behalf of a private individual or a consultant, who then enters into a contract with the recipient agency. For example, suppose that you are a consultant in the health care field and want to provide training to paramedics within hospitals. First, you find a grant to provide the funds to do such training. Then you find a fiscal agent that can be authorized as a recipient, such as a private, nonprofit hospital. When the grant funds arrive, you and the hospital work out a contract by which you design and deliver the training. You get the work you want to do, at the fee you want. What does the hospital get out of the contract? Obviously, it gets the training—but it also gets more.

Typically, fiscal agents skim the top of the grant. They take 10 to 12 percent of the grant for *overhead expenses* or *grant administration expenses*. That percentage can represent a substantial figure if a major university or hospital is involved. If a large university can land, say, $10 million worth of grants, the university will receive a million dollars or more just for administration expenses. Writing grants entails great economies of scale, since a grant that is ten times as large as another rarely entails ten times as much work. Time is a key factor in obtaining grants. If the password is patience, then the countersign is perseverance. The federal government, for example, typically takes at least three months—often five to six months—to give you the money after you identify the available funds. The largest foundations—such as the Rockefeller or Ford—are even slower in most cases than the federal government. Smaller foundations respond more quickly, typically in three weeks to two months. Remember that the funds are available. You only need the time and patience to wait for them, assuming you have a viable use for the funds that meets the objectives and purposes of the granting organization.

Successful grantsmanship requires skill at proposal writing and political awareness. Ironically, proposal writing, which some often view as expensive and time-consuming, is not the most important factor in getting a grant. A good proposal is vital, of course, but not enough.

The actual writing of the proposal is only a nominal part of the grant process. Yet many grant writers spend a lot of time on their proposals, perhaps a great deal more than is warranted. The average amount of time spent by many review committees on a proposal is about 25 minutes. In less than half an hour, a decision is made on a piece of work that cost you three weeks of hard labor. Stacked in a pile of other proposals, your best effort becomes just one of many. About all the proposal team member might remember is that the proposal with the orange cover was a good one. So, although you have spent weeks dotting the *i's* and crossing the *t's*, the committee rarely, if ever, gets to that level of detail. The point is to learn how to make a proposal look good without spending an inordinate amount of time writing it.

Information in the Private Sector

Thousands of technical and business publications are produced every year in the United States. You will undoubtedly find dozens of them that pertain to your field of interest. As you follow the business news in your specialty, you should ask: What information in this article suggests a demand for my consulting services? You can unearth scores of opportunities just by keeping abreast of events in your field. As you see opportunities develop, contact firms that need your services, and let them know about you. You have every reason to expect signing a consulting contract.

Consortiums

There is a vast market of clients who need more information for decision making in an increasingly competitive economy but who do not have the dollars to spend on getting that information. The consortium research project enables you to serve this market. In consortium research the consultant combines the research and information requirements of several clients into one project. The fee for the project is then paid collectively by the clients served.

Suppose that all the hospitals in a given market area could save money or otherwise benefit by hiring persons who have not had formal education in a variety of health care support activities. Such positions might include X-ray technicians, autoclave technicians and medical records technicians. The hospitals' motive might be to save costs or to make up for a shortage of trained labor. A research project can be designed to find out whether high school graduates would be suitable for those positions. The project would determine whether limited on-the-job training and the use of instructions on hospital procedures would provide sufficient training for these people to fill the vacant positions. Let's say the study costs $75,000—more than any single hospital is able to pay. However, seven hospitals might find this a reasonable and prudent investment on a collective basis, each hospital contributing according to the number of its beds.

The opportunities for consortium research are common and frequent. Usually the consultant needs to identify a specific research activity that would be of interest to a group of clients. At times an opportunity presents itself when a client expresses a need for work but does not have the money to fund it. In such situations look around for potential co-sponsors.

A good consortium research idea has two main characteristics. First, the information to be researched should not touch upon the business strategy or the prop   ary interests of your clients. Not only are these areas confidential, but consortium research on them may be precluded by federal legislation. The second characteristic is that the ideas should contain the germ for an ongoing product or service. For example, a one-time report on consumer buying intentions might be rolled over into a quarterly update. The circulation of the service might even be expanded beyond the original sponsors. To safeguard the subscriber/sponsors' proprietary interests, you might publish generic data, keeping more specific information confidential.

One university-based, part-time consultant developed the proprietary idea of a city-wide bimonthly study of consumer buying and saving expectations. A sharp marketer, he signed up 35 mercantile, service and financial institutions (at monthly fees of from $800 to $1,400) within 17 months. These corporate clients received the bimonthly report and the opportunity to ask confidential and proprietary questions pertaining to their business planning.

Formal consortiums, formed for a specific, even one-time activity, might become the grant development arm for a number of organizations, such as small colleges. Small public and government agencies frequently lack the financial ability to hire grant development personnel. By acting on behalf of a group, you can apply the consortium research idea to grants.

Professional Associations

Your creativity in discovering consulting opportunities is the only limit you have in finding new markets. For example, starting and administering a professional association is not such a wild idea as you might think. The feasibility of the project is demonstrated by the following true story.

A successful administrator of a national professional association gave up his position to move to a new city because of an excellent career opportunity for his wife. After discovering that the positions in his new locale did not offer the income that he was used to earning, he struck upon the idea of organizing his own professional association.

For the market test he selected a field that was not represented by an association—students attending law schools in the greater New York area, including neighboring states. Out of 700 students solicited, 43 mailed in checks for the membership fee of $45 each, a healthy six percent return. With 11,000 such students in the target market, the assumption was that the capture rate would be nine percent on the first promotional round with a follow-up campaign. A total number of 990 memberships could be expected at $45, producing total revenue of some $44,550 per year. After the cost of operating the association was subtracted, the sum of $27,000 would be available for the director's salary.

The funds collected from the test were returned to the 43 student participants. Another group that could afford higher dues was selected for the actual market. After one year 1,301 members were each paying annual dues of $75 for total revenue of $97,575. The dollars available for director's salary and unrestricted reserves exceeded $70,000.

The professional association was operated as a not-for-profit organization, but others have been set up as profit-making companies. A professional association offers many other ways to obtain income: outside consulting by the director, rental of exhibitor space at the annual meeting, sale of the tape-recorded presentations at the annual meeting, library subscriptions to the journal or newsletter, charges for participation in the annual meeting, and so on. If you wish to represent the interests of a group in this society, no law says that the group must be formed prior to your taking an interest in it.

Tips

Imagination and the willingness to look at a situation from a new point of view are your best assets in uncovering new consulting opportunities. The next chapter will show you how to sort out the *profitable* opportunities so that you can use your talents to the fullest.

5

Turning Opportunities into Profits

Selecting the best consulting opportunities for yourself is a matter of intuition. However, you can take certain measures and use specific guidelines to make the most advantageous choices. If you're planning for long-term success, you are looking for the consulting opportunity that gives you the edge over most or all other consultants.

Process Orientation

As discussed in Chapter 1, consultants may be broadly divided into two groups—those who are process-oriented and those who are task-oriented. Process-oriented consultants take a skills approach toward the market. Based on their general skills and talents, they seek out opportunities for consulting in different types of organizations, situations and environments. They go anywhere that they believe their talents can be usefully applied. Task-oriented consultants see themselves more narrowly than process-oriented consultants, seeking out consulting opportunities in organizations similar to those where they have used their know-how in the past. If you are task-oriented in your approach, you are looking for the type of assignment you had before. You must wait for an opportunity that suits your abilities. That opportunity may arise often or only rarely. In any case the amount of work you get is too often beyond your active control.

Uncovering consulting opportunities requires broadening the range of your services. A process-oriented approach enables you to offer your consulting skill in many environments, not just one or a few. You can actively seek out and service markets that are less crowded and competitive. You can go to markets. You don't have to wait for the markets to come to you.

Another distinct advantage to being process-oriented lies in its diversity. When you are narrowly task-oriented, all of your potential clients tend to be more or less competitive with one another. A client may want to tie you up, withhold you from the market. This makes building a practice more difficult. A process-oriented consultant normally has clients from many different industries or markets. A client's desire to prevent the consultant from serving direct competitors has little or no effect if the practice is process-oriented.

Some consultants have reservations about being process-oriented. They feel they might be seen as *false prophets* and unmasked by potential clients. Perhaps you feel this way. You should not feel any qualms of conscience, as long as you observe two policies:

1. Truly understand what the client is buying from you, the consultant.

2. Represent yourself to prospective clients correctly and ethically.

What the Client Buys

Clients are not as concerned with the theoretical comprehensiveness of your skills as they are with your practical experience and your ability to get the job done and done well. You may have a string of degrees after your name, all notable accomplishments. But if you cannot satisfy the needs of your clients, you have not done what a consultant is supposed to do. The client is paying for results, not academic achievement. If, in a given field, you can accomplish what needs doing, you should not hesitate to hold yourself out as an authority.

Consultants suboptimize. They are concerned with practical results, not with an academically perfect or theoretically correct solution to a problem. The optimal solution may exist, but it almost always costs too much in terms of money or time to be practical. A business can go bankrupt trying to be perfect. Consultants work in the real world, which involves looking for the best solution that can be produced within the budgeted time and money. That solution is usually both suboptimal and satisfactory.

Ethical Representation

Just because you are bringing your talent into a new field, you should not feel hesitant about representing yourself as an authority. As a process-oriented consultant you are applying your particular expertise to new problem areas that often call for unfamiliar technology. Indeed, the application of technology or knowledge to a new situation is a strong and highly respected talent. Just as engineers applied the aerospace technology of the 1950s and 1960s to education and health care in the 1970s, industry needs consultants who can apply the current technology to problems and needs in the 1990s.

You may represent yourself as a problem solver or as someone who produces accomplishments. You are bringing two factors to bear on the client's need: a body of knowledge and your individual ability to apply that knowledge. The client has neither that knowledge nor that talent. As a result the knowledge you bring into the application is gratefully and usually uncritically received. You are rendering your clients a valuable service, and you have every right to call yourself an authority. Naturally, you must have or acquire enough knowledge to offer a genuinely helpful service to your clients.

The first step is matching your skills with an area of need that can benefit from them. Your knowledge and skill may come from many different sources—formal education, on-the-job training, practical experience, field research, interviews, self-study, and so on. As long as you have the necessary information to fulfill the client's need, any of those methods is perfectly acceptable.

Much of the knowledge you bring to a client is available from sources other than consultants—books, training programs, articles, etc. You may think: If an area is well-documented, the information is as available to my potential clients as it is to me. Why do they need *me*?

Sources of Need

Clients need you for two reasons. First, in practice people are too busy or too lazy to become self-sufficient. For example, a book on raising the level of giving in a church may be *available*, but not many church leaders are going to read it even if the topic is important to them.

To convince yourself of this fact, consider that there are over 350,000 churches, synagogues and temples in the United States, according to the *Yearbook of American and Canadian Churches*, 1991. A book on fundraising normally doesn't sell more than a few thousand copies. Even if a church leader happens to read the book, the leader may still value your services highly because you have the ability to apply it. Besides, the church leader usually hasn't the time or inclination to master the information and apply it. In addition, the client may be lacking the energy and discipline you have to tackle the problems at hand.

The second reason is an offshoot of the first. Having the information about a subject does not produce the ability to generate accomplishments or solve problems. Your talent is the ingredient that produces results. This talent, coupled with hard data, is the marketable service. Your clients want to buy your result-producing capability.

Educating the Client

An unrecognized need is the same as no need. Some consultant services are needed, demanded and understood even before consultants are available in the market to deliver such services. It is far easier to sell your services when the prospective client recognizes the need for them and values them. Such is the case for a consultant who knows how to raise venture capital. Other services that a consultant might provide have no such built-in ready demand.

For these services it is not obvious to the potential client that a need exists or that the client would benefit from the consultant's efforts. In such cases it is necessary to educate the client about the desirability of the service.

Educating the market, an activity usually indulged in by only large firms, costs time and money. IBM created a huge market for itself by educating its markets during the early years of the computer industry. A large firm can afford to make that sort of expenditure. As a small business you may not be able to. In fact, you could go broke trying to convince clients of their needs. If your clients don't see why they need you, you can get shuffled from one unaware decision maker to another and never close a business deal. Or you can *advertise* your services all over town, and the response might not cover the cost of the *advertising*.

The small consulting practice faces pitfalls in trying to educate clients. Uneducated clients can drain your time and money, causing you to spend your resources inefficiently and create a market for other consultants. Once you awaken prospects to the need for your consulting assistance, you've created a market for any consultant who can win over the prospects. Even if you do convince potential clients of their needs, you still run the risk of losing some or all of your opportunity to other consultants who decide to cash in on your efforts. By that time you might not have any budget left to survive the ensuing competition for the actual contracts.

Some consultants have succeeded in creating a market by educating clients. This strategy works when the consultant is offering services based on unique talents —talents that cannot be copied by competing consultants—or when the consultant does a good job of protecting the turf. If you have a promising approach to a problem that requires the investment in client education, be sure you can put a working *copyright* on your ideas to keep others from poaching on your territory.

On the other hand, when a group of potential clients is already aware of their need, you can devote your time and money to persuading them to choose you over others.

If your clients have been suddenly awakened to their needs by a dramatic, newsworthy event, much of the education process is done by the media. In effect, other people will spend their money to create your market. For example, around the time that the United States Supreme Court freed lawyers from bar association restrictions on advertising, the lawyers' trade journals wrote about legal advertising in almost every issue. The press invariably tends to devote the greatest attention to simple, dramatic events, which in this case was the Supreme Court decision. The professional publications made the topic more than important; they made it hot!

Given an event like this, you can use the media not only to promote your specialty but also to make the market aware of *you*. If you announce your specialty just as media interest is rising, the media will give you enough coverage to build a reputation for free. You don't have to spend a cent or talk to one prospect. Of course, you have to spend some money on promotion, but the money will be well spent. In addition, you can take advantage of the Low-Cost/No-Cost methods for self-marketing discussed in Chapter 6.

Despite the fact that some consultants know full well that having an informed, interested client makes their marketing task much easier, they are intrigued by the challenge of creating demand or building a market where none exists.

You must care about the efficiency of your promotion. How much response do you get for each dollar or hour you spend building your consulting practice? If your promotion is aimed at a narrow group with highly focused interests, it is usually more efficient than one aimed at a larger group. By using subsets of mailing lists and even small advertisements in specialized publications, you can get a much better return on the dollar than with a larger promotion. When you have a narrow focus, you will find it easier to get profitable speaking engagements at gatherings of your potential clients. The same rule holds true for articles you write for the publications read by your potential clients.

As an independent entrepreneurial consultant, you have an advantage over large consulting firms by entering new markets. You can establish your authority within months of the developments that make clients aware of the need for your type of consulting. Six months after the Supreme Court decision that opened up advertising to lawyers, one consultant had absorbed all the printed material available on the subject of marketing professional services and was consulting with lawyers on the marketing of their services. A larger organization would never have acted this fast. Typically, a large firm must have major new ventures approved at several levels of decision making, and all the decision makers seek to protect themselves from later recrimination if the venture goes bad. A large organization normally takes twice as long to *decide* to enter a new market as it takes you to actually *enter* it.

When you are beginning to work with a market that has been suddenly and dramatically educated, you are often giving advice in an atmosphere of controversy. You can actually turn your small size and previous lack of connection with your potential client group into evidence of your credibility. In effect you are saying to the client: This is my only business; I have no other interests to serve here outside of giving you the benefit of this field of knowledge. No larger organization can possibly make this claim, and even solo consultants who have had previous contacts with the client group cannot claim the extreme degree of specialization and credibility that you can.

You can cultivate the image of a lone, pioneering researcher in an uncharted area, seeking the best advice for your client group. This approach, with its public-spirited tone, improves the power of your promotion, enabling you to get information from live sources more easily.

Identifying Opportunities in a Newly Educated Market

Opportunities in a newly educated market are generally found through publications in both the private and public sectors. A wealth of information is available at low cost or no cost about changes in many areas. In just a few hours of reading a week, you can generally be well-informed and specifically knowledgeable about the events that affect your potential clients. Figure 5.1 contains a sample of the opportunities culled from reading a few months' worth of *The Wall Street Journal, Business Week* and the *Harvard Business Review*. A description of the group that could benefit from consulting is listed in the left-hand column, with the affected fields of consulting specialization listed in the right-hand column. As you see from Figure 5.1, you may discover several promising opportunities for every hour you spend

Figure 5.1   Some Opportunities in Newly Educated Markets

Issue That Creates the Opportunity	*Group That Is Affected*
Blocking cuts in federal spending	Lobbyists
Cash flow problems resulting from economic downturn	Small businesses
Increasing burden of government paper-work requirements	Small businesses
Dissatisfaction with schools leading to home teaching of children	Parents
Changes in bankruptcy law and need for creditor relations and financial planning	Candidates for personal bankruptcy
Membership drive creating need for fundraising and organizational motivation	Unions
Need to increase motivation and morale of sales staffs	Companies having problems with sales
Job stress related to air traffic control	Air traffic controllers
Problems with productivity of high-level employees and professionals	Organizations having upper upper level productivity problems
Need for grants to provide computer-based aids for the handicapped	Firms providing such
Lawsuits related to personnel files	Firms needing better security
Need for help in gaining consent from executive families for relocation	Large businesses with several major offices
Federal tight credit policy creating need for cash management	Small firms
Firms paying more attention to their quarterly reports and needing help with graphics, print production and public relations	Companies concerned with public image and financial community
Interest in buying condominiums for office space	Professionals and small businesses

Figure 5.1   Some Opportunities in Newly Educated Markets (Continued)

Issue That Creates the Opportunity	*Group That Is Affected*
Corporations seeking to dispose of surplus real estate	Real estate brokers
"Nonpromotable" managers needing career counseling and training	Various organizations
Mergers and buy-outs creating need for legal advice and intercorporate gamesmanship	Corporations vulnerable to take over
Recruitment of managers to firms that seem to offer limited advancement opportunities	Family-owned businesses
Need for organizational development consulting in firms with a predominance of mainly members at the top	Family-owned businesses
Estate planning to pass control of businesses on to family	Founders of businesses
Security and protection against Mafia influence	Businesses at risk
Need to increase meeting productivity	Managers
Need for understanding Japanese culture and business practices (or other countries where American companies are doing business)	Firms doing business in Japan
Desire to involve workers in management functions to increase productivity	Factories and companies wanting to improve worker morale
Need for international geographical, political and economic knowledge	Companies interested in locating abroad
Finding defective products and dealing with customers and public relations	Companies needing to recall products
Need for computerized cost control	Business that have recently become big enough to benefit

Figure 5.1   Some Opportunities in Newly Educated Markets (Continued)

Issue That Creates the Opportunity	*Group That Is Affected*
Shift from outside data processing and purchasing	Companies desiring to save money on that share of their budget
Health care cost control	Companies confronted with rapidly increasing health benefit costs
Dealing with journalists	Executives facing hostile media
Employment counseling for retired people forced by inflation to look for work	Government and private agencies
Defending or improving children's TV programs	Corporations sponsoring children's TV programs
Need for general institutional management skills for hospitals which are failing due to lack of management sophistication	Hospital managers
Loans for energy management and development of alternative sources of energy	Banks

reading current business and professional publications. Your problem is having too many opportunities from which to choose.

Generally, there is a time lag between the dramatic appearance of new conditions and an awareness by potential clients that the changes apply to them and that they need your services. This is true even if the need existed before events underlined its existence. You can use this lead time to learn the information and develop the skills you need. For example, lawyers needed marketing advice long before they were widely aware of this need. The few who took marketing seriously enough to seek expert advice benefited handsomely. The importance of the Supreme Court decision is not that it created a *need* among lawyers for marketing advice but that it created an *awareness* of the need for marketing advice.

More than three years after the decision, fewer than five percent of all lawyers actually used advertising. Remember this example to avoid choosing a consulting specialty that you value but that your potential clients have yet to appreciate. Look instead for events and/or media coverage that focus the attention of potential clients on their need for a certain kind of service. In other words, look for the development of a new solution for a problem that may have been long-standing among a class of potential clients.

Because of the lead time involved, you do not have to be able to deliver the needed services now. You do, however, have to be able to combine your problem-solving and results-producing abilities with the relevant area of technology. The only requirement is that you can quickly master the solution, given your problem-solving abilities.

Danger Signals

Even when an opportunity meets all your requirements, you may have to walk away from a client if you detect one or more danger signals. These signals, listed below, indicate that for one reason or another, the opportunity is not turning out as expected:

1. The presence of meaningful direct competition.
2. Doubts about the potential client's ability to pay for your services.
3. Doubts about the potential client's awareness of the need for your specialization area.
4. Doubts about the value of your consulting to potential clients.
5. The unsuitability of your talents or temperament to the client.
6. Inefficient promotional channels.

There is another side to these danger signals. If a potential opportunity passes all of these tests, you have a good chance to develop a new market for your consulting talents. If there is no direct meaningful competition and potential clients are able to pay for your services, if they are aware of the need for them and see them as valuable, and if they get along with you well and are easy to reach, how can you lose?

Meaningful Direct Competition

To be *direct*, your competitors must not only be doing what you're going to do; they also must be planning to do more of it. Most consultants who look like possible competitors have better things to do than expand into the narrowly specialized area that you have selected. Their current involvement, if any, in the specialty you are considering is not part of an overall plan, but incidental to their main business. So your investigation of the competition must be done in two stages:

Stage 1: *Make a list* of all your possible competitors. Sources for competitors are:

- *Trade publications* directed to your prospective client group   You will find possible competitors among the advertisers and authors of the articles in these publications. Look especially for those who are listed as sources of advice or of support services that are especially designed for your potential client group.

- *Consultants and Consulting Organizations Directory, Directory of Management Consultants, Dun's Consultant Directory*   See the Consulting Directories and Reference Works section of the bibliography for details on these and other references.

- *Yellow Pages of Telephone Books*   Check under the appropriate listings: management/business consultants, training consultants, etc.
- *Newsletters in Print, Oxbridge Directory of Newsletters* and *Encyclopedia of Association Periodicals* (see the bibliography)   These references list newsletters and other publications for your potential clients. Their publishers and editors may be possible competitors themselves. If they are not, they would certainly know who the competitors are!

Stage 2: *Determine how involved* these competitors are in the field you are considering. Also ascertain their plans for involvement. This research entails telephone interviews with your possible competitors, those who know about them, your potential clients and newsletter editors in the field. If potential competitors are reluctant to talk with you about their activities or plans in the area of your specialty, they may see you as competition. Perhaps they are interested in expanding into the specialty you are discussing. (And perhaps they are not making any plans, especially if they are unresponsive on all the topics you bring up.)

If you find a direct competitor and the opportunity is otherwise a very attractive one, you must compare the significance of the competition to the size of the market. Maybe the market is big enough or complex enough to support both of you, or there may be different subspecialties for each of you to concentrate on. Limited competition may be healthy, particularly if you can identify certain weaknesses in the competition. Another alternative is to join forces with the competitor! After all, if joining forces to dominate a market were not often more advantageous for the parties than competing, the antitrust laws would be unnecessary.

Client's Ability To Pay

Regrettably, some clients in an otherwise viable market simply cannot pay for consulting services. Consider the client group consisting of recent college graduates looking for jobs. They constitute an ideal client group in almost all respects. They know they need advice on marketing themselves to American industry. A large and easily accessible literature covers the kind of knowledge they need. The consulting you provide would unquestionably be very useful. And you have a highly efficient promotional channel for your consulting—the help-wanted pages of the newspaper. But they don't have the money to pay for one-to-one consulting.

Client's Lack of Awareness of Need

This signal is as deadly as the client's inability to pay, but the death is slower and more painful. A good example is the reaction of prospering physicians in highly specialized fields to the offer of marketing advice. Because they have plenty of patients, they don't think seriously about marketing. Physicians generally recognize their need for outside help in managing their practices. In fact, having management consultants is considered fashionable in some circles, and some marketing advice occasionally slips in through the back door with these consultants.

Yet some physicians close that door to marketing consultants. They neglect to plan for dangers to their prosperity, such as socialized medicine, malpractice claim increases, DRGs or more competition from specialists practicing in their field. They don't feel the need to fine-tune their images to get exactly the kind of patients they want. By long tradition, they are reluctant to consider self-marketing, and no small consultant can afford to overcome such an obstacle. As the competition continues to increase, however, more physicians will consider marketing, just as many dentists have.

Value of Your Services

Sometimes your solution turns out to be exotic and untried. It may be the type of answer that could be recognized nationally if it is successful—or that could make a tombstone out of your letterhead if it is not right. Perhaps your answer for low productivity and morale is to have workers' pay levels voted on by fellow workers. The effect of this innovation could mean quantum leaps in productivity and profitability or one small leap into bankruptcy. The chance of success is very slim, too slim to justify betting your client's interests and your own survival. Instead of an exotic, untried approach, you might consider a more orthodox solution or even withdrawing from the area.

The rationale for greater orthodoxy is simple. Without word-of-mouth momentum, not even the most sophisticated promotional campaign can help you grow as a consultant. Betting on the momentum of a highly experimental solution entails more risk than you need to take. Conversely, with so many opportunities available, a prudent withdrawal from an exotic approach does not mean a loss of business. If you happen upon some unusual, innovative service that becomes widely and highly valued, that is fine. Not only are you likely to have a built-in *patent* on your ideas, but someone will probably write a book about you. The chances for this kind of success, however, are slim and probably not worth the risk.

Unsuitability of Your Talents or Temperament to Clients

With the abundance of consulting opportunities, there is no reason to deal with people you don't like. Sometimes the personality of the client group makes it almost impossible for some consultants to work with them. Some consultants are freewheeling, and others are controlled and careful. Different client groups are comfortable with different styles of consulting. Accountants, for instance, want to work with no-nonsense, detail-oriented people. Higher levels of management are usually not interested in discussing the details of new discoveries in engineering or science. They are more comfortable with generalists. It is difficult for physicians to take advice from anyone except another physician, especially in matters even remotely related to the way they practice medicine.

Yet some consultants tend to give their so-called unsuitability so much importance that they often pass up excellent consulting opportunities. Perhaps they mistakenly think that they don't have the proper abilities. Or maybe they don't have the courage to present themselves to a class of consulting clients with whom they are not socially comfortable.

Don't overrate this danger signal. You have only to take two precautions when you sense this danger signal. First, be certain that you don't pass up an opportunity because it calls for a talent you forgot you had. Some of your most powerful talents may be *invisible* to you. Second, don't pass up an opportunity merely because you doubt your own authoritativeness in dealing with a potential client group. If the clients are truly aware of the need for your consulting and if you are certain of its value to them, your fear is groundless.

The real factor to look for is the extent to which your potential clients don't like you— or you don't like them.

Inefficient Promotional Channels

A client group may have all the other earmarks of a splendid market. Yet if you can't reach it, you have no real opportunity at all. In this age of seemingly endless market segmentation and specialized mailing lists, you are not likely to find any market group inaccessible. If gaining access to a group and communicating with it is difficult, you might find a quick and efficient alternative promotional method. If you cannot, you might be better off foregoing the opportunity.

Effective marketers, including successful consultants, select a reachable market and then package their services to be both attractive and desirable to the market. A reachable market is one that can be promoted cost effectively and efficiently. Dentists, for example, are easily identifiable, limited in number and inexpensive to reach. They represent a reachable market. Contrast that market with people interested in improving the interface between worker-machine systems in the work environment. They are all over the place, but they are hard and expensive to identify and reach.

Concentrating on a particular market can create tremendous opportunities. One marketing consultant had an unusual start in the consulting business. At 29 years of age, he left a company where he had served successfully for four years as sales manager and later as vice president of marketing. He had studied marketing, lived marketing, thought marketing and practiced marketing. And he was smart enough to realize that the world could survive without another marketing consultant. He systematically reviewed five industries in which he had an interest. He noticed that for one of these industries, there seemed to be no *marketing authority*. Granted, it was a new and young field but one filled with opportunity.

This consultant established a goal for himself—to be the nationally recognized authority in this industry within three years. He was successful! He writes a regular monthly marketing advice column in the industry's leading trade magazine. He speaks at the national and three regional industry conventions. He charges $1,500 a day for his services and at this writing has a backlog of 87 days of consulting services to be delivered. He is quoted, interviewed and sought after on a regular basis by the powers that be.

How did he achieve this? By systematically applying the proven principles of marketing strategy and theory to a specific situation and market. True, he is a generalist—but one who is smart enough to promote himself as a specialist!

Saying No to Bad Business

If any of these danger signals appear, you may have to turn away a client. Since you have hung out your shingle and are in business, a flat turndown is not good promotion. It is almost insulting. There are several better ways to say no. You can adopt one or more that suit you.

One is to say, "I would love to work with you, but I don't offer that particular service." Then give a referral, making sure that the referred person can handle the project. A bad referral is almost as bad for you as a mishandled project. When you do not have a sure referral, offer the client several names, and state that you are not certain of their abilities. That response throws the obligation of the evaluation onto the client.

Saying you are too busy can create a false impression about your fee. When you are too busy, clients and some consultants may infer that you will soon raise your fees. If you are truly too busy but would like to do some work for the client later, you may not get the chance. Word may get out to other clients that your fees are high and that you are too busy. That impression, however false, hurts your chances not only with the one client but with others as well.

If you *are* too busy, be sure that any attempted refusal will work. Don't use a refusal technique that might corner you into taking on more work—no matter how high the fee is. The following techniques are designed either to avoid taking on a project or to get the work on your own terms:

Redefine the problem, and accept the job on your own terms. For example, a county office of education was hoping to start the third year of a federal grant to do a curriculum development program, and it needed an external evaluation, as federal programs often do. The project was about a year behind schedule, and the county office was concerned about getting the funds for the third year. An outside consultant who was offered $3,000 to do an evaluation contract decided that too much had to be done for the money and that the evaluation was too late to do any good anyway.

Instead of directly refusing, the consultant decided that a pilot study contract would be more appropriate. The consultant asked a series of questions that were calculated to embarrass the office director: What are you going to do about sample size? What are you going to do about the lack of a control group? These questions were deliberately designed to surpass the director's ability to answer. If he wanted to be hired for an evaluation, the consultant would never have asked such questions. In fact, he knowingly killed his chances of being hired for that contract.

Finally, the director asked the consultant what he would do. The consultant answered the director's question and then was asked if he would be willing to take a contract to do this pilot study if someone else did the evaluation. The consultant received a $23,000 contract to do the field study, and the director hired someone else to do the evaluation report. The consultant had redefined the problem on his own terms.

This consultant understood that the client did not know a great deal about the problem at hand. Such is usually the case. Look at it this way. When clients don't know a great deal about their problems, they are likely to feel all the more compelled to maintain control. They must let the consultant know that they are not going to be hoodwinked. In actuality clients typically formulate their strategy for two minutes on the elevator following lunch, just before they meet with you. In such a case the first thing that clients have to do is impress you with how much thought they have given the problem. Some consultants are intimidated by this strategy and fail to propose alternative solutions.

When face-to-face with clients, just tell them, in some way, that they will have control. All you have to do in most cases is say: I hear you. . . I understand you. . . I know you want control. Then propose your alternative solution. As long as you have properly communicated your understanding of the clients' need for control, they are usually willing to accept another solution. Without saying so they think that you are an expert—and they haven't given the problem more than two minutes of thought anyway. They have no confidence in their own approach. They just want to avoid being taken advantage of.

High-bid the project. This strategy is not suitable to pedestrian consulting assignments because you come off looking just plain expensive. The project should involve a technical element or a judgmental area. You have to render a conclusion on how the job is to be done or on the quality of the job. In such instances you can high-bid the work in order to turn it down. The desirable feature of this approach is that you can't lose. If you go high and the client still wants you, the high fee is a sweet consolation for having to take on the work.

Misdefine the problem. Again, this approach works only in technical areas. If you misdefine a routine problem, you look dumb. When you misdefine a technical problem, however, the client figures you have a different approach, judgment or philosophy. In most technical fields people misdefine technical problems all the time. Frankly, no one knows whether you are right or wrong. Everyone has a different approach to a problem. Misdefining a technical problem, therefore, should not reflect unfavorably on your competence as a consultant, though you should exercise this strategy with discretion.

Accept only a portion of the project. Sometimes clients want to make their managerial duties easy by hiring one consultant to do everything. As the consultant you might take on the assignment if you are willing to hire other consultants, staff or resources. If you don't enjoy managing other consultants and staff, suggest taking a piece of the project. Suppose a client wants a marketing study that includes billboards, experimental designs and the supervision of field staff. You might offer to take just the experimental design part of the project. You really can't lose. If the client turns you away to avoid having another consultant to manage, you have said *no* to the business. If the client accepts your counterproposal, you have business on your own terms.

Conflicts of Interest

Conflicts of interest crop up in a number of ways. Suppose you are working full-time for a business organization, and one of its customers asks you to do some consulting. You are a natural for the work, but you might be taking business away from your employer. In such cases you have to assess the potential conflict and the attitude of the organization. Some are very rigid, almost paranoid, while others have relaxed policies.

Another potential source of conflicting interests may arise if you are working for two or more clients who are competitors. You have two ways to handle this situation. As long as there is no conflict of interest in your estimation, inform each client of your work for the other. Tell both that no information or advantage can leak from one account to the other. On the other hand, if you have a consulting opportunity that could grow into a conflict, your obligation is to turn down the new work. Inform your existing client that you have received an offer of work that you perceive as a conflict of interest. Usually, the client agrees. State that as long as you are working for the client, you will not take on work from the competitor. These steps are necessary both for the client's protection and for yours. The best protection for your reputation is honesty with all parties concerned.

When You Don't Have the Resources

Consultants sometimes have to pass up good opportunities because they don't have the resources to properly execute the assignment. Perhaps they don't have a high-powered enough computer, the staff or the necessary facilities. If a project is actually beyond your capabilities, you can hurt your reputation by taking it on and botching the job. Some projects are so big that they require a large team of consultants. If you can't manage or assemble such a team, perhaps you can recommend a leader and work as a team member. Other projects may call for skills you don't have. You can recommend another consultant who can handle the job, or you can work with one and use the skills you have.

In general don't let an opportunity go by for the lack of resources. Today, you can usually get any kind of business service on a short-term basis at very favorable rates.

A consultant was once offered a national marketing survey for a large company. Although the total fee was almost $4,000, she didn't have the capital to do what was required, which was the installation of an inward and outward WATS telephone service. The investment was $1,100 to $1,200. On the advice of an associate consultant, she found a company that was marketing an inward (800) WATS toll-free source. The firm offers WATS telephone service almost as a regular answering service. For $300 up front and some monthly guarantees, the consultant got the kind of phone service she needed and kept the job.

Don't give up consulting jobs because you lack the resources to do the job effectively. Go out and rent whatever you need!

Add-On Opportunities

Following the guidelines in this book you should have no trouble enlarging the size of your clientele. At the same time selling additional services to your existing clients is the kind of opportunity that you can handle more efficiently and that can produce greater profit than a new account.

With new accounts consultants spend a great deal of time establishing relationships instead of handling the problem that they were hired to solve. With an existing client you don't have to spend time on such preliminaries as familiarizing yourself with the client's operation, meeting the people affected by your proposals or marketing your services. You can spend more time dealing with the problems and justifiably receive more money for solving them.

While the add-on opportunity accompanies every account to one degree or another, some clients require add-on services more naturally than others:

- Some consulting has to be done on a continuous or periodic basis. For example, consultants in educational psychology to the sponsors of children's TV programs have an ongoing role.

- Some clients have a number of problems that call for modifications of the same solution. For instance, a changeover from the English to the metric system might have been so successful that the client will call upon the consultant to handle a change in accounting procedures, customer relations policies or other transitions.

- Sometimes a very large client organization has a widespread problem that manifests itself in piecemeal fashion, and the consultant might be called upon to apply the same solution repeatedly. If a consultant successfully teaches the middle managers of a headquarters corporation to hold more productive meetings, that consultant could then be contracted indefinitely to train the middle managers of all the corporation's branches.

Add-on opportunities are the bread and butter of a consulting practice. Add-ons do not require the expense involved in marketing yourself to new clients, and they will enhance your reputation as a problem solver. You will be seen as someone who can tackle a variety of problems, and that makes you a real asset to any company that retains you.

Tips

The opportunities in consulting presented in Chapters 4 and 5 offer a new perspective on how to identify and exploit a broad range of possibilities. Too many consultants look only at what they have done in the past as a guide to the future. They ignore the new possibilities and needs that arise every day, and the result may be that they never use their talents to the fullest. By identifying opportunities and testing them against the danger signals for viability, you can broaden your horizons in the business world almost overnight.

Once you have identified the opportunities that you want to take advantage of, you have to market yourself. The next chapter shows you how to set up an effective marketing strategy and sell yourself so that you can turn these opportunities into real income.

6

Low-Cost/No-Cost Marketing

In the consulting business, as in most others, the billings tend to rise or fall in direct relation to the energy, enthusiasm and creativity invested in marketing. Yet many consultants simply do not see the need for it. Why not?

Two attitudes toward developing a consulting practice prevent consultants from properly marketing their services. Some consultants rely on their reputations to attract clients. Others are fascinated with the technical side of consulting and simply don't care about marketing. These attitudes and inclinations, as natural as they may be, can nullify the benefits of all your other work. If you really want success, you must make marketing—active, aggressive, effective marketing—a part of your practice.

Consultants who rely on their reputations for selling assume that if they simply take care of their reputations, their reputations will take care of them. This rule-of-thumb is partially true. A poor reputation can undermine all your other efforts to grow. So a good reputation is the foundation for increasing business. However, it is only a foundation. It cannot yield the results that an active marketing plan produces.

A reputation does not take care of itself. You must take care of it as you would a plant. Waiting for your reputation to develop as a natural consequence of your consulting activities will shortchange you in a number of ways:

- Your reputation may become outdated, giving you a high rating on abilities that no one needs anymore.

- Your reputation spreads haphazardly, and it probably does not reach the prospective clients you want.

- Your reputation may become distorted through word of mouth. You may not be credited with the kind of expertise that best suits your marketing approach.

- The passive approach does not bring a new consultant those first crucial clients and keeps the established consultant from getting the most desirable contracts.

Marketing often takes a backseat to the technical aspects of a consultant's work. Challenged and energized by apparently insoluble technical problems, most practitioners are frustrated when confronted with basic marketing responsibilities. They tend to put off the marketing work because they are *too busy* at the moment or because they have *plenty of work already.*

To be a competent consultant, you must be technically proficient, but you don't necessarily have to be adept at marketing. To be a competent and *successful* consultant, however, you must learn to be effective at marketing. At the same time, your services cannot be marketed like Coca-Cola or IBM computers. You want to *sell without selling* so that prospects come to you instead of you chasing after them.

Figure 6.1   Marketing Strategies Used by Consultants

Marketing Strategy	All Consultants	Pretax Income Greater than $110,000	Pretax Income Less than $55,000
Cold personal calls	58.5%	14.4%	70.7%
Direct mailing of brochures/ sales letter to cold lists	70.6	20.8	71.3
Provision of no-charge diagnostic services to prequalified leads	42.7	19.8	58.1
Promotion to similar clients on basis of referrals or names obtained from clients	60.5	71.6	22.9
Lectures to civic, trade and professional audiences	17.8	40.1	9.6
Writing articles, books, news- letters for trade, professional, civic audiences	18.2	37.6	8.3

Source: *Economics of the Consulting, Training & Advisory Professions, Consulting Fees, Incomes, Operating Ratios, Marketing Strategies*, May 1991. Reprinted by permission of National Training Center.

Figure 6.2　Earnings Curves of Consultants

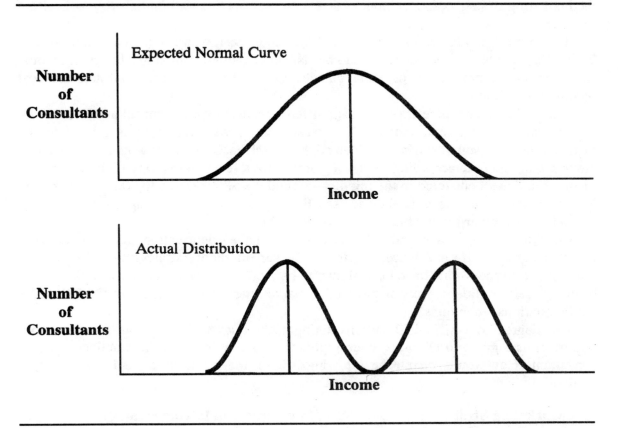

This chapter will help you meet the challenge of marketing. Fortunately, the most effective approaches to selling yourself are also the least expensive. We will see that the most successful consultants use these *Low-Cost/No-Cost Techniques*, which have an effective track record for building viable, profitable consulting practices.

Planning Your Marketing Approach

The marketing strategies that consultants use have a profound effect on their chances of success. As advocates of indirect marketing techniques for the consultant, we believe that the direct, hard-sell techniques that some consultants use are not as effective as indirect strategies, which are more like public relations activities. As an added bonus, these indirect, Low-Cost/No-Cost Techniques are much less expensive.

In a recent semiannual study of the economics of the consulting profession, consultants were asked several questions about the marketing strategies they use. The results were correlated with the consultants' income levels (see Figure 6.1). The data, which clearly demonstrate the value of different approaches to marketing, can serve as a guide to selecting the marketing strategies and techniques that are most effective for building your consulting practice.

This survey, conducted in February and March of 1991, was based on a sample size of 7,328. The data have been determined to be statistically significant at the .05 level. Income figures reflect net personal income after business expenses and before federal, state and local income taxes, if any.

You will note that there are significant differences in the kind of consultants' marketing techniques based on their income. The reason for these differences is related to the distribution of consultants' incomes. You might expect that consultants would be distributed along a normal curve according to their income, with a few making very high or very low incomes and most clustered in the middle—around the $30,000 to $40,000 income range. However, the actual curve is skewed (see Figure 6.2), with one group clustered below $30,000 and another group clustered above $40,000.

Consultants in the lower end of the scale seem to have a deprivation mentality. Lacking in self-image and self-confidence, they follow the very marketing strategies—cold calls and other indirect types—that have been shown to be ineffective. Successful consultants, who have high self-confidence, rely on productive marketing strategies—the Low Cost/No-Cost public relations techniques.

The degree to which different marketing techniques are successful is even more important as a guide to choosing your approach to marketing than the practices of other consultants. How would *you* rate the following different marketing strategies in terms of their productivity?

Marketing Strategy	**How Successful Is This Strategy?**		
	Very	*Somewhat*	*Not At All*
Cold personal calls			
Cold mailings			
Free diagnosis			
Cold phone calls			
Writing articles			
Giving free seminars			
Contact marketing			
Fee for diagnosis			
Giving seminars for fee			
Prior client reference			
Newsletter publishing			
Speaking engagements			

In fact, cold contacts and giveaways are the least successful techniques. Speaking, newsletter publishing and referrals are the most successful. These successful approaches, also the least expensive, and activities like writing articles and giving seminars are the Low-Cost/No-Cost Techniques. They are the indirect, public-relations type approaches to marketing that successful consultants use.

The Low-Cost/No-Cost Techniques

Most of us are familiar with traditional marketing methods: ads in *The Wall Street Journal* or in professional publications, direct mail campaigns, cold-call solicitations, joining the country club, and so on. Although a few consultants have achieved success with such methods, I don't recommend them as primary marketing techniques. A less traditional approach—the Low-Cost/No-Cost Techniques—more closely suits the nature of consultants.

Most consultants are technicians who find marketing challenges frustrating. They don't enjoy the process and don't do well at it. To be successful at anything, you have to enjoy it. The LC/NC Techniques help consultants enjoy marketing because they are more *technical* in nature.

Pursuing clients in the traditional way puts consultants in an unfavorable position. Ideally, consultants should have clients come to them. However, if they do make the initial contact with potential clients, they are in a far better position if the clients already know about the consultant, if they are *pre-sold*. The LC/NC Techniques help either way by causing clients to seek you out or by paving the way for your acceptance when you approach them.

These techniques are more technical than traditional marketing methods, yet they have profound impact on obtaining business. They bring the market to you and allow you to enjoy building a thriving practice. Here are the Low-Cost/No-Cost Techniques:

- Requesting assistance in research
- The rubber chicken circuit—becoming a speaker
- Public and professional meetings
- Directories
- Newsletters
- Magazine and journal articles
- Letters to the editor
- Teaching
- Working the press

Let's address these techniques one by one.

Requesting Assistance in Research

Since you are a consultant, the assumption is that you can bring a well-documented body of knowledge to the market of your choice. Remaining an effective consultant means staying current with developments in your field. You can turn this obligation into a three-step marketing tactic (see Figure 6.3):

1. List the important organizations and people in your field.

2. Write to each name on your list, asking to be kept abreast of any developments related to your field.

3. Publicize your research efforts, and market yourself and your abilities.

There are several sources for your list: news clippings about key people and organizations in your field, directories of associations, research organizations, publications and rented mailing lists.

Once you have assembled your mailing list, send a letter to each individual on your list. A letterhead with a prestigious, public service name will enhance your professional image. The most natural thing in the world is for recipients of your letter to keep you informed of their activities in this field, even at some trouble and expense.

On the other hand, those you interview are looking to get information from you too. They expect an exchange with someone who is in touch with the latest trends in your area. They may get more information from the interview than they give you. This is acceptable, since you want them to find out that you are competent and knowledgeable. Your aim is to establish yourself as an authority who offers the state of the art in your consulting specialization.

Your research efforts should be well publicized. When you make your knowledgeability generally known, you are self-marketing. Your purpose is to make yourself and your abilities known to as many influential people as possible. As people begin to associate your name with your specialty, prospective clients will start coming to you. You can achieve this result by using the other Low-Cost/No-Cost Techniques.

You can make your list of information sources do double-duty by pulling out the names of the most important sources—key company executives, trade association officers, trade publication editors, and the like. These key people tend to be the most influential names on your list. As such, they are also the busiest and least accessible.

If you contact these key people just to get general information or—worse—referrals, you are nothing to them but an unprofitable nuisance. On the contrary, if you approach them for their insights and thoughts for an upcoming article, book or lecture, you become someone who can enhance their prestige and nourish their reputations. You are a source of important information who may be an *authority* with valuable insights to offer.

Your contacts become unwittingly involved in your future success. Since you will be delivering their thoughts to the world, they will make sure that those thoughts are properly recorded and that they receive the appropriate attention.

No matter how famous or important your contacts already are, they are flattered that their thoughts are important enough to be sought out for publication. So they may even give you

Figure 6.3   Requesting Assistance in Research Form

Important Organizations and People	Address and Phone	Date Initial Contact Made (Notes on Contact)	Dates Information Received	Date Thank You Letter Call/Sent/Made

information that they might not dream of disclosing if they weren't allured by the platform that your book, article or speech offers.

Your key contacts may provide personal referrals to other important people, including potential clients. Their initial reluctance to talk with you is an attempt to avoid wasting time with unprofitable nuisances. Once you establish yourself and your specific platform for their views, they will do everything they can to help you—and themselves.

Two shrewd publishers recently launched a small textbook empire using these techniques. They had virtually no campus salespeople, and their competitors were giant publishing houses with scores of campus reps. In producing their first college textbook, they sought the advice of dozens of prominent educators. They produced an excellent textbook *and* involved educators in its success.

By the time the book appeared, the professors couldn't wait to get their hands on it. They talked about it with their colleagues, and they adopted it for their classes. It was, after all, partly their own creation! Within two years this text was the leading introductory text in the field—an incredible marketing coup.

The lesson is clear: When you involve influential people in your research efforts, they invariably become contacts. Whenever your contacts have the opportunity to recommend services of the type you sell, they are almost compelled to think of you favorably. They have a personal investment in your success.

The Rubber Chicken Circuit—Becoming a Speaker

Ours is an organized society. We group together on the basis of professions, business interests and community affairs. Thousands of professional, technical and civic organizations are in the United States. Hundreds meet every day. Every major hotel in this country rents its meeting rooms out each day to groups of professionals and business leaders for their weekly, monthly, quarterly or annual meetings.

Organizers of these meetings share two characteristics: They almost always serve chicken at these meetings, and they use a great many speakers.

One out of three consultants who make more than $75,000 actively seeks out writing and speaking engagements, but only one out of every 20 consultants who make less than $40,000 does so. When the others in the less than $40,000 range are asked why they resist such publicity, they usually reply that articles and speeches are burdensome responsibilities. They are missing out on some powerful ways to sharpen their edge in the marketplace. Long after people have forgotten exactly *what* you said or wrote, they recall that you *did* it. Their natural assumption is that you are an authority.

Writing and speaking opportunities are two of the most effective ways to attract consulting clients. Prospective clients are favorably impressed with a good performance, as are those who are in a position to refer business your way. Therefore, you should think twice before turning down these opportunities.

If you want to gain exposure to local business leaders and bankers, spend time talking before such organizations as the Chamber of Commerce or Lions Club. If you are interested in members of a particular profession, you can meet them at the appropriate professional and technical association meetings. Members who frequent these meetings are the most likely prospects for your services. They seek out the association and attend the meetings because they are looking for help, cooperation and insight.

Speaking before these prospects is time well spent. People who speak before a group are presumed to be authorities! As a result, you gain a lot of professional exposure and stature. You also should get a lot of consulting business.

If you have ever belonged to an organization or, worse yet, been a program chairperson, you know how difficult it is to find good speakers who can say something of value to the membership. The demand for speakers always seems to outstrip the readily available supply. Perhaps the reason is not so much the dearth of speakers as it is the abundance of organizations.

In addition to professional, trade, business and civic meetings, thousands of corporate and business training sessions are held each year. Being invited to present at a regional or national training session provides a golden opportunity to make contacts and get referrals. Speaking at a national meeting gives you the stamp of approval from the central office in the eyes of regional and local managers. Additionally, the company usually pays a fee for your work— sometimes a substantial one.

If you are not already in contact with organizations in your area that need speakers, look in *The Encyclopedia of Associations* or *The National Trade and Professional Associations of the United States and Canada* (see the bibliography). These directories list the addresses of each organization's national headquarters. A call or letter to headquarters gets you the names and addresses of those who head up the local chapters in your community. Simply contact these local leaders and let them know about your interest and availability.

Invariably you find ample opportunity to gain professional exposure before prospective clients. This exposure is enhanced if you are invited to speak at some of the many regional or national conventions, meetings or trade shows.

At the local level, many organizations are unwilling to pay for your services as a speaker. Don't limit your exposure to those organizations who are willing to pay you. If you want to use the lecture circuit to make money directly and immediately, other approaches would likely be more profitable. Also, when you are compensated for your efforts as a speaker, your tendency is to feel less free to market your services as a consultant.

When speaking before organizations, don't hide the fact that you are a consultant from your audience. Tell them what you do. Include descriptions of consulting situations with which you have been involved without disclosing confidential information. Let members of your audience see how they can benefit from your services as a consultant.

Hand out something of real interest that contains your name, address and phone number. The members of your audience may not need your services as a consultant today, and they may not need you for six months or a year. Anything that will help them remember you is to your benefit.

To be prepared at all times, create one or two talks about 20 to 25 minutes in length, keeping them ready for presentation whenever the opportunity arises. In selecting a topic, remember that broad, familiar subjects are more interesting to your listeners than a specific, time-sensitive, once-only kind of talk. Listeners almost always prefer to hear known information presented in a new fashion.

Public and Professional Meetings

You don't have to be the speaker at a meeting to create marketing opportunities—all you have to do is show up and circulate. If the meeting is in any way related to your area of interest, you can make your services known to others in attendance. Some of them might be looking for your kind of consulting right then and there. The best opportunities, however, come from your active and significant involvement in the power structure of the organization.

Public meetings sometimes present business opportunities. These meetings include any get-togethers by local agencies, such as the school board, the sewer district and the city council. Although you would probably be wasting your time by attending all of them, those that deal with issues and areas of interest to you are worth your attention. Even the relevant meetings don't require your attendance from beginning to end.

To make the best use of your time at these meetings, confine your attention to the people who represent business opportunities. *Professional citizens,* for instance, show up at public meetings simply to satisfy themselves that their government is doing a good job. They cannot be considered prospects. Entrepreneurs and small business owners, on the other hand, represent potentially rich opportunities. Don't make the common mistake of thinking that all consulting work comes from large corporations or big government agencies. Actually, a great deal of it is found with small business and entrepreneurs.

Professional organizations also provide the opportunity to make your services better known and to contact people who can benefit you professionally. As you work with other members, they come to recognize your skills and expertise. When they have a need for consulting services, you're a *natural* in their minds.

Membership in organizations is a low-cost but highly effective self-marketing technique. Yet it is worth little if you're not active. Merely joining and paying dues is not enough—you have to be a worker. Since you should plan on devoting time to the organizations of your choice, join only one or two. Then select the two most important, active committees, and become involved.

Membership in a professional association enabled one young training director in private industry to get his career started. Extremely introverted, he didn't come off well when he first met people, and he was having trouble convincing prospective employers of his worth. After bouncing around from one job to another, he considered leaving his hometown, Minneapolis, for a larger city where he felt that opportunities in his chosen field would be better. Instead, acting on the advice of a friend, he became active in the local chapter of the training professionals association, working on committees and participating in the association's affairs with a number of people. Potential employers got to know him and his skills. He overcame his introversion as he got to know these people and eventually landed a better job with one of the association members.

Which organizations are for you? Review such publications as *The Encyclopedia of Associations* (see the bibliography), and select organizations whose membership would likely include candidates for your services. Attend a few meetings, size up the group and make your selection.

Directories

Another Low-Cost/No-Cost marketing approach is to be listed as a consultant in one or more association directories. In about 40 percent of the cases, the listings are free. Roughly another 30 percent offer listings in the form of paid advertising spots about the size of a business card with a message about your service. Although the other 30 percent of the directories do not offer either paid or free listings for consultants, they might accept general advertising, and you should consider listing in these directories as well.

Most consulting professional associations publish directories or rosters of their members. Perhaps the best known and most comprehensive directory of consultants is published by Gale Research Inc., located in Detroit, Michigan. There is no charge for being listed in the directory, which is found in the collections of major public, academic and corporate libraries. Updated periodically and brought out as a new edition, the directory provides an excellent means of exposure for consultants (see the bibliography for more information).

Use *The Encyclopedia of Associations* or *The National Trade and Professional Associations of the United States and Canada* (see the bibliography) to identify the associations related to your market. Then simply inquire about the nature and availability of their directory listings.

Newsletters

More than 25,000 newsletters are published in this country. According to *Hudson's Subscription Newsletter Directory*, 10th Edition, more than 4,300 of these are business and professional newsletters. As instruments of communication, they channel a great deal of information to large numbers of people—often at a low cost to both the editor and the recipients. As business enterprises, some of them make a lot of money for their publishers.

More than half of the newsletters published in this country are given away free as extremely effective, high-level marketing devices. Consultants often give them away to potential clients, selling either single copies or subscriptions to others. Basically, they find a few hundred people who are good prospects and send them a free newsletter. With the newsletter they establish a medium for technical, professional dialogue about a variety of topics. As an added feature, the publication permits them to mention their consulting activities.

Most newsletters are done on a personal computer with a simple word-processing program and shipped out for a quick, limited printing run. The most important consideration is that the news be relevant and highly interesting to the readers. Usually, content bears more weight than appearance. See the sample newsletter in Figure 6.4.

Newsletters are superb marketing instruments that have worked for many consultants. If you feel that a newsletter is right for your consulting specialty, you want to select subjects for the newsletter that don't reveal your proprietary information. You can concentrate on

Figure 6.4   Sample Newsletter

The Professional Consultant

Issue # 1515

ISSN 0272-8559

Paul L. Franklin, Editor
National Training Center
123 NW Second Ave., Suite 405
Portland, OR 97209 USA
Telephone 503/224-8834
Facsimile 503/224-2104

The Professional Consultant newsletter serves as the official publication of the Academy of Professional Consultants & Advisors (APCA) and is included as a part of membership dues.

Issues of *The Professional Consultant* are distributed to members of the Association of Independent Consultants (AIC).

Subscriptions: $120 per year (12 issues) may be paid by Visa, MasterCard, American Express, Discover or check made payable to National Training Center. Air delivery beyond North America add $18. Single issues: Subscribers & APCA members $8, non-subscribers $12, Survey issue $29. Telephone and fax subscription orders accepted.

The Professional Consultant is available by fax. For information and pricing contact Faxitron, Inc. at 213/475-4901 or fax 213/475-1368.

Postage paid at Portland, Oregon. Postmaster: send address changes to: *The Professional Consultant*, Paul L. Franklin, 123 NW Second Avenue, Suite 405, Portland, OR 97209.

THE PROCESS COUNTS, TOO

I recently read synopses of two studies conducted on the consulting enterprise. The studies were of clients and their satisfaction with their consultants. The results of both were interesting and confirmed some beliefs I have long held.

In sum, both reports indicated that clients typically had less complaint about the end results consultants achieved than they did about the road their consultants traveled to get the results.

The complaints? First, many clients indicated that their consultants failed to create a relationship with them.

Second (and related to the first), they lamented that consultants did little to keep them abreast of their progress from the start-to-finish of an engagement.

Building relationships with clients and keeping them well-informed as a consulting project unfolds are to consulting what consistently high quality customer service has become to highly competitive sectors of the marketplace. That is, they are easy to talk about and what every conscientious consultant wants to attain with clients. But, too often the time does not get allocated to give clients the attention they deserve.

Creating and maintaining a relationship with clients is like fostering any other relationship: it takes commitment and time. So, too, does keeping clients informed. Both activities tend to compete with the consultant's yearning to "find more clients" and "bill more time".

This attitude is obviously shortsighted. The adage "your best customers are your current customers" applies to selling consulting services as much as it does to selling cars.

Write it off to marketing, if you must justify taking the extra time to build a real relationship with clients.

Write it into your contracts (i.e., progress reports), if you must have extra impetus to keep clients informed.

Remember, too, that it is almost always easier to sell your services to someone who has experienced your good work and likes you than it is to drum up new business.

Figure 6.4   Sample Newsletter (Continued)

The Professional Consultant

Paul L. Franklin, Editor • 123 NW Second Ave., Suite 405
Portland, OR 97209 • USA • Telephone 503/224-8834
© 1992, National Training Center and Howard L. Shenson

LET OTHERS TELL YOUR STORY

Prospects are more likely to be persuaded by hearing of the results you have produced for clients than they are by your description of your services. Citing your track record in solving problems that look like theirs is far more convincing than a laundry list of consultative services.

To exploit this tendency, you will want these three products in your marketing toolbox:

• Two or three good consulting success stories that demonstrate your capabilities;

• Testimonial paragraphs or letters; and,

• A current client list.

A good success story captures the essence of your work. Brief and to the point, the story emphasizes the **benefits** or **results** you produced for the client. Preferably, benefits are quantified, capturing the impact of your work to the client's bottom-line. Following results is how you achieved them, followed by the original problem your client was experiencing.

It has been said that great salespeople "do nothing but tell great stories". The same can be true in marketing consulting services if you have success stories to use in describing what you can do for prospects. Use the stories whether meeting with a client directly or writing a letter. In fact, use them at every opportunity.

Always ask satisfied clients to provide a testimonial letter that describes the benefits of your work to their organization. Ask that they focus on the bottom-line results produced as a result of your services and, secondly, how you helped achieve them.

If you know the client well, you may suggest that you prepare the draft of such a letter that they can then edit. Most clients prefer this approach since it simplifies the task for them, and they retain editorial control.

Use the developed testimonials in your capability statements, flyers, brochures and sales letters. Remember, prospects find more compelling others touting your services than they find you doing so.

Finally, a client list is a good way to demonstrate the breadth of your experience and the likelihood that you have a suitable "track record". Put the focus on company/organizational names not on individuals. Use the power of the computer to keep your list current.

A good format for the list is to use an attention grabbing headline, listing the clients below. It is worth noting that former clients are rarely contacted. Having the list will often, however, supplant the need for references. And, it reinforces your image as a savvy and seasoned consultant.

Incorporate your client list in brochures and/or capability statements. Always leave the list with a prospect when you meet with them. Few can avoid taking a look to see with whom you have consulted previously — even though they may ignore all the rest of the material you handed them.

Success stories, testimonials and a client list are excellent ways to let your past successes tell your story. Be sure to develop these powerful marketing tools.

2

Figure 6.4   Sample Newsletter (Continued)

The Professional Consultant

Paul L. Franklin, Editor • 123 NW Second Ave., Suite 405
Portland, OR 97209 • USA • Telephone 503/224-8834
© 1992, National Training Center and Howard L. Shenson

PROPOSAL WRITING CHECKLIST

Writing effective and winning proposals is part art and part science. As a result, it is not uncommon to have streaky success ... you win for awhile and lose for awhile. Writing proposals that consistently win is the obvious goal, however.

One way to attain consistency is to develop a checklist that covers all of the essentials you want in every proposal. Use the checklist as a final review tool of drafts, fine tuning parts that do not measure up.

Included below is such a checklist that we have used and has proven useful to other consultants, as well. To see how your proposals "measure up", pull out a copy of your last proposal, read it and score it.

Score each item 1 to 7, with 7 being high.

____ The proposal has a statement of assurances. It informs the client about what assurances/guarantees I make about the quality of my services and the result I will produce.

____ It reflects that I have obtained information about the problem(s) to be addressed from the client and/or the client's staff.

____ It demonstrates my thinking and analysis of client needs.

____ It contains both goals and objectives.

____ General goal statements reflect the overall purpose and direction the project (and my services) will lead the client.

____ The objectives communicate specific and precise results that will be achieved by retaining my services.

____ These goals and objectives are clearly the goals and objectives the client is expecting based upon our pre-proposal conversations.

____ I have put the focus on what I will do, not on how I will do it.

____ I have not given away services in advance of an agreement.

____ The plan outlined (scope of work) has the highest probability of meeting the project objectives within the time and financial constraints the client is expecting.

____ I have included the results, activities, and accomplishments that will not occur as a result of the project.

____ I have specified the client's responsibilities in helping to meet the objectives as clearly as I have my responsibilities.

____ I have demonstrated as graphically as possible how the processes and techniques to be utilized will produce the anticipated results. All steps in the work plan can be seen as essential to producing the results, not as "fluff".

____ There is a specific timeline or schedule which clearly communicates the sequence of events and the approximate times that these events will take place.

____ There is information on how the results can be evaluated or success otherwise measured.

____ There is a meaningful capabilities statement that identifies the strengths and resources that I bring, or my staff or subcontractors bring, to the project. These capabilities are related clearly to the needs/problems of the client and the results to be achieved.

____ The statement of capabilities is motivat-

3

Figure 6.4   Sample Newsletter (Continued)

| *The Professional Consultant* | Paul L. Franklin, Editor • 123 NW Second Ave., Suite 405
Portland, OR 97209 • USA • Telephone 503/224-8834
© 1992, National Training Center and Howard L. Shenson |

ing and involving and underscores my commitment to the results to be achieved (i.e., it is more than a resume, brochure or standard capability statement).

___ The statement of capabilities does not dwell on past events of little import to the project, such as my education, employment or professional appointments.

___ The costs of my services are fully disclosed, including expenses for which the client will be responsible and my expected schedule for payment.

___ I have taken care to provide all of the financial information the client requested in a format that she will understand and accept.

___ The tenor, language and financial information included in the proposal demonstrates to the client that cost estimations are in line with the financial information they have provided and with the results to be produced.

___ The proposal is attractive and interesting. Its format invites readership, and its language is direct, succinct and absent jargon.

___ The format allows the client to move around the proposal and to find information needed with ease.

___ The client is given a specific avenue to obtain additional information, if it is needed.

___ The proposal is written for a broader readership than the client contact, recognizing that others may read it and be involved in the decision making process.

TALLY YOUR SCORE. If your total is between 140 and 182, your proposal is probably fine. A lower score suggests a need to sharpen your proposals.

FIXED PRICE CONTRACTING TIPS

Research on the consulting enterprise relentlessly shows that those who use fixed price contracts make more money than those who charge on a daily or hourly rate basis. There are many reasons why fixed price contracts are more profitable. A big one is that quoting a fixed price puts the risk on the consultant and not the client. As a result, fixed price contracts are much easier to sell.

There are other marketing advantages to fixed price contracts, including:

• They allow you to focus on costs directly associated with achieving specific results. You do not need to sell those costs plus your daily or hourly rate (which may seem exorbitant to a prospect).

• They typically require you to be more precise in proposing, planning and budgeting, which is not only good business but helps to demonstrate your professionalism to clients.

• It makes decision making easier for the client. Either they think the results to be delivered for the cost are worth it or they do not.

Add the following three strategies to your use of fixed price contracts, and you will extend further their marketing advantage.

1. Don't round your cost figures. Leave (or make) the cost you quote something like $33,417 — not $33,400. Quoting an odd number rather than a rounded one tells the client that you worked with actual costs, not approximate ones. This subtly reinforces that you have planned carefully — and with a sharp pencil. Even if your actual cost estimate comes out in a round figure, say $10,500, quote an odd number, say $10,503. The dollar

4

Figure 6.4   Sample Newsletter (Continued)

The Professional Consultant   Paul L. Franklin, Editor • 123 NW Second Ave., Suite 405
Portland, OR 97209 • USA • Telephone 503/224-8834
© 1992, National Training Center and Howard L. Shenson

amount is insignificant, and you will buy credibility. Resist the tendency to round. Even if you round down the client is apt to suspect you did the reverse.

2. <u>Make the last number in your price quote be an odd number.</u> Not only don't round your quote, but make it end in an odd number, preferably 1, 3, 7, or 9. Research shows that people ask fewer questions about figures ending in these numbers than if ended in 0, 5 or an even number. Odd numbers are not easily divisible and less apt to be mulled for a relationship to some variable that may dilute the credibility of the overall figure. Again, you have subtly reinforced the credibility of your quoted figure.

3. <u>Don't negotiate the cost.</u> Negotiating a proposed fixed cost is the same as saying that your proposed figure has no direct relationship to the work to be performed. Rather than negotiate the price, negotiate the scope of work and provide a new cost based upon the reductions in the scope of work to which you and the client agree.

• • • • • • • • • • • • •

COMMUNICATIONS BRIEFINGS AVAILABLE FOR FREE DISTRIBUTION AT SEMINARS AND WORKSHOPS

Free copies of *Communication Briefings* are now available to training, seminar and workshop presenters who would like to distribute the newsletter to program participants.

Communication Briefings is an excellent monthly newsletter with more than 200,000 readers at a regular annual subscription rate of $69. Each eight-page issue is full of practical business information and ideas,

making it a useful handout for anyone presenting on marketing, public relations, management, advertising, human resources or business communications topics.

Copies for distribution can be shipped to your office or directly to a seminar location. For details, contact Ms. Cecca McClay, Seminar Services, *Communication Briefings*, 700 Black Horse Pike, Suite 110, Blackwood, NJ, 08012. Phone (609)232-6380.

• • • • • • • • • • • • •

THE MERITS OF PROGRESS REPORTS FOR CONSULTING

Hopefully, the article on page one of this issue convinced you to take added care in staying in touch with clients during consulting engagements. One strategy for staying in touch — and rendering a service — is providing the client with periodic, written progress reports during the course of an engagement.

Surprisingly, many consultants do not provide progress reports to clients. They write them off as too cumbersome or too time consuming, despite the fact that these reports reinforce that you are diligent, making progress and rendering high quality service. Progress (or interim) reports particularly help to set the client at ease when you do not have considerable personal contact with them during the course of a long project.

As the name implies, these reports chronicle progress in attaining the ultimate project goal(s). But, keeping the client informed is only one use. Other good — and appropriate — uses include:

• They can be used as <u>milestones</u> and written

5

Figure 6.4 Sample Newsletter (Continued)

The Professional Consultant Paul L. Franklin, Editor • 123 NW Second Ave., Suite 405
Portland, OR 97209 • USA • Telephone 503/224-8834
© 1992, National Training Center and Howard L. Shenson

into the contract as payment points. Clients are often more willing to pay out significant portions of a contract as it progresses if they get something tangible along the way.

• They can also be used to inform the client of project problems that are occurring and to suggest specific adjustments to the project timeline or scope of work.

• Pledging to provide progress reports gives you prescribed time frames for stopping, assessing project progress and adjusting the scope of work, as necessary. They provide a framework for planning and scheduling the work as you go. And, they help you avoid the all too easy trap of falling further and further behind when you do get "out of sync" with the negotiated timeline for completing the scope of work.

What to include in a Progress Report

Reports can be short, long or in between, depending upon their frequency and the complexity of the project. Usually they are submitted at the completion of a given project phase or at regularly prescribed intervals (e.g., monthly).

They generally should contain:

• The work completed to date;
• The benefits derived from the completed work;
• How what has occurred sets the framework for the next project phase(s);
• Any problems that have occurred and what was done about them (or needs to be done); and,
• Any recommendations to be made or decisions that need to be made to enhance the overall success of the project.

Reports should also document any decisions made-to-date that shape or alter the next phases of the project. And, they document any substantial deviations from the original scope of work, including the rationale for the departures.

Progress reports have benefits to both the client and the consultant.

Benefits to the client, include:

• They will appreciate being kept informed, particularly in long projects and/or when there is limited personal contact with the consultant;
• Reports give the client a sense of control over the project;
• The report can be shared with others, including superiors, providing the client with valued reporting information;
• Regular communication with clients tends to increase their investment in a project, acceptance of the consultant, gratitude for the work being performed; and,
• In the event of a dispute, reports provide written proof of what has been said and done.

Benefits to the consultant, include:

• Reports force you to discipline yourself during the course of a project;
• They require you to stop at prescribed junctures, assess progress and adjust if necessary and appropriate;
• They extend the impact you make during a project and enhance your image and reputation;
• They provide the same proof for you in the case of a dispute as they do for the client; and,
• They provide justifiable billing points.

For both the client and the consultant, there are many more positives than negatives when it comes to progress reports.

6

Figure 6.4   Sample Newsletter (Continued)

| *The Professional Consultant* | Paul L. Franklin, Editor • 123 NW Second Ave., Suite 405
Portland, OR 97209 • USA • Telephone 503/224-8834
© 1992, National Training Center and Howard L. Shenson |

PERILS OF PARTNERSHIPS

The idea of forging a partnership may sound like a good way to extend your consulting capability. Having someone to share the work and expenses is very appealing. Taking on a partner may also seem a good way to fight professional isolation, expand into new markets or simply re-energize your practice. Nonetheless, it is my belief that partnerships are not in the interest of the consultant about 95% of the time.

Partnerships are fraught with problems in their own right. There is the question of contingent liability. There are cumbersome decision protocols and resource allocation issues to work through that add to administrative overhead, and so on.

While maintaining a viable partnership can be difficult in any business, they are particularly troublesome in the consulting enterprise. This is because a bad or unhappy partnership destroys the assets of the consulting practice — a fate not common to many other businesses.

For example, if two people decided to go into partnership and open a retail computer store, the assets of the business are computers and peripheral equipment. The assets still have total value if the owners decide to dissolve their partnership.

Conversely, if two people decided to go into a consulting business and it does not work out, they have a serious problem because they are the assets of the business. Their ability to get along, work together and be synergistic is the real asset. If they do not get along or produce more together than they would individually, then the asset has little or no value.

BUT, there are ways to gain the benefits of a partnership without the potential liabilities. One good way is for consultants to associate — or ally — with one another. Increasingly, we are seeing consultants forging associations that have all of the advantages of partnerships (and often more) without any of the distractions. This kind of arrangement can take on many forms.

For example, it is increasingly common to see two or more consultants share offices, split rent and secretarial costs while maintaining their individual, independent businesses. Associating consultants are marketing each others services for a fee and sub-contracting back and forth among themselves. Yet, they retain the freedom to walk away and take the assets of their business with them if they do not like the way the game is being played.

The letterhead of a friend's law firm lists six names along the side. At the bottom, it is mentioned (in slightly larger type) that the firm is "an association" of independent professional corporations.

All the attorneys in this "firm" are in business for themselves. They share rent, the costs of secretarial support, a law library and a conference room. They refer clients back and forth, and they cover for each other during vacations or illness on a sub-contract basis.

Yet, they are all free to come and go as they want. They set their own income goals, business priorities and even type of law they practice. They stay together because there is mutual benefit not because of a binding partnership agreement. They are all clear that they each have the right.

Associations, alliances, affiliations—call them what you may — hold more promise for consultants than does a more conventional partnership arrangement. Before taking on a partner, seriously consider affiliating in a more informal way.

Figure 6.4 Sample Newsletter (Continued)

The Professional Consultant

Paul L. Franklin, Editor • 123 NW Second Ave., Suite 405
Portland, OR 97209 • USA • Telephone 503/224-8834
© 1992, National Training Center and Howard L. Shenson

MILLION DOLLAR CONSULTING

Million Dollar Consulting — The Professional's Guide To Growing A Practice is the title of an excellent new book written by Allen Weiss, CPC. The founder and president of Summit Consulting Group, Inc., Weiss shares his perspectives and insights gained from 20 years in practice.

Written in a useable "how-to-do-it" format, Weiss' book is brimming with checklists, guidelines and case studies. The book breaks down important elements to success, explains the "how tos" in detail and then provides useful examples to reinforce points. This alone makes the book worth having. But, there is much, much more.

I particularly like Weiss' orientation to the consulting enterprise. He asserts, rightly in my mind, that consulting is first and foremost a relationship business. He asserts that niching is the worst thing most consultants can do because doing so detracts from building relationships and puts the focus on the buying and selling of specialty services.

In relationship-based consulting, the buy decision is a collaborative one between client and consultant. The client trusts the relationship with the consultant sufficiently to bring problems forward and seek advice. The consultant honors the relationship sufficiently to tell the client what she can and cannot do for the client, including finding another resource person more suited to the task.

All in all, Weiss's work is a must have (and read) for consultants. Published by McGraw-Hill, the hardbound price is $24.95. You may order a copy with a credit card by calling McGraw-Hill at 1-800-722-4726.

You may also order directly through Weiss, and he has promised to personalize copies for those who mention that they are APCA members. Check, VISA, Mastercard or money order can be sent to Weiss (add $2.90 for shipping) in care of: Summit Consulting Group, Inc., Box 1009, East Greenwich, RI 02818.

Paul L. Franklin
123 NW Second Ave., Suite 405
Portland, OR 97209

First Class Mail
U.S. POSTAGE
PAID
Portland, OR
Permit No. 637

subareas in your field of specialization—judicial decisions, legislation, new products and services, book reviews, and so on. If you feel that a newsletter is a good marketing tool for you, the next question is: How do I get started?

If you plan to use the newsletter as a promotional vehicle, just send copies to all groups who are prospective clients. If you want to make a profit on the publication, you have to identify a group that needs information that is currently unavailable from any other source. Scout out the competition by checking publication listings and the *Newsletters in Print Directory* (see the bibliography). Get sample copies from publishers of newsletters and magazines in your area. Before starting a for-profit newsletter, make sure that the intended reader group is willing to pay for it and that they are easy to identify.

Since your newsletter will probably offer highly specialized information, your market will be narrow, allowing you to use articles on precise topics. If the material is too broad, it is not apt to hold your readers' interest. By concentrating on subjects such as new books, research results, patent news, judicial decisions and new legislation, you can provide information that is publicly available and yet not worth your readers' time to track down. You perform a service without giving away information that is a profitable part of your consulting practice. With this approach the topics and ideas will be easy to research and write.

Your newsletter should target those who are actually interested in its contents. Start with those who know you and are interested in what you have to say, then extend your readership by renting inexpensive mailing lists for a direct mail promotion. Consider obtaining prequalified leads from small space ads in publications.

The experience of some newsletter publishers suggests that the most effective way to market a newsletter is to provide prospective readers with one or more sample copies. You might send prospects sample copies once a month for three months. With the first two copies simply solicit a subscription order. In the final copy inform readers that this is their last chance to get the newsletter unless they subscribe.

Getting the News   You want to accumulate more news than you could ever use. Get on everyone's mailing list. Cull through every article and column, focusing on material related to your area. Then focus what you write down. If your newsletter deals only with legislation affecting the oil industry, select material focused on that area.

Pay attention to people news. People love news about others who got promoted, demoted, born, done in, ripped off, convicted, released or otherwise caught in the limelight. Your subscribers are a great source of news, and they invariably enjoy the opportunity to assist you.

Writing the Newsletter   If you have done everything correctly up to this point, the rest is a downhill glide. Your news-prospecting tactics should have filled your mail with hundreds of potential news items. You have only to sort out the items that will be of the greatest interest to your readers. Follow these three rules:

1. Select regular news categories as ongoing features in all issues. Topics such as industry meetings, conventions, new products and merger news are appropriate. Devote a half to a full page to each topic, and your newsletter will be organized and blocked out.

2. Be terse and concise. Use a crisp, catchy writing style.

3. Design an easy-to-use format. Keep it simple—to give the impression that it is hot off the presses and to make your job easier.

Now that you are ready to go, start writing the news.

Keeping Readers/Subscribers Happy   After your readers have completed your newsletter, you want them to think: *This was better than I expected.* If the publication is supposed to promote your consulting practice, a sharp format with good information reflects favorably on your competence. If you are publishing for profit, keeping your readers happy attracts subscription renewals and new subscribers. Communicate with your readers. Find out what they like and what they don't. Give them what they want.

You need to set a competitive subscription rate on a for-profit newsletter. Because you are setting a price for a product, you must contend with the elusive volume-price relationship. In some markets the price has a direct bearing on the volume you sell. If the market is *elastic*, high prices can turn off part of your readership. If it is *inelastic*, it yields higher profits in proportion to higher prices and is comparatively insensitive to high prices. How do you find the right price? Unfortunately, no formula can give you the answer. You have to keep testing the market to find out the effects of various prices on your subscription volume.

Publishing Magazine and Journal Articles

More than 7,000 technical and professional publications and 9,000 house organs are published in the United States. More than 80 percent accept unsolicited manuscripts on topics of direct interest to their readers. These publications are usually desperately short of good articles and often pay a modest sum to the writer. Take advantage of this scarcity.

Publishing articles gives you valuable professional exposure and recognition. Yet to gain actual consulting opportunities, you must place your articles with the right periodicals. In some cases an article might fail to generate business because it did not contain any information of value. More likely the article did not work because it was published in a periodical that was largely or exclusively academic or theoretical. The readership is just not in the market for consulting services.

Few people other than professors and graduate students read the theoretical journals. You really can't expect much response to articles in such publications. Furthermore, with so many professors trying to get published, the backlog of articles is up to three years for some journals. Of course, the exception always crops up to defy the rule. The first article I published appeared in a rather erudite journal. The article was about impulse buying and led to some calls to do consulting. One of the major factors in my getting the business was that so little had been written on the subject. The need was so great that even business people were reading the academic journals. By a peculiar set of circumstances, publication in an academic journal generated some business.

In general publish your articles in periodicals that are read by practicing professionals and businesspeople. Be certain your articles contain solid information of value to the readers. Let them know you are a consultant. To drive your point home, include actual experiences or cases (without disclosing names or confidential information). Include a biography of yourself with enough information to enable readers to get in touch with you. You might even express an interest in hearing from people who wish to pursue the topic in greater depth. Also include a picture of yourself—publications like to use photos to break up long blocks of type, and a photo with your article enhances your professional image.

Some writer/consultants get a lot of mileage out of their writing efforts. A consultant in one of my seminars recently provided me with an excellent case in point. He published 65 articles in various house organs in one year! Although that many articles might sound like a full-time job in itself, the fact is that he wrote only four basic articles. By changing the industries' and companies' names, he multiplied the four into 68, of which 65 were published. With each article he required that his standard *bio* be printed. It included his name, photo, address, the fact that he is a consultant, the kind of consulting he does and some of his experience. He was deluged with more business opportunities than he could handle.

Success stories like this one give rise to the next question: Where do I get published? For professional and technical publications, try *Business Publications' Rates and Data* for the names of suitable publications. Also try *Encyclopedia of Association Periodicals, The Working Press of the Nation: Volume 2-Magazine Directory,* and *Scientific and Technical Organizations and Agencies Directory* (the latter lists and describes the organizations' publications). Some people find *Writer's Market: Where & How To Sell What You Write* an excellent starting point due to the list of technical and professional journals provided. For publishers' addresses and telephone numbers, consult *Literary Market Place* or *Publishers Directory.* All of these books are referenced in the first section of the bibliography. When you have the names and numbers of the publications that suit your purpose, call or write to each to ask for a copy of their manuscript requirements.

Pay attention to what topics are being written about in your area. Write about controversial subjects or areas where there is a genuine need for information. With enough good material and a little persistence, you should be able to place several articles.

Letters to the Editor

Letters to the editor have more effect than most people think. Exposure in newspapers and trade and professional periodicals has benefited many consultants. Invariably a group of zealous readers—about 30 to 40 percent of the total readership—follow letters to the editor to keep abreast of what people are saying and thinking. Writing a letter is an excellent way to show off your good ideas. See the sample letter in Figure 6.5.

Teaching

If you are inclined toward teaching at all, this option deserves serious consideration. While teaching opportunities with universities do not abound, many organizations—school districts, libraries, major corporations and YMCAs, for example—are entering the field of education for reasons of their own. Don't pass up the chance to teach or to create such an occasion.

You often meet and develop prospects in teaching. If your prospects are past students, you have an advantage because they have seen your competence in the classroom. Doing business with students while they are a member of the class can be compromising. However, former students often discuss their classes with their employers, which may inspire them to pursue the consultant for an assignment.

The seminar business, one of the nation's fastest growing industries, provides tremendous potential for the consultant. A profit center in its own right, a seminar can be a highly effective vehicle for the marketing of consulting services. Consultants who regularly market their services in seminars report that they convert one out of every eleven seminar participants into clients. It is important, however, that you not waste participants' time by directly selling your services during the program. Effective marketing of consulting services in seminars requires a low-key, indirect, unobtrusive approach.

Working the Press

A passive approach to consulting—hanging out a shingle and waiting for business to walk in the door—presumes that potential clients know who you are and accept you as an authority in your field. However, unless you are already a well-established authority whose contributions are widely known, this presumptive attitude is not likely to produce the desired results.

One way to increase your exposure and establish yourself as an authority at little or no cost is to become a *news maker,* to stimulate media interest in your opinions and activities. Getting the press to notice you takes more than just handing out a few press releases. You need to be aware of how periodicals work, what reporters and editors are interested in and what makes the news. Just like you, most publications are in business to make money. Editors want material that will interest readers and increase subscriptions. While some newspapers and magazines are predisposed toward sensationalism and controversy, the trade press generally prefers practical, how-to information—the kind of information that you, as a consultant, can provide.

The first step in becoming a news maker is to target the trade publications in your field. Study them for content and style. What issues and topics are currently being featured? What slants are given to the articles? What is their editorial policy? Specific knowledge of what the trade journals consider to be newsworthy and a feel for how this material is presented will help you to create effective press releases that will enhance your reputation as an authority.

Using the information gathered during your review of the publications, you can prepare a press release using one of the following approaches:

- Discuss economic, political and social trends and their significance for your field.

- Comment on the relevant research and opinions of economists, politicians and authorities in your field.

- Present and analyze data collected in a survey or questionnaire. (This needn't be a sophisticated or lengthy treatment—just enough to stimulate discussion and get your name before the readers.)

Press releases, in and of themselves, may not generate new business. But they will help to give your name an aura of authority, to establish you as a prominent figure in your field.

Your opinions will become sought after, both by the press and by other people in your field—you will become newsworthy. An offshoot of this free publicity is invitations to submit articles and speak to professional associations and civic groups, which should increase your exposure tenfold. This exponential effect of well-placed, carefully timed press releases is achieved at little or no cost—and should contribute to a profitable practice.

In making yourself newsworthy, you must be careful to create a positive image. If you are perceived as being too controversial, too far removed from the mainstream of opinion, you could be labeled as a pariah, reversing the exponential effect of publicity. Instead of being helped by it, your practice could be seriously harmed. This is not to suggest that you should avoid controversy altogether. Indeed, one of the surest ways to get your name in the news is to take a firm position on a controversial issue. But these opinions should not stray too far from accepted norms and standards—or you may find yourself becoming the person everyone loves to hate. Look over the samples provided in Figures 6.6 through 6.8.

Tips

The principles underlying these nine Low-Cost/No-Cost Techniques are the same. Each one establishes you as an authority in your field. They all encourage clients to come to you or send you out to contact clients you are informed about. The uncomfortable cold contact is eliminated. The economic payoff is that, compared to expensive ads or direct mailing campaigns, these techniques are all low-cost/no-cost or even make you money by themselves! And they work—any successful consultant will testify to that fact.

If you are beginning your consulting practice or if you are interested in expanding, you may want to supplement your Low-Cost/No-Cost marketing techniques with some form of advertising to get your name in front of as many potential clients as possible. The next chapter will show you how to get the most out of your direct marketing dollar by using the same principles that underlie the nine Low-Cost/No-Cost Techniques.

Figure 6.5   Sample Letter to the Editor

Howard L. Shenson

January 26, 1984

Editor, Letters to the Editor
Los Angeles Times
Times Mirror Square
Los Angeles, CA

Dear Sir:

Mr. James Flanigan's article (Wednesday, January 25, 1984) on the consulting business was most interesting but in one regard misleading. It states that total consultant billings in the United States are equal to $2 billion annually and cites **Consultants News** as its information source. This dollar figure refers only to management consulting and excludes other types of consulting.

Total consultant billings, including legal and accounting services, is actually a $43 billion-a-year business. If you exclude the fees earned by attorneys and accountants, total consulting sales are actually calculated to be some $21 billion. Of this total, $9.5 billion is for business. Thus, management consultants account for only some 20 percent of total business consulting. Financial, marketing, data processing, engineering consultants and others need to be included to gain an accurate picture of the dollars expended by corporate America on outside consultants.

Also of note in Mr. Flanigan's article is the statement that the average daily charge of the 30 largest management consulting firms in the United States is about $400 a day. My own research indicates that the average daily billing rate of management consultants in the United States is $640; and for consultants in general—$631. These figures are derived from a national study of 6,315 consultants.

How does one explain the discrepancy between $400 and $640? It is, I believe, a function of the fact that most consulting practices are small. While the largest 30 management consulting practices employ vast numbers of staff consultants who bill out at lower rates, smaller practices do not.

You might find it of interest to know that 91.6 percent of the consulting practices consist of one or two professional personnel. Further, 79.2 percent of all consulting practices in this country are solo/one-person operations.

I am enclosing a summary of my own research.

Sincerely,

Howard L. Shenson

HLS:cc
Enclosure

20750 Ventura Blvd., Ste. 206 • Woodland Hills, CA 91364 • Telephone 818 / 703-1415

Figure 6.6 Sample Press Release

Corporate Public Affairs
Financial Relations
Market Planning
Counsel

For: Howard L. Shenson, Inc.   Contact: Michael Baybak or
        20121 Ventura Blvd.   Michael Graves
        Woodland Hills, CA 91364
        Contact: Howard Shenson
                   President
                   (818) 703-1415

Income and Business Expectations Rise for Professional Consultant of All Types According to National Shenson Study

LOS ANGELES, Calif.--Professional consulting of all types is a high growth business despite--or perhaps because of--the economic downturn, according to the sixth semiannual national study of the consulting profession, scheduled for release next month by the nationally operating "consultant's consulting firm," Howard L. Shenson, Inc., of Woodland Hills, Calif.

Nearly three-quarters of professional consultants surveyed in July reported they "expect an increase in business over the next six months."

Net pretax income for consultants of all types showed 61.9 percent earning $28,000 to $56,000 a year and 14.6 percent earning from $56,000 to more than $96,000 a year.

A total of 77.2 percent of survey respondents who have been in practice for more than two years also indicated their 1980 income rose by 5 to 29 percent over the prior year. For another 7.1 percent of these respondents, net pretax income rose by more than 29 percent.

However, one adverse sign of the times brought to light by the survey is slower payment by clients. Survey respondents reported that 60+ percent of receivables due were beyond 30 days, with 40.1 percent in the 31-day to 60-day category.

The semiannual Shenson survey is the only comprehensive study in its field of the economic conditions and economic health of the consulting professions. The study is based on a randomly selected respondent group of 4,021 consultants and heads of consulting practices throughout the U.S., out of a total of 52,444 professional consulting practices identified.

Thirty-two fields of consulting professions covered include:

Management	Personnel	Investment Advisory
Finance	Insurance	Data Processing
Aerospace	Engineering	Training
Education	Advertising	Public Relations
Marketing	Real Estate	New Business Ventures
Communications	Planning	Arts and Culture
Meeting Planning	Travel	Psychological Services
Health Care	Publishing	Hotel/Restaurant/Club
Broadcast	Municipal Service	Grantsmanship
Design (Industrial)	Production	Executive Search
Scientific	Graphics/Printing Trades	

(More)

Figure 6.6 Sample Press Release (Continued)

The just-completed study is scheduled for October publication in the Shenson firm's industry newsletter, "The Professional Consultant," which is also the official newsletter of the American Society of Professional Consultants, of whose board of governors Shenson is a member.

"In general, the attitude among consultants is that any government approach that tries to balance the budget and make people more self-reliant is good," said Howard L. Shenson, president of the firm releasing the study. "The attitude is that business will either learn to live with the interest rates or that the rates will come down. If things get really bad, the government will tend to bail out the economy by increasing spending on study contracts, of which consultants are the prime beneficiaries."

Other highlights of the study:

The average consultant charges $447 per day for his or her services.

The top five consulting fields in terms of earning power, on an average per-day fee basis, are:

1) Scientific, $624 per day.

2) Advertising, $567 per day.

3) Aerospace, $552 per day.

4) Engineering, $544 per day.

5) Executive Search, $527 per day.

The lowest-paying five out of a field of 33, on an average per-day fee-basis are:

1) Public Relations, $389 per day.

2) Data Processing, $388 per day.

3) Arts and Culture, $388 per day.

4) Insurance, $376 per day.

5) Communications, $367 per day.

The survey shows that 84.2 percent of consultancies are full-time practices and 15.8 percent are part-time.

A total of 59.6 percent have been in business four years or more, indicating major expansion in the consulting ranks in recent years.

According to survey figures, more than 5,700 consultancies have joined the ranks in the past year alone.

Asked to explain the surge in the ranks, Shenson said, "In today's tougher economy, many salaried people are very worried about job security. They find that, in converting from salaried professional to professional consultant, they are able to exert more control over their financial future."

Shenson is the former chairman of the Department of Management at the California State University at Northridge.

In the past five years he has trained over 15,000 people in becoming professional consultants.

####

Figure 6.7   Sample of Printed Survey Results

The Professional Consultant   ©1991, HOWARD L. SHENSON • 20750 VENTURA BOULEVARD
WOODLAND HILLS, CA 91364 • USA • TELEPHONE 818/703-1415

AVERAGE (MEAN) ANNUAL INCOME OF PROFESSIONALS
After Business Expenses and Before Income Taxes For The 12 Months Ending March 31, 1991

	1991	1990	1989
All Professionals	$104,188	$ 99,873	$ 96,001
Accounting	$107,553	$103,875	$ 99,887
Advertising	$105,482	$102,833	$ 98,776
Agriculture	$ 74,220	$ 71,886	$ 69,210
Aerospace	$110,375	$104,441	$ 99,122
Arts & Cultural	$ 62,911	$ 58,999	$ 56,780
Banking	$100,026	$ 96,122	$ 92,349
Broadcast	$ 99,902	$ 96,842	$ 92,987
Business Acquisition/Sales	$103,348	$101,985	$101,335
Chemical	$ 97,454	$ 93,180	$ 88,767
Communications	$ 70,997	$ 68,207	$ 65,396
Construction	$ 94,035	$ 92,994	$ 89,533
Data Processing Consulting	$ 92,290	$ 87,998	$ 84,778
Data Processing Programming	$ 66,036	N/A	N/A
Dental/Medical	$111,098	$105,111	$100,004
Design-Industrial	$ 77,909	$ 73,225	$ 70,094
Economics	$ 98,852	$ 93,846	$ 95,550
Education	$ 66,023	$ 63,001	$ 60,341
Engineering	$109,343	$105,444	$101,042
Estate Planning	$ 88,671	$ 87,948	$ 84,668
Executive Search	$104,556	$102,336	$100,296
Export/Import	$103,285	$ 99,707	$ 96,113
Fashion/Beauty	$ 60,483	$ 59,824	$ 57,499
Finance	$110,772	$106,366	$102,318
Franchise	$100,386	$ 98,121	$ 93,612
Fund Raising	$ 75,311	$ 72,500	$ 70,320
Grantsmanship	$ 66,004	$ 63,377	$ 61,888
Graphics/Printing	$ 79,660	$ 74,993	$ 72,571
Health Care	$113,458	$109,032	$104,002
Hotel/Restaurant/Club	$ 80,036	$ 74,869	$ 72,235
Insurance	$ 79,982	$ 77,041	$ 73,266
International Business	$105,440	$102,995	$ 99,873
Investment Advisory	$108,229	$107,134	$102,641
Management	$103,811	$ 99,980	$ 96,112
Marketing	$104,920	$100,096	$ 95,874
Municipal Government	$ 83,776	$ 78,645	$ 73,090
New Business Ventures	$ 85,030	$ 81,203	$ 76,482
Packaging	$ 95,674	$ 92,469	$ 91,366
Pension	$ 98,884	$ 95,177	$ 93,734
Personnel/HRD	$ 78,997	$ 74,555	$ 71,889
Production	$105,446	$ 99,644	$ 95,999
Psychological Services	$ 88,778	$ 85,870	$ 83,108
Public Relations	$ 80,048	$ 76,412	$ 73,157
Publishing	$ 86,671	$ 84,113	$ 80,446
Purchasing	$ 93,383	$ 90,337	$ 86,500
Quality Control	$103,885	$ 99,359	$ 94,233
Real Estate	$ 85,986	$ 84,983	$ 84,007
Records Management	$ 87,008	$ 83,018	$ 79,659
Recreation	$ 70,817	$ 67,785	$ 65,222
Research & Development	$121,349	$118,808	$112,886
Retail	$ 79,662	$ 75,774	$ 73,369
Scientific	$125,092	$119,572	$113,740
Security	$ 93,860	$ 91,126	$ 87,668
Statistical	$ 86,552	$ 83,662	$ 80,762
Telecommunications	$101,543	$ 99,265	$ 94,447
Traffic/Transportation	$ 88,222	$ 82,974	$ 80,123
Training	$ 84,818	$ 81,647	$ 78,581
Travel	$ 77,027	$ 74,782	$ 72,473

Source: *Professional Consultant & Seminar Business Report*, 1991. Reprinted by permission.

Figure 6.8 Sample Article

Page B6   *NATIONAL BUSINESS EMPLOYMENT WEEKLY*   February 10, 1991

BUSINESS OPPORTUNITIES MONTHLY

How to Sell Your Talents as an Independent Consultant

Twelve steps to help market your services to clients

BY HOWARD L. SHENSON

Professional consulting — providing advice and information in exchange for a fee—is one of the fastest-growing segments of the economy. Many persons engaged in consulting don't, of course, call themselves consultants. They've adopted other titles—financial planner, accountant, attorney, trainer, consulting engineer, psychologist, adviser, architect, designer, etc.

Regardless of what they call themselves, they're linked by the need to identify a client, package their know-how into a saleable service, deliver advice and information in a fashion that satisfies the needs of the client, and be compensated in relation to the value of their time or service.

Marketing professional consulting services is unique. It's fundamentally different from marketing products. Indeed, it's even distinct from the methods employed to market other types of services. Those who are able to master the art of marketing a professional practice not only benefit economically, but enjoy a level of personal satisfaction that usually is the envy of their less successful peers.

Some consultants mistakenly think that just being good at what they do is sufficient to build a profitable practice. Others are shackled by the feeling that marketing is beneath them or somehow unprofessional. Selecting and implementing inappropriate marketing strategies can destroy a professional firm. But so too can avoiding the necessity of marketing.

For a professional, marketing is much more like a carefully orchestrated symphony than a buffet dinner. Irregular implementation of seemingly effective strategies used by others can be more damaging than helpful.

To build and maintain a viable professional firm, marketing must permeate every activity. The successful don't worry about marketing only on Monday or Friday; they worry about it 24 hours a day, seven days a week. Every action of the professional affects the acquisition of future business. Unlike products or even

Mr. Shenson is a management consultant in Woodland Hills, Calif., and has written seven books on consulting, including "Shenson On Consulting: Success Strategies from the 'Consultant's Consultant'." (1990, John Wiley & Sons), from which this article is adapted.

other services, the work product (professional service) cannot be separated from the delivery vehicle (the professional).

Research clearly indicates that those most successful in marketing professional or consulting services share the following characteristics:

1. A dedication to a market orientation. Ours is a market-driven economy. Those who prosper in the market, including professionals, develop services (or products) responsive to market demand. Take care to avoid the practice that has toppled so many who seemed destined for success—creating elegant solutions to nonexistent problems. Always start with the market and work backward. The ability to determine what the market desires through research, testing or intuition is the most basic and fundamental principle of consulting services.

2. A commitment to target and niche marketing. No consultant can be all

> *Some consultants mistakenly think that just being good at what they do is sufficient to build a profitable practice*

things to all clients. Success is a result of carefully defining the services to be provided in terms of market segments. This point is perhaps best illustrated by the following story:

New to private practice, an experienced marketer planned to set up shop as a consultant. He had worked for a large manufacturing firm, and informed the seminar leader that he now had to make his most difficult decision—on what and for whom he would consult. He selected a new but rapidly growing industry. Within three years he had established his firm as the leading authority and resource in this specialized, niche market. He had more business than he could handle, contributed articles to trade magazines serving the industry, gave speeches, conducted seminars and was regularly contacted by the press for his views on issues regarding this narrow specialty.

The selection of his market niche was, in a sense, accidental; he could have

elected to serve a different segment. His success, however, was the result of target and niche marketing. Being good at what he does is important and helpful, but not causal; there are many generalist consultants who are good, though not successful.

3. A devotion to client interest, above and beyond any other. More than anything, clients retain consultants with the assumption (hope) that they will be dedicated to placing the client's interest and well-being above any other interest. For the most successful, this goes far beyond avoiding obvious conflicts of interest, such as simultaneous service to competitors on proprietary matters, or adherence to professional society ethics. It permeates every decision and action. It means that a client willing to generate billable hours will sometimes be told to spend his money elsewhere. And it may mean great personal sacrifice to serve a client today rather than next week. From time to time it also will mean running the risk of losing a client who must be told the hard facts.

An accountant selected a computer and software package and negotiated the lease for her client. She received a fee for doing so. Several weeks following installation and training, the vendor sent the accountant a letter of appreciation and a check for $500. She could have deposited the check; it's likely no one would ever have known. Or she could have returned the check to the manufacturer. Instead, she had the good sense to endorse the check over to her client and deliver it, indicating that the client had obviously been overcharged by $500. The good will and favorable word of mouth that followed was worth far more than $500. Placing client interest ahead of any other interest isn't only the right policy, but one that's often rewarded in unexpected ways.

4. An ability to generate rapport before attempting to sell. Successful professionals invest time and energy in building a meaningful relationship with prospects prior to marketing and selling them. The best clients are those with whom a significant and genuine relationship has been established. Given a choice, people do business with those who they believe have their sincere interest and well-being at heart. They don't want to be sold; they want to be helped. Consultants unable to

Continued on Next Page

Figure 6.8   Sample Article (Continued)

February 16, 1991   NATIONAL BUSINESS EMPLOYMENT WEEKLY   Page B7

BUSINESS OPPORTUNITIES MONTHLY

Twelve steps

Continued From Preceding Page

communicate that their services are motivated by desire to aid client will either fail or be far less successful than they could be.

5. A dedication to developing a marketing strategy based on creating image and reputation. Those in need of professional services are far more likely to retain consultants they regard as knowledgeable, resourceful authorities than those they look upon merely as salespeople. Being perceived as state-of-the-art, cutting-edge, respected, informed, sought-after and even well connected should be the foundation of any marketing plan. The most successful have worked hard to establish a reputation as the leading authority within their niche market or specialty.

6. An ability to market results not technology. Many professionals limit their success because they fail to sell results and benefits and instead concentrate on selling technology. They hide behind jargon and a technical approach. However, clients rarely care about what's inside the "black box;" they buy results and benefits. Thus, the successful consultant develops the art of communicating with the client in those terms.

It's much like a dining experience in a five-star restaurant. As a patron, you expect to be served a fine meal with decorum and taste. The frantic conditions in the kitchen are not your concern, nor should they be.

7. A commitment to avoid creating an impression that one is hungry and needy. No one wishes to do business with someone perceived to be needy, hungry or unsuccessful. The most successful professionals avoid any appearance of needing the business. Obviously, clients and others recognize that the professional needs clients to stay in business, but they'll be far less inclined to do business with someone they feel is in need of their business.

The consultant needs to appear more like a busy surgeon than a desperate used-car dealer. Being too available, too bending, too negotiable, too flexible is never in the consultant's interest. Despite this, the professional must not be perceived as uncooperative and uninterested. A subtle balance must be struck. The prospective client should come to recognize that he needs the professional more than the professional needs the client. Accordingly, the consultant must establish policies for doing business that are appropriate for his or her practice and insist that those served adhere to those policies. Obviously, such policies must be reasonable and acceptable.

8. An ability to create the impression of accessibility and helpfulness. Those who feel they may have a need for professional or consulting services are often unwilling to contact a consultant because of two fears. First, they fear they'll be perceived as uninformed, inexperienced or incapable. Second, they're concerned

that they'll become obligated for (high) fees prior to determining whether they need assistance. Marketing success requires that the consultant always be perceived as open, helpful, nonthreatening, accessible and willing to discuss the benefits of retaining his or her services. Although it isn't required that the professional avoid being compensated during the needs analysis stage, it's often helpful to business development. In any case, it's always important that the prospective client be informed of the nature of the financial obligation that will be incurred.

A plastic surgeon found that much valuable time was being wasted with initial consultations that resulted in the patient's decision not to retain his services. So he established a policy of charging for the initial consultation. When they sought appointments, patients were informed of the policy. Approximately 18% elected not to make an appointment. The policy not only compensated the plastic surgeon for his time, but also served as a screening device to deter the less serious.

9. A recognition of the important distinction between marketing and selling. Consultants must engage in both marketing and selling to build viable practices. Success requires that the professional understand the difference between these two

No one wishes to do business with someone who is perceived to be needy, hungry or unsuccessful

activities. Marketing involves all activities that are designed to establish the image and reputation of the consultant and to make the market aware of the availability of his or her services. The opportunity to sell results from successful marketing and involves all activities that cause an interested prospect to engage the services of the consultant. Some professionals feel they need do only one or the other. Both are vital. And the ability to know when one is engaged in marketing, as opposed to selling, is crucial.

Marketing makes the task of selling easier; it sets expectations, it informs, it educates. Consider the speed with which the modern shopper wheels through a 35,000-square-foot supermarket. In 15 or 20 minutes the shopper arrives at the check-out counter with $100 worth of products piled high in a shopping cart. Such speed of decision-making and self-service has been made possible by marketing. Imagine how much slower and more expensive the shopping process would be if the proprietor of the general store still had to personally convince (sell) us on each product.

While this is obvious with respect to products, many professionals miss the significance of this analogy for their own practices. The better they can inform the market of the value of their services, the needs they can solve and the results they'll produce for a client, the easier the

selling job. Client awareness of and appreciation for the image and reputation of a particular consultant can be created through either indirect, public-relations-type marketing activities or direct marketing strategies, or both. But even the most effective marketing doesn't eliminate the need for selling, for selling involves the art of demonstrating to interested and informed clients the wisdom of engaging the professional's services and allows the professional the opportunity to customize in relation to the prospect's specific needs.

10. A discipline that allows you to bury your ego. Professionals, like everyone else, love to be recognized and honored for their achievement. However, success often requires that the professional avoid the limelight and allow others—the client and the client's staff—to obtain recognition for successes. This is difficult and requires discipline, for professionals tend to be more egocentric than others; high educational attainment and a long track record of successes often contribute to their egocentricity. They also are often viewed as a threat to the careers and objectives of those with whom they work.

In taking credit for results and accomplishments, professionals can elevate this threat to such a degree that it has the potential to hurt client satisfaction, future business and referrals. Developing humility and the skill of sharing credit while still making sure that those who are important know of the professional's contributions is important for building a successful practice.

11. A devotion to the value of referral marketing. In most cases, a successful professional can, in relatively short order, develop a practice in which more than 80% of all business comes from referrals. There is no more cost-efficient business development strategy than referral marketing. But to be effective, referral marketing must be sophisticated and strategic. Assiduous attention to the objectives and proven-effective methods of referral marketing are really the lifeblood of the most successful professional practices.

12. A commitment to the consistency and regularity of marketing. It's often been said that the best time to borrow money is when you don't need it. If this is true for getting credit, it's even more true for marketing professional services. The time to market isn't when you don't have business and are desperate. To be effective, marketing must be constant and ongoing. Successful consultants must treat marketing with the same dedication as they treat their most valued clients.

Many professionals attempt to avoid marketing, preferring to spend their time doing the work that marketing makes possible. The press of client obligations becomes, for then., the best excuse for not marketing. Nothing is more damaging to building a successful practice. The professional must limit the amount of time expended on client work and charge a sufficiently high fee to ensure that consistent and meaningful marketing is an integral part of practice management.   ●

7

Effective Direct Marketing

Given the myriad of indirect, Low-Cost/No-Cost marketing techniques available to the consultant and their effectiveness in building a profitable practice, you may be tempted to ignore the whole issue of direct marketing. Yet direct mailing of brochures, space ads in newspapers and magazines, and other types of direct promotion of your services do have a place in your overall marketing plan. Primary emphasis should be placed on indirect marketing techniques but not to the exclusion of direct low-cost techniques such as advertising.

Effective advertising resembles the Low-Cost/No-Cost Techniques in that costs are kept down and you achieve the maximum results for your output of energy and money. This chapter discusses how you, as a consultant, can design and implement an effective, low-cost ad campaign by overcoming clients' fears about using a consultant.

Fears and Concerns of Clients

The seven Low-Cost/No-Cost Techniques described in Chapter 6 establish a personal, professional relationship with potential clients. In using these approaches, you don't have to be as concerned with clients' fears about hiring a consultant because they know you and respect you. If you sense that a client is afraid of retaining a consultant, you can deal with that concern directly in a face-to-face meeting.

In advertising you are at a disadvantage because those who read your ad don't know you and therefore are strongly influenced by concerns and fears about consultants. You have to anticipate and dispel those fears if your promotional campaign is to be successful.

Clients' major fears and concerns about using the services of a consultant, listed below in order of priority, were determined by a survey of 576 clients conducted by *The Professional Consultant* newsletter:

1. *Fear that the consultant is incompetent.* Many respondents indicated that consultants talk a good line but may not have the know-how to back up their talk.

2. *Fear that the consultant is incapable of being properly managed or directed by personnel of the client organization.* Some respondents perceived consultants as being competent but too controlling, too self-directed. Those respondents are concerned that they will lose control of their management prerogatives from a take-charge consultant.

3. *Fear that the fee charged by the consultant is too high.* While fewer than 21 percent of the respondents shop or compare fees, many are concerned that they may be paying too much for the services that are being provided.

4. *Fear that the consultant is too busy with other client work* to expend the time required or provide the resources necessary for doing the job right in the time allotted. Some respondents indicated that consultants spend a great deal of time in the marketing stage of the consultant-client relationship trying to impress the client with how busy they are and how important their client list is.

5. *Fear that the need for a consultant is an expression of the client's own failures or limitations.* In some fields it is fashionable to use consultants. In others needing a consultant is still viewed as an admission that something is wrong.

6. *Fear of loss resulting from the disclosure of sensitive proprietary data to someone who is a relative stranger.* There is a serious concern, especially among small corporate clients, that consultants will not be discreet with the information obtained as a result of interaction with the client organization.

7. *Fear that the client has not properly diagnosed the problem.* Interestingly, it is not the *consultant's* diagnosis that concerned some respondents but rather their own. These clients are concerned that their incorrect or incomplete information will result in the consultant's spending a lot of expensive time without results.

8. *Fear that the consultant will not be impartial.* There are two issues of concern here. The obvious one is that the consultant will have some priority other than the client's interest, which will color the consultant's objectivity. True professionals never allow their evaluations and decisions to be governed by any objective other than the client's best interests. However, even the most ethical, disciplined consultants are prone to see the solution to all problems in terms of more consulting. This tendency is so pervasive that a consultant can recommend unnecessary add-ons without being aware of this bias.

9. *Fear of developing a continuing dependency for the consultant's services.* Respondents expressed a minor concern that they would never rid themselves of the need for the consultant's unique service.

Don't make the mistake of thinking that a denial of these concerns is all that is required to be successful in selling your services. Laying these fears to rest is the beginning of marketing. This chapter will show you how your direct marketing campaign can reduce fears and induce clients to come to you.

Approach to Direct Marketing: The Free Offer

Direct marketing of consulting services requires a special approach suited to the nature of your services and the needs and concerns of your clients.

As a small or medium-sized consulting practice, you are not competing in the same market as sellers of shampoo and tires. Your goals, sales points and target audience are all different. You can achieve your results with a relatively small budget, perhaps even more efficiently than with larger expenditures.

Your goal in direct marketing is very simple—to get prospects to contact you. Having prospects come to you obviously is preferable to pursuing and persuading them. Your direct marketing promotions should sell without selling, obliging prospects to think of your name when the need arises. On one level you must assure prospects that you are *not* selling consulting services. On another, unspoken level, you must compel them to seek those very services.

Achieving the delicate balance between selling and subtlety requires a special type of promotion that prompts prospects to contact you without stirring up their anxieties about retaining a consultant. One effective technique is a direct mail piece or space ad in a newspaper or magazine asking readers to get in touch with you for free advice on some matter or free help with a minor problem. You respond to the requests with a short booklet or brochure that solves the problem and gives the reader ample reason to contact you for more help and information—without obligation, of course.

This approach, known as the *Free Offer*, draws clients to you because it sells without selling. All the Free Offer sells is the suggestion that readers contact you for assistance on some matter that you happen to know about. If the Free Offer has to do with your field, fine. Just be sure not to give *everything* away. Save a few items, and sprinkle the Free Offer with references to them. Suggest that, if readers need more information, they should call you. Almost anyone who can be considered a potential client will find some question to call about.

The ad merely asks readers to take a small, inconsequential, nonthreatening action. The promise is simply to solve the problem for free, with no implication that your consulting is needed to help the solution along. Your ad should offer a solution that is *complete* and *self-contained*.

You must be careful not to offer to solve too big a problem. If you do, your readers simply won't believe it is possible to offer so much for free. Figure 7.1 gives some examples of potential Free Offers.

By using a Free Offer like the ones in Figure 7.1, you may attract as many as 50 inquiries for every $100 you spend on advertising. This level of response broadens your prospect base,

Figure 7.1   Sample Free Offers and How They Work

The Free Offer	Help You Can Offer
For groups seeking to block federal funding cutbacks, a booklet, "How To Make Your Congressman Aware of Your Federal Funding Needs."	People in Washington to call with information requests. What to do when there is no meaningful response to a communication with a congressman. Where-to-buy service that facilitates mass mailings.
For small businesses with cash flow problems, a report, "43 Things You Wanted To Know about How To Behave Around Your Banker, But Were Afraid To Ask."	Where to get information on federal small business assistance. What to look for in your accountant's work to increase your loan-worthiness. Loan sources that have been lending money recently to small businesses.
For Firms seeking to improve the morale and prestige of their sales forces, a booklet, "How To Attract a Better Class of Applicants for Your Sales Openings."	Which local employment agencies have been doing work on sales jobs recently. How to tell if a job applicant is lying. The most frequent employment interview violations of the federal equal employment laws.
For small businesses confused by the rapid introduction of new facsimile transmission equipment, a free short-term subscription to "Facsimile Equipment Digest," a monthly digest of new-product announcements.	Product introductions that are reliably rumored to be coming soon (from your inside sources at the companies) that have not been officially introduced. How to handle delivery backlogs. How to handle user satisfaction survey results.
For firms manufacturing expensive computer-based prosthetics for handicapped people, a booklet, "How To Keep Current on Federal Aid for the Handicapped."	How to fill out a particular kind of grant application form. Where the federal money has been going lately in this area. What private sources of money have been doing lately in this area.
For real estate developers seeking to sell condominiums as professional offices, a research report, "How To Get a Doctor To Open the Mail You Send Him."	Names of successful office condominium developers for developers interested in expanding into that area. Names of banks and bank officers heavily involved in office condominium deals.
For small companies seeking free publicity for their new products, a survey report, "The 22 Best Outlets for Free Product Publicity."	Success stories in the reader's own industry. The best advertising or public relations agencies for the reader's particular situation
For corporation executives facing hostile media, a booklet, "How Six Prominent Executives Handle Hostile Journalists."	How your clients handle hostile journalists. How six prominent corporations prevent hostility from arising in the first place. Names of the best public speaking coaches.

providing you with additional marketing opportunities. In summary, a Free Offer should have the following characteristics:

- The offer is *free*.
- The offer gives a *solution* to a prospective client's problem.
- The problem is *related to your consulting area*.
- The problem does *not appear too difficult to solve*.
- The solution is *complete* and *self-contained*.

Why the Free Offer Works

A properly designed Free Offer communicates to the prospect that you will not deliver a high-pressure pitch for your services. While most prospects realize that you are not spending money for the benefit of humankind, they will be more apt to contact you if you assure them that you are just giving away a bit of valuable knowledge. Of course, you don't say this directly. Your offer of some useful information in a booklet or brochure in itself assures the reader of your professionalism and low-key approach, encouraging potential clients to contact you for additional information.

Prospects can call you with the confidence that they can back off without hesitation or compunction. They know that you are selling your services, but they need the comfortable fiction that the call is only for information. Once they respond, your ad can be considered a complete success.

After the initial contact, both you and the potential client can conveniently forget the suggestions in the ad. Your prospects can talk with you freely without the threat of a sales pitch and pressure to close. With this understanding, the client very often leads the conversation to buying your services. You should not be surprised if you are asked to take on a large, complicated and expensive assignment at the initial meeting.

Developing Your Free Offer

The purpose of your Free Offer is to get a client contact, generally leading to a face-to-face meeting. Therefore, it should avoid any topic that evokes clients' concerns. It should seem only to define in general terms what can be done for the client. It should raise clients' confidence in themselves and in you, encouraging them to ask for your services.

While most Free Offers are in the form of a brochure or booklet, you should not limit yourself to the printed medium. If your voice is a vital ingredient in your presentation, your "booklet" might consist of an audio cassette tape. A consultant in the computer field might program a message on a floppy disc for display on the prospect's computer screen. Give some thought to all the media.

The Free Offer consists of three parts:

1. Delivering the goods.

2. Involving the client.

3. Providing necessary information.

As we review each of these sections, an example Free Offer will be outlined. You can use the worksheets in Figure 7.2 to develop an offer related to your consulting specialty.

Keep the nine fears and concerns of your clients in mind as you construct your Free Offer. The first fear—that the consultant is incompetent—is an opportunity to display your expertise. If your services involve creativity, your offer should show imagination and flair. If you are a graphic artist, the graphics in your booklet had better be good. You are showing off your talents, so make it good, and the client will believe in your competence.

Delivering the Goods

In your ad state that you will produce valuable information on some worthwhile and interesting subject. Begin your booklet by outlining the problem and providing the promised information.

If you don't deliver the goods, potential clients will lose respect for you and expect the same kind of frustration in dealing with you. Make sure that whatever you offer is valuable, even though it relates to a limited topic, and that you come across with useful information. You want the reader to believe in you and trust you.

For example, say a consultant who writes grant proposals wants to make a Free Offer. Many proposals are written for government grants. The consultant in our example wants to get inquiries from potential clients without offering too much and without giving away services.

If the offer is for a booklet entitled, "How To Write Winning Proposals in Five Easy Steps," prospects simply won't believe it. They've had enough experience with the government to know that it can't be that easy, and they will expect either a useless collection of generalizations or a direct sales pitch. The other problem with this offer is that the consultant would be offering to tell them how to do what he does for a living. If he could actually deliver on the promise, he would be giving away his services.

A topic such as "Finding Unclaimed Federal Grant Money" has a much better chance of succeeding. Potential clients are interested in finding grants, and the offer sounds plausible. The consultant can deliver the information without giving away free work. This is an interesting and credible Free Offer.

The booklet on unclaimed federal grant money can begin with a short outline of the topic, describing how hundreds of millions of dollars' worth of federal grant money is left unallocated because no one applies for certain grants. Then the consultant can describe how easy it is to locate these grants, which are matters of public record, and list the written sources to look up and agencies to contact. Also he can list a few of the actual unclaimed grants. At this point the consultant has delivered the goods; he has made good on his promise.

Now, pick a possible Free Offer connected with your consulting specialty—something that is interesting and limited in scope like the one in the example. Write it down on the worksheet in Figure 7.2, then list the information that will fulfill your promise. Concentrate on offering help and information that is not identical to your specialty but is interesting to your potential clients. As you write down the actual information to be included in the booklet, make sure that it is valuable to your clients and fulfills the promise in the ad but does not give away proprietary material.

Involving the Client

After you have delivered the goods, you want to involve your potential clients by giving them a reason to contact you. The reasons should relate to the Free Offer alone, not to your consulting specialty.

One way is to describe a couple of vignettes in which clients contacted you for help related to the Free Offer. The consultant in our example could describe two occasions where clients came to him for help in finding grant money and were successful.

This approach builds up the client's confidence along with evidence of your ability to be helpful. You want to depict clients as competent and independent, not as helpless and in constant need of your advice. Also, do not specifically identify clients, as this may seem to be a breach of confidentiality. Use terms like *a major manufacturing company* or *a national accounting firm*. Your discretion will not go unnoticed.

Another way to involve the client is to list some obstacles to using the advice you gave in the first part of the booklet. These obstacles should relate to clients' lack of confidence in their ability to be creative or use new resources. In telling potential clients that they have all they need except confidence, you are building them up by emphasizing how much they already have.

Then you proceed by providing the solution to the obstacle, which involves contacting you and getting a little advice or help. If the prospects lack confidence, you can show them how to use the information in your Free Offer to get the most out of their abilities and other resources. The solution should involve only an hour or so of your time. Anything more than that implies that you are already beginning a major consultation—an impression that you want to avoid.

The consultant in our example could list some obstacles to tapping into the millions of dollars in grant money that are waiting for the right organization. One obstacle could be matching available talents with existing grants. An organization could have hidden talents or might not see how its business could be applied to a particular grant. This technique builds the potential client's confidence by focusing on potential and hidden talents rather than on incompetence and failure.

Another potential obstacle could be not knowing the right people to talk to in some government agencies. After all, who has enough time to run a business and know the ins and outs of thousands of government agencies? Our consultant, however, can give guidance and support in the difficult process of finding the right people to contact, providing the prospective client with the benefit of his experience in working with the government. He is not saying that the prospect is incompetent but that the demands of real world business don't leave enough time to do everything.

A third way of capturing the prospect's interest is to add an enticing comment or two on a related subject. For example, the Free Offer on unclaimed federal grant money can also raise the issue of unallocated money available from private nonprofit organizations and from state and local governments. In mentioning these sources, our consultant can state that he is available for consultation on these matters without giving any details. Thus the promise on federal grants is fulfilled and new possibilities are raised, giving prospects a reason to make personal contact.

Take the remaining worksheet in Figure 7.2 and outline some potential obstacles to using the information you have provided in your Free Offer. Sketch out a couple vignettes that show how you helped those who contacted you for information—without mentioning your consulting specialty or saying that these contacts signed up for your services. Finally, write down some areas related to your Free Offer that would also interest potential clients. In effect, these are additional Free Offers requiring face-to-face contact.

Keep in mind that you want to build up the client's confidence and allay any fears of becoming permanently dependent on you for help. You are simply giving the client an opportunity to get in touch with you for a little more advice and guidance on your offer.

Combine the vignettes with the obstacles and solutions by listing the obstacles and solutions first (of course, all the solutions involve a consultation with you—again at no cost) and then giving a vignette in which someone contacted you and had a satisfactory outcome. As part of the vignette, you do not want to say that the prospect became a client of yours. Simply outline the free advice you dispensed, and describe how it was useful. Also emphasize that the information was delivered in a short time. Potential clients are not going to believe that you gave away a day of your time just to improve the economy.

Include the additional items as part of a vignette or separately as further information you can give. A vignette describing how a company contacted our consultant for more information on federal grant money could also state that the matter of private grants came up and leads were developed that led to valuable contracts.

The obstacles and solutions, vignettes and additional items give the prospect a reason to contact you in person—and that is where the actual sale will take place. In the first section you delivered the goods, and in the second section you gave the prospect a reason to contact you. Having completed the contract you made in your ad, you created a sense of incompleteness to give the potential client a reason to contact you.

Providing Necessary Information

Your booklet should conclude with basic information about yourself and your services: your address, phone number and a short description of the kind of consulting you do. You also can list your policies on billing, contracts, confidentiality, and so on. You might say that you believe that consulting should be cost effective, or you might declare your willingness to enter into performance contracts. Basically, you want the client to know you are a businesslike professional.

This section should be short—preferably one page. Too much information about yourself makes the booklet look more like a sales pitch and less like a simple offer. Clients who write for more information can get your brochure that lists your accomplishments and abilities.

Figure 7.2   Worksheet for Free Offer

Delivering the Goods

Your Free Offer
The Information That Delivers the Goods

Figure 7.2   Worksheet for Free Offer (Continued)

Involving the Potential Client

Obstacle to Using Your Advice	Solution to the Obstacle
Obstacle to Using Your Advice	Solution to the Obstacle
Obstacle to Using Your Advice	Solution to the Obstacle
Obstacle to Using Your Advice	Solution to the Obstacle
Obstacle to Using Your Advice	Solution to the Obstacle
Obstacle to Using Your Advice	Solution to the Obstacle

Figure 7.2   Worksheet for Free Offer (Continued)

Involving the Potential Client

A Vignette Describing How You Helped Someone

Another Vignette

Figure 7.2   Worksheet for Free Offer (Continued)

Involving the Potential Client

A Related Item or Area of Interest

A Related Item or Area of Interest

A Related Item or Area of Interest

A Related Item or Area of Interest

A Related Item or Area of Interest

A Related Item or Area of Interest

The procedure for developing a Free Offer is similar to that for producing a brochure. After you have written your copy, you need to consult a printer and/or design specialist to set up the actual format. You may want to engage professional help in writing the brochure as well as the design of the layout and any graphics involved. Remember that this booklet is a display of what you can do, and you want it to show off your abilities. The expense involved in quality printing on good stock and in good graphics is more than offset by the result in potential sales. With a successful offer you will probably be sending out only a few hundred brochures, perhaps fewer. The response to your offer need not be massive to be successful because those who do inquire are very likely to need and want your services.

Following Up on the Free Offer

Paradoxically, a Free Offer may be *too* effective, cutting off prospects from comfortable entry to the consultant. Prospects may be disappointed in a sense to find that the consultant has kept the promise made in the ad. The offer turns out to be exactly what the ad said it would be—a self-contained solution to a modest problem. At the end of the piece is simply a line that reads: *For more information, or a consultation contact* _____. If the prospects are still interested, they have to contact the consultant cold, just as if there had been no ad. They are up against the same old uncomfortable feelings. This Free Offer has failed in its essential purpose—opening the way to a face-to-face meeting between the prospect and the consultant.

A good Free Offer gives some valuable information and shows that the consultant is competent or even creative. However, it only gives hints or an outline of parts of the solution. To get the whole story the prospect has to make contact with the consultant. That way if the prospect is interested, it is easy to call and ask for more information.

Writing the Ad Copy

After you have selected your topic and have your booklet ready to go, you need to compose your ad. The rules for composing a Free Offer ad are the same as for any good ad. If you decide to use more conventional ads, you can use this section as a guide. But the focus here is on constructing an effective ad for a Free Offer.

Gauging the effectiveness of advertising for an immediate response is very simple. For each ad or for each mailing the question is the same: Did the dollar value of the immediate responses exceed the cost of the ad by enough to make the desired profit?

This emphasis on immediate response means that you don't have to use complex and expensive devices to influence delayed responses (which you probably can't afford anyway). It does impose a harsh discipline on you, a discipline so harsh that the best frame of mind for writing advertising is *desperation*. Imagine that you are drowning. The 50 to 100 words you have left will be the last ones you utter—unless you get the lazy, indifferent, impatient reader to act *now*. You don't have time to be funny or clever, to glorify your business or to justify your appeal. You have only enough time to clearly describe the benefits of responding immediately.

You do this by:

1. *Using the present tense and the second person* (you).
2. *Appealing to the reader's senses.* Give as physical a description as you can of the benefits of responding.
3. *Using short, simple words in short, simple sentences.*
4. *Urging the reader to respond.*

If this advice strikes you as extreme or overly simplistic, observe how you read ads in a newspaper. Notice that a strong, simple and direct appeal is much more apt to make you stop scanning and actually read the ad.

As a professional offering a high-quality service, you may have developed a dislike for advertising, finding it crass or distasteful. As a result your own ad copy may read like an announcement in a church bulletin. But any reticence or self-effacement in your copy is apt to undermine the purpose of your ad—to get responses.

Direct mail professionals attest to this fact based on their experience with hundreds of millions of pieces of mail—each designed to get a simple, immediate response. Even when they are appealing to the most jaded, sophisticated audience, these professionals are bold and straightforward. Follow their example by being as direct as possible in your advertising, without resorting to hype or obvious overstatement.

Designing Your Ad

Especially when you are using small newspaper or magazine ads, where every square inch must earn its keep in direct responses, the mail-order style is apt to be most effective. In mail-order, an ad, a direct mail piece or an entire advertising campaign can be judged quickly and easily by the number of responses it produces. Through thousands of scientific tests, direct mail professionals have discovered that you attract attention with white space, headlines and pictures. See the sample in Figure 7.3.

White space is expensive, but it gets attention. Test your market to see if it works for you.

Headlines should be short and punchy, promising the reader a quick, easy-to-understand benefit. Use words like *New, Now, How To, Announcing, At Last* and *Free*. Using a specific date in the headline is often effective.

A picture of your Free Offer is an excellent attention-getter. You should test it to see if it is worth the money you pay for the space it requires.

Figure 7.3　Sample Ad

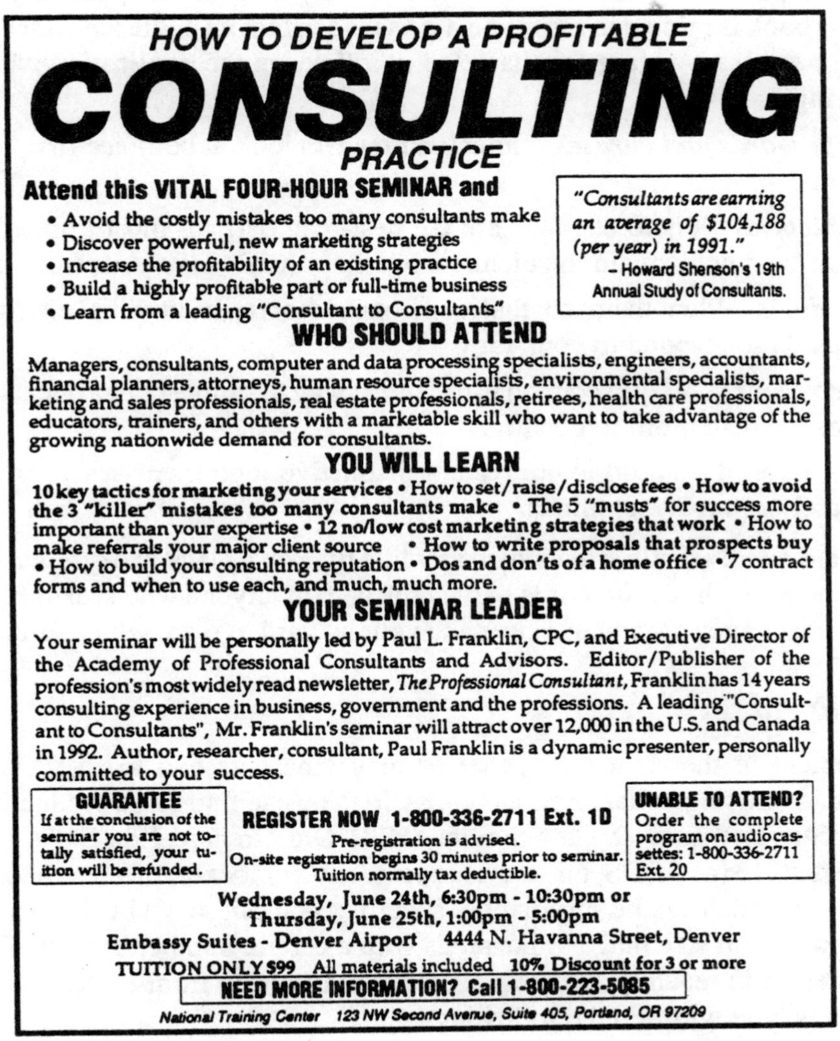

Layout

The slightest visual obstacle may prevent readers from completely reading your ad. In your layout use:

1. *Short paragraphs*   Indent the first line of each paragraph. Use six lines or less, even if you have to break the formal rules of paragraph structure.

2. *Ordinary, popular typefaces*   Use serif type if your audience generally is older than 35. This book is printed in serif type. Use sans serif for an audience under 35. The type should be at least as large as that used in articles in the publication where the ad is appearing.

3. *Boldface words and phrases*   Impatient readers look at boldface first to get the gist of your ad.

4. *Small pictures*   Photo captions are the best-read parts of most printed matter. The captions need not explain the pictures, but they should give your sales message.

5. *Subheadings*   Plan them so that someone who reads nothing else gets enough information to respond to your ad.

6. *Reply coupons*   A reply coupon is the surest way to bring about a decision. Ads with coupons are read more frequently.

7. *Logos*   Even if your ad is not read, a distinctive logo increases your prestige and acceptability in readers' minds.

You want to *avoid* artistic effects such as white type on a black background—except for a headline of no more than four words. Avoid the help of anyone who seeks *self-expression* through your ads. Fancy special effects make your ad hard to read, which turns off readers.

Placing Your Ad

Ad placement in the right newspaper or magazine gets two to five times as many responses per advertising dollar as poor choices do. You can find those productive media by checking the Standard Rate & Data Service (5201 Old Orchard Rd., Skokie, IL 60076). Commonly referred to as SRDS, this service provides a number of different books for media and mailing lists, which can be surprisingly specific. You can select business executives of companies of a certain size range or hospitals with a certain number of beds. For example, if you're interested in reaching firms with problems resulting from employees postponing their retirements, you will find the following:

Magazines: *Business and Heath, HR Magazine, HR News, Human Resource Executive, Personnel Journal* (from *Business Publications Rates and Data*)

Mailing lists: 92,000 personnel executives; 80,000 personnel administrators; 27,000 personnel and benefits executives (from *Direct Mail Lists Rates and Data*)

With this kind of guidance, you can target the most appropriate periodical or newspaper in which to advertise or the best mailing lists to use for direct mail campaigns.

The Rules of Advertising

Years of experience with advertising, both good and bad, have taught us four rules of thumb that you may not find in textbooks.

Effective and Cost-Efficient Advertising Is Specific Advertising

Advertising can be effective but not cost-efficient. It can bring in prospects, but it can cost too much to do so. Specific advertising costs less because the audience is smaller, and you can concentrate on magazines that reach your audience or use a small mailing list. An ad in *The Wall Street Journal* costs a lot more than an ad in a professional journal.

Test, Test, Test and Test Some More

Careful testing is the only proven avenue to success in advertising. Testing provides the feedback you need to develop ads and to protect yourself against the whims of inspiration.

If you are located in a major metropolitan area and elect to try newspaper advertising, test your ad in a smaller neighboring community before investing big dollars in the local metro daily. You can save up to 80 percent of the money needed for a test in a metropolitan area. Pick a community that resembles yours demographically and has a newspaper with similar reader characteristics. You can exercise the same caution with radio, magazine and direct mail campaign. For example, send out 1,000 direct mail pieces, not 20,000. This market test enables you to determine whether it is worthwhile to spend money on the larger campaign.

Extensive testing may be required, as a number of variables are involved, including:

- Frequency with which advertising appears.
- Dates and times when advertising is run.
- Promotional message being used.
- Size or length of advertising.
- Media in which advertising is placed.
- Price or fee charged by different outlets.

With so many variables, if one attempt fails, it doesn't mean the idea is bad. It might work with a different combination. Testing enables you to find out at minimal expense.

Keep track of the variables that affect the response to your ads. Placement on the page, size of the ad, the headline, the absence or presence of a coupon can all affect results. Record the response by ad and date so that you know how long it takes to get the full response to an ad. You might discover that for a daily paper 60 percent of the ad's total response comes within two days after it is run, 20 percent on the third day and 10 percent on the fourth. With this type of information, you can tell within a few days whether an ad is a winner or not. You can then purchase your advertising accordingly.

If you are running ads simultaneously in different publications, make sure that you can tell which ad is responsible for which responses. If you offer a free booklet, one way to trace responses is to code the request with a line such as: Ask for booklet NP-3.

If your early ads do not pull their own weight in immediate billings, don't abandon the whole concept of advertising. Experiment with different media, themes, Free Offer, graphics and other factors. If you keep at it, you will learn which combinations produce results. Treat each failed ad as a valuable investment in knowledge. You can then build on your successes and avoid failures.

Emphasize Immediate Response When Your Budget Is Limited

If your budget is limited, design ads that produce an immediate, direct response. This kind of ad proves or disproves itself quickly. The cash flow also may be improved because immediate-result ads usually turn revenue more quickly, reducing the amount of cash that has to be tied up in advertising.

Spend Only Enough To Get the Job Done

Consulting almost always requires individualized, one-on-one selling. So most consulting advertising is designed to create an inquiry, not a sale. Since consultants must talk with potential clients prior to making a sale, they need not make a large investment in advertising space to sell the service. It is cheaper to get someone to make contact than to make a sale.

Tips

If you follow the nine Low-Cost/No-Cost marketing strategies and use an effective Free Offer in combination with a good brochure, you likely will find yourself inundated with contacts. Once the potential client is in your door, you have to make the sale. Selling involves the same indirect strategy that you used to generate contacts—to sell without selling. At the same time you need to be skilled at asking for a close—actually getting the potential client to commit. The next chapter will cover this topic, showing you how to win contracts from your face-to-face meetings. An important element in entering negotiations and making a sale is knowing what the project will entail. If you can't make reliable estimates, you will end up badly underpricing or overpricing yourself—and either practice will hurt your consulting business. A good estimate leads to a good proposal—and a good proposal is an excellent way of selling yourself.

8

Selling Your Services

The very notion of selling is anathema to many consultants. It conjures up an image of a sleazy man in a checked suit haranguing customers with an obnoxious sales pitch. The traditional hard sell, which turns off many people and has given selling a bad name, certainly has no place in the sophisticated arena of the consultant.

Modern selling strategy eschews the hard sell in favor of a client-oriented approach. Rather than cramming a product or service down consumers' throats, today's sophisticated sellers determine the needs of their target markets and dovetail their product or service to fit those needs.

This modern approach is particularly well suited to consultants, whose services are built around clients' needs. Emphasis is placed not on imposing services on unwilling prospects but on providing solutions to problems and enabling clients to take advantage of opportunities.

During the selling phase of your marketing plan, you present yourself face-to-face with the prospect. The skill and confidence with which you handle the presentation will determine the eventual outcome—either a lost opportunity, or a contract and the possibility of additional business.

Controlling the Presentation

The key to a successful interview is control, which is your ability to exercise subtle restraining or directing influence over your prospect. The purpose of control is not to overpower the prospect but to exercise authority. Without control your chances of getting the contract are significantly decreased. In fact, control is the essence of selling, which can be defined as helping the prospect to identify his or her needs and demonstrating that you are in a unique position to satisfy those needs.

Most clients want to speak with you, a consultant, because they have a problem. They may or may not have given the problem much thought, even though they claim to have done so. Your ability to assess the problem quickly and succinctly will establish you at the outset as an authority, placing you in control of the situation. Don't wait for your prospective client to tell you when you can start exerting control. Instead, make controlling statements and requests, such as:

Could you sit over there, sir?

I will first demonstrate the outcomes that will be achieved. Then I will show you how. . .

Ask your prospect questions; start to give directions; keep control over your sales literature or examples. Show them to your prospect when you are ready.

Speak forcefully and with confidence. When your behavior indicates that you know what you are doing, your prospect will think that you know what you are doing and relinquish the control to you. A weak voice or tentative manner will undermine your authority. Don't say, *I want to give you some information.* Say, *I am going to.* . . Don't say, *I think.* Say, *I know.* Don't say, *This might.* Say, *This will.* Just remember that confidence should not be confused with boastfulness or arrogance.

Here are some tips on controlling a presentation:

- *A good first impression.* A strong and forceful (but not too forceful) greeting is a good start. Be firm and confident, from handshake to opening statement. Your dress and style should suggest command and authority without being intimidating.

- *Use your personality.* Don't be someone you're not! It won't work. Figure out your unique strengths and let them work for you. Be comfortable with who you are, and display your satisfaction with yourself. It has been said that the true sign of maturity is an acceptance of who and what you are. This maxim doesn't mean that you can't change or that you're not interested in change. It does mean that you accept yourself for what you are at the present time and that you can capitalize on it.

- *Think positive.* Have you ever gone to see a prospective client saying to yourself: I hope to get a contract? That mental posture, while not necessarily wrong, does not predispose you psychologically to making a sale. You are not as apt to succeed if you think in terms of *hope, might, maybe, perhaps.* Instead, think in terms of *can* and *will.* Always say to yourself: I'm going to get this contract. This person needs my services, and I intend to close the sale.

- *A smooth sales presentation.* Your prospect will not be as likely to interrupt if you give a logical, flowing sales presentation. A smooth presentation reduces your need to exercise outward control. It is always in your interest to maintain an aura of control without actually having to exert it.

A well-planned presentation answers all the major questions and objections. It demonstrates that you are in control and reduces the prospects' objections and concerns. Dragging out the presentation or meandering detracts from the main point and gives your prospective client a chance to ask questions out of sequence. When that happens, you lose control.

The Inexperienced Interviewer

Going into a meeting with a prospective client can be a disaster through no fault of your own. The prospect who does not know how to conduct a proper interview may receive a poor impression despite your best efforts.

The interviewer who slumps in the chair across from you and says, "Well, tell me about yourself," has just set the course for disaster. What do you talk about? What can you say to turn the prospect on to your services? You don't know what the client needs, so you can't speak to anything in particular. In such an open-ended void, simply say that you will be glad to talk about yourself, but that you would first like to ask a question.

After the prospective client agrees, ask him or her to describe the specific outcomes, benefits and results required for the project under consideration. Next, ask the prospect to describe the specific qualities that he or she is looking for in a consultant to handle the assignment. While both questions are being answered, take careful notes, either mentally or in writing. You can then formulate your response to the original question, should it arise again. Now you can match your specific capabilities to the client's needs.

You also want to know what experiences the client has had with other consultants in the past. Fundamentally, the question is whether the relationship was a good one. If not, what specifically did the client dislike? In what fashion have past consultants been compensated? The next thing to determine is whether the client expects to compensate you for this initial meeting.

Payment for the First Meeting

Consultants often have difficulty deciding whether or not to ask clients to pay for the first meeting during which a proposed project is discussed and before the contract is signed. Maybe that's an unreasonable expectation, and maybe it's not. Experience shows that roughly 20 percent of the clients anticipate that they are going to pay for the first meeting. So during that initial meeting, determine the client's attitude on paying. Clients who have not used a consultant before may fully expect to be billed for the meeting. Those who have used consultants before may realize that the first meeting has a marketing objective and that payment would be unreasonable.

The main drawback to requesting payment for the first meeting is that the client usually expects tangible results immediately instead of waiting for a plan of attack from the consultant. I recommend that you inform the client that the initial contact is an opportunity to get to know each other and to explore the project under consideration—and that it is customary not to charge for the initial contact. In the cost calculations presented later in this chapter, an initial contact is computed as part of your marketing expenses so that the client is paying for the initial meeting as part of your overhead.

Focus on the Problem

Of course, the main piece of information you will elicit during the interview is the client's understanding of the problem to be solved. Don't ask the client to tell you what you ought to do. The solution is your job. Instead, ask clients about their experience in working on the problem or situation. The emphasis is on the client's observations.

Ask the client what is supposed to look different after the consultation? What question is going to be answered? What situation is going to be changed? What thing is not going to be happening anymore? Try to uncover the client's concerns. Suppose the client says that the company would like to get personnel turnover down from 44 percent to 20 percent a year. You now know what is troubling the client and what would prove that the consultation was a success.

All these techniques set the stage for working with clients. You let clients know that you are interested in their situation, that you understand their problems and that you want to deal with them in a way that has meaning for them.

Making the Sale

Consultants have a hard time getting clients to say *yes*. The reason is usually that consultants are good technicians, but rarely good salespeople. However, you can decide to do one thing at an appropriate time with the client—ask for the contract.

Asking is one of the most important techniques in sales. A major midwestern university conducted research into professional sales techniques. In an analysis of the behavior of sales personnel, the study revealed that the 15 percent of the salespeople who were most effective, the ones who wrote the most orders and had the biggest book, were the ones who asked at least eight times for the order while giving their sales pitches. They repeatedly found different ways to ask for the order. They asked questions like: *When would you like this installed? Will it be all right with you if we install it next Wednesday?* They keep taking the aggressive role. On the other hand, the 19 percent who represented the least successful sellers never asked for the order. Some comment by the prospect during the sales presentation would indicate to them that the prospect didn't want to buy. Rather than risk being turned down, they never asked for the order. The study concluded that the most effective way to get the order was to ask for it in a number of different ways on a number of different occasions.

Asking is a good way to overcome the prospect's inaction. Press the point with statements like: *I think we have a good understanding of what needs to be done. I will start a week from today, and I will stop by tomorrow with a letter of agreement for your review and signature.* With such a statement, you have asked for the contract. You have made a definite proposal. The client has either to accept your offer or say *no* to you.

Inaction can be deadly. It can kill an otherwise lively deal. If the buying decision has not been made, you want to concentrate your efforts on getting it made in your favor. Keep selling. If the client has decided to buy your services but for some reason postpones implementation, don't spend time trying to sell the client any longer. Concentrate on finding out why the prospect won't implement.

Usually, clients fail to implement because they don't know how. They want you, and you want them. They like what you are going to do, but they don't know the mechanics of getting started. Many people who retain consultants don't pay for them. They don't even write purchase orders. When they need a widget, they ask for one, and someone else writes a purchase order. So you have to be prepared to implement for them, at the same time easing their embarrassment at not knowing how to implement. You develop the contract or letter of agreement. You specify the wording for the purchase order.

Another reason for postponing implementation is a lack of funds. You may have to help them find the funds, maybe a grant, to get the contract. Or you show them how they can generate the funds internally. If the funds are in the organization's coffers, but not available for the project because it doesn't seem important enough, you might demonstrate that the project has a higher priority than the client thinks.

Finally, some clients fail to implement simply because they get cold feet. Everyone hesitates before making a major purchase. People who buy consulting services experience the same last-minute reluctance. The only thing to do is to reassure the client that the decision is the right one and recall all the benefits of the consultation.

Body Language

Many sales authorities take careful note of nonverbal communications. Here are some typical nonverbal signals and what they communicate:

Folded Arms
Very defensive. . . Prove it to me.

Crossed Legs
Bored and defensive.

Hand Stroking the Chin
I'm thinking about it. . . . I haven't reached a decision.

Putting Something (Like a Pencil) in the Mouth
Give me more information. . . . What's in it for me?

Touching or Rubbing the Nose
I doubt it. . . . I don't believe you. . . . Doesn't make sense.

Rubbing the Eyes
Convince me. . . . I really don't know. . . . Tell me I should.

Sitting on the Edge of the Chair
I'm interested. . . . I'm cooperative.

Unbuttoning of Coat/Jacket
I'm opening up to you. . . . I believe you.

Tilted Head
I'm still interested.

Short In and Out Breaths
  Frustration and disgust. . . Get out of here, now!

Tightly Clenched Hands
  I'm tense. . . not relaxed. . . . I'm getting hostile.

Palm to the Back of the Neck
  Defense. . . Uncertain and apprehensive. . . Are you through?

Clearing Throat
  Uncertain and apprehensive.

Fingers Positioned To Make a Church Steeple
  Confident. . . I'm very sure of what you are saying.

Tugging at Ear
  I want to say something. . . . I want to talk.

By paying attention to body language you can sharpen your sales skills. The key to sales is control of the situation. If you know what your prospect is thinking about you and your presentation, you have a definite advantage.

Ego and Control

Letting your ego control your reactions to clients can have an adverse effect on your sales efforts, as illustrated by the following example. A university professor received a call from a consulting firm interested in having three *smart* graduate students do an image study of the firm. The students, who didn't know very much about image study, were flattered and worked to become conversant in the subject.

In a meeting at the consulting firm, the president and vice president explained what they wanted done. The students in turn explained their enlightened approach. The president and vice president said that was not exactly what they had in mind, and they again explained how they wanted things done. The students became insulted and left without the consulting job.

The students let their egos get involved. They would not compromise their professional standards (so newly acquired) for the crass approach suggested. Since they could not be in control, they refused to be associated with the job. If you think the client is denying you sufficient control over the project, ask yourself whether you really don't trust the people in control—or is your ego getting in the way? Most often, you will find that it is your ego.

Consulting can be defined as the art of the possible. Realistic, successful consultations result from shared objectives and approaches between clients and consultants. An unwillingness to subvert your ego to the requirements of the job can only end in disaster.

Estimates and Sales

The foundation of your relationship with your clients is your ability to accurately estimate the needs of the client and the situation. This estimate guides your proposal and your estimate of costs to the client. Without a thorough understanding of what is involved in a particular assignment, you will be unable to draw up an effective and fair contract. Your estimate and description of a given project form the basis of your proposal, which can be a very effective sales instrument. If you can't make solid believable cost estimates, you can hardly expect to impress prospects with your efficiency and professionalism.

Estimating is a matter of time and discipline. It calls for thought, work and calculation. Yet if you take the time and do the work, you should be able to come up with very accurate estimates. Admittedly, the first one or two estimates may not be as close to the actual costs as you might like. But as you do more of them, you collect detailed feedback, and you can be more accurate on future estimates.

Seventy-six consultants polled by *The Professional Consultant* were asked questions about fee setting, contracts and estimates. They were asked to cite the cause when costs exceeded estimates. In reply, 73 percent of those who used a fixed-price contract and 59 percent of those who used a daily rate contract reported poor estimating as the cause.

The consultants working exclusively on fixed-price contracts also evaluated their ability at estimating. Of those who ranked themselves as *very good,* costs exceeded the original estimates in only 14 percent of the cases. Of those who evaluated themselves as being *not very good* the percentage of overruns was 29 percent. The key to profitability in fixed-price contracts is reliable estimates.

Preparing a reliable estimate entails:

- Mapping out the entire project to identify its components.

- Assigning detailed cost estimates to each component.

- Totaling the costs for all components.

- Applying the overhead rate and profit.

The Functional Flow Diagram (FFD)

To visualize the project as a whole, construct a pictorial flowchart of what must be done. Review it, revise it and redraw it until you can't think of anything else that can be done. If you are uncertain about your comprehensiveness, ask someone to review the diagram. Sometimes a fresh pair of eyes sees things that you don't. Suppose a client needs a training program in sales and product maintenance for branch office personnel. Your first step would be to construct what is called a functional flow diagram (FFD), such as the one shown in Figure 8.1.

The FFD is made up of a series of lines and boxes:

- Each box represents a major component of project activity, indicated by a label in the box. These labels should begin with action verbs, such as *administer, analyze, compute, design, determine, tabulate.*

- Every box must have an input and an output. See Figure 8.2. In the course of designing your FFD, additional activities may have to be added. In Figure 8.2, for example, you may decide that the names of persons to be surveyed will have to be determined. The result of this activity or step would have to feed into Box 2.

Figure 8.1   A Typical Functional Flow Diagram

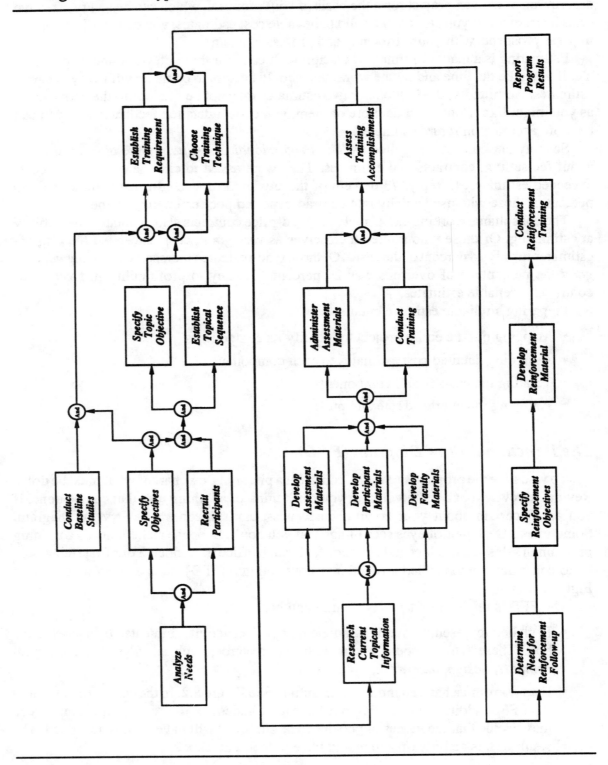

Figure 8.2   Example of Input/Output Elements

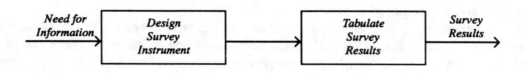

Figure 8.3   Example of "And" Connective

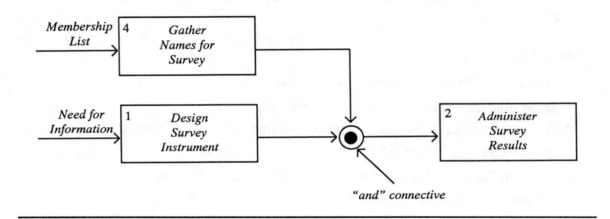

Figure 8.4   Example of "Or" Connective

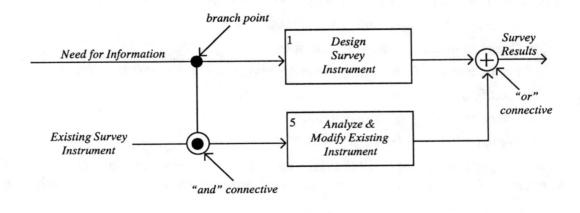

Figure 8.3 indicates how you would make this addition. The added symbol is called a *connective*. There are two kinds of connectives: "and" connectives and "or" connectives. In Figure 8.3, the "and" connective is used to demonstrate that the result or output of both Functions 1 and 4 is required to proceed with Function 2.

The "or" connective indicates either a *choice point*, when used on the input side of a function, or a *branch point*, when used on the output side of a function. Suppose that in this particular project you could modify the survey instrument used by the client last year rather than design a new one. The benefit of doing so remains to be studied. Figure 8.4 describes this future option.

Consider using such options liberally. They anticipate decisions so that you don't have to make up your mind suddenly on the basis of limited data. These options enable you to demonstrate to your client that full consideration is given to all viable alternatives. This point may be particularly useful in a competitive situation since it demonstrates that a part of your bid, estimate or fixed price includes a series of decisions involving choices between viable alternatives.

Itemized Estimates

As you review Figure 8.1, you can foresee having to:

1. Determine trainee information requirements.

2. Assess competence of trainees relative to information requirements.

3. Develop training objectives.

4. Select indicators/measures that ensure objectives have been met.

5. Determine training requirements.

6. Formulate training outlines.

7. Create training agendas.

If you've done similar projects before, perhaps this degree of detail is enough. If not, you probably should itemize each activity further. Take the first entry: *Determine trainee information requirements*. The detailed breakdown might look like this:

1a. Develop management interview guides.

1b. Create branch office survey instruments.

1c. Conduct test of face validity for interview guides/survey instruments.

1d. Modify interview guides/survey instruments.

1e. Interview management personnel.

1f. Write preliminary findings report.

Although this degree of detail is usually enough, you can break each of these items down even further. The second entry, *Create branch office survey instruments*, might look like this:

- Determine type of questionnaire to be used.
- Select questionnaire items.
- Develop scales or measures.
- Write questions to be used.
- Develop survey instrument shell.

You may continue to break down the components of a job until you feel familiar enough with the subdivisions to make reasonable "sub-estimates." For subcomponents that are still difficult to estimate, ask for some advice. Perhaps a business acquaintance or someone you work with can help you with that part of the estimate.

Assigning Costs

For each component assign precise, detailed estimates, using a pricing sheet such as the one shown in Figure 8.5. This form enables you to cover all possible sources of cost for each component of the project, even the smallest or most remote. It also makes estimating easier by enabling you to work on one relatively small part of the project at a time. For example, estimating an engineer's time on one inspection tour is much easier than estimating time on the project as a whole.

On the pricing sheet, the costs are categorized as either *Direct Labor* or *Direct Expense*. Your needs may warrant additional or different classifications. You can make up your own sheet, modeling it on this illustration.

To calculate labor, estimate the time, in hours or days, that each category of personnel is likely to spend on the subcomponent. Then note the rate to be applied for that type of employee. If you have a specific individual lined up for the job, use that consultant's rate.

Do the same for direct expenses. In some cases you can estimate units, such as the miles driven in an auto. In other cases you simply have to put down a lump sum. Let's say that you're estimating on the final report. When you get to *Printing/Photocopying*, you know that the report has to be roughly 50 pages and that you need 25 copies. If you pay 10 cents a copy for your photocopying, your cost here is $125 (50 pages x 25 copies x $.10).

Let's say the project calls for three plane trips to the factory. Under *Auto*, you would insert three times the mileage to and from your local airport, as you'll have to drive your car to the airport and back three times. The cost of the three plane tickets goes into the box for *Air*. And, if the client does not provide transportation at the airport near the plant, insert under *Rental Car* the cost of car rental for three days.

As you can see, very few, if any, costs can escape this system. Having a stack of preprinted pricing sheets makes the estimating process all the easier. The breakdowns for our training program are shown in Figure 8.6.

Totaling the Pricing Sheets

This step is simply a matter of arithmetic. Take a blank pricing sheet and label it: *Total Pricing Sheet*. Then go through all your subcomponent pricing sheets and total each type of

Figure 8.5   Pricing Sheet

Project Title _____

No. _____

Component _____

Direct Labor	Days/Hours	Rates	Total
Senior Consultant(s)	_____	_____	_____
Junior Consultant(s)	_____	_____	_____
Clerical Personnel	_____	_____	_____
Drafting Personnel	_____	_____	_____
Subtotal			_____

Direct Expenses	Units	@	Total
Auto (in miles)	_____	_____	_____
Phone	_____	_____	_____
Postage	_____	_____	_____
Air	_____	_____	_____
Hotel (per day)	_____	_____	_____
Rental Car (per day)	_____	_____	_____
Printing/Photocopying	_____	_____	_____
Subtotal			_____

Overhead   _____

General and Administrative Expense   _____

Profit   _____

Total   _____ expense. In the example in Figure 8.6, you would add up the number of days spent by senior consultants on the whole project:

1a. Develop interview guides	1/4 day
1b. Create branch survey instruments	1/2 day
1c. Test face validity	0 days
1d. Modify guides/survey instrument	1/4 day
1e. Conduct interview	1-1/2 days
1f. Write final report	2 days
Total senior consultant's time	4-1/2 days

You would repeat this step for *all* the pricing sheets for *all* the subcomponents of the job. The 4-1/2 days for component 1 (a through f) would be added to the subtotals for other parts of the project. When you have collected all the hours for senior personnel, place the total in the appropriate box on the total pricing sheet. Then multiply that figure by the daily labor rate (in our example, $300) for the total labor cost for senior consultants. Repeat the process for all personnel. Add the totals for each category of labor to derive the cost of all direct labor for the project. Next, enter the total costs of all direct expenses (auto, phone, and so on), and add these figures for total direct expenses.

In our example the total for direct labor totals $3,840, while direct expenses total $949. The cost of the job to you (including your own daily labor rate) is therefore $4,789.

Applying the Overhead Rate and Profit

This calculation is simple. The overhead rate is applied to the direct labor rate. The profit percentage is applied to the total charges. In our example the calculation is as follows:

Direct labor	$3,840
Overhead rate (85%)	3,264
Direct expenses	949
Subtotal	$8,053
Profit (18%)	1,450
Total	$9,503

With this estimate you need to be sure that you have broken down your project into specific enough segments and that your overhead is really 85 percent. If these two points are firm, then you should be quite safe in assuming that the $9,503 will yield the profit you seek.

Normally, the client sees only the total figure. That is, the client knows that the total fixed price for getting the job done is $9,503. Your labor rates, overhead and rate of profit are confidential. However, if the client is a government agency, they may require that your proposal include a line item budget. If so, you can then enter these figures in a spreadsheet, which gives you an overview of the entire project and clearly demonstrates to the client that

Figure 8.6 Estimates by Components

1a. Develop Interview Guides

Direct Labor	Days	Rate*	Total
Senior Consultant(s)	1/4	$300	$ 75
Junior Consultant(s)	1/4	200	50
Clerical Personnel	1/4	60	15
Drafting Personnel	1/2	80	40
Subtotal			$180

Direct Expense	Unit	@	Total
Auto			$ 0
Phone			10
Postage			0
Air			0
Hotel (per day)			0
Rental Car			0
Printing/Photocopying			4
Subtotal			$14

*Note: Rate refers to daily salary, not billing rate. See Chapter 9.

1b. Create Branch Survey Instruments

Direct Labor	Days	Rate	Total
Senior Consultant(s)	1/2	$300	$150
Junior Consultant(s)	1	200	200
Clerical Personnel	1/2	60	30
Drafting Personnel	1/2	80	40
Subtotal			$420

Direct Expense	Unit	@	Total
Auto			$ 0
Phone			15
Postage			0
Air			0
Hotel (per day)			0
Rental Car			0
Printing/Photocopying			5
Subtotal			$20

Figure 8.6   Estimates by Components (Continued)

1c. Test Face Validity

Direct Labor	Days	Rate	Total
Senior Consultant(s)	0	$300	0
Junior Consultant(s)	1/2	200	$100
Clerical Personnel	0	60	0
Drafting Personnel	0	80	0
Subtotal			$100

Direct Expense	Unit	@	Total
Auto	75mi	.20/mi	$ 15
Phone			10
Postage			0
Air			0
Hotel (per day)			70
Rental Car			0
Printing/Photocopying			5
Subtotal			$100

1d. Modify Guides/Survey Instrument

Direct Labor	Days	Rate	Total
Senior Consultant(s)	1/4	$300	$ 75
Junior Consultant(s)	1/4	200	50
Clerical Personnel	1/4	60	15
Drafting Personnel	1/4	80	20
Subtotal			$160

Direct Expense	Unit	@	Total
Auto	75mi	.20/mi	$ 15
Phone			25
Postage			0
Air			120
Hotel (per day)			100
Rental Car			50
Printing/Photocopying			10
Subtotal			$320

Figure 8.6   Estimates by Components (Continued)

1e.   Conduct Interview

Direct Labor	Days	Rate	Total
Senior Consultant(s)	1-1/2	$300	$450
Junior Consultant(s)	0	200	0
Clerical Personnel	0	60	0
Drafting Personnel	0	80	0
Subtotal			$450

Direct Expense	Unit	@	Total
Auto	75mi	.20/mi	$ 15
Phone			25
Postage			0
Air			120
Hotel (per day)			100
Rental Car			50
Printing/Photocopying			10
Subtotal			$320

1f. Write Final Report

Direct Labor	Days	Rate	Total
Senior Consultant(s)	2	$300	$600
Junior Consultant(s)	3	200	600
Clerical Personnel	2	60	120
Drafting Personnel	1/2	80	40
Subtotal			$1360

Direct Expense	Unit	@	Total
Auto	75mi	.20/mi	$15
Phone			20
Postage			5
Air			0
Hotel (per day)			0
Rental Car			0
Printing/Photocopying			135
Subtotal			$175

you have not produced your figures out of thin air. One of the client's concerns is that a consultant's fee is based more on imagination than reality since there is no *solid* product like a car or a building. For the client there is something a little mysterious in the entire consulting process, and a spreadsheet with figures you can explain and justify lends an element of reality to an otherwise mystifying activity.

Flexibility

One of the major advantages of this approach is your ability to be flexible with the client. Let's assume that you have presented your proposal to the client, who likes everything about it except the total fixed price. Your client informs you that the budget for this training program is only $9,000. Probably the worst thing you could do is to agree to do it for $9,000. With this reaction you tell the client that your estimate contains at least $503 worth of fat.

Instead, go back to your bid sheet, and pick out some less important item(s) that could be cut from the project. Then go to your client and say, "If we eliminated the testing for face validity of the questionnaire and survey instruments and cut the follow-up training to two days rather than three at each branch office, we could do the project for $9,000." Now the decision is with your client. Making such changes is easy when you have done a good job of estimating with a bid sheet.

In the larger consulting practice, a number of individuals are likely to contribute to a given project. In such a case perhaps the bid sheet should be put together through the joint efforts of several individuals. The person who is responsible for the component of the project should usually bid it. However, one person, probably you, should coordinate and control the efforts of the bidding individuals. You want to ensure that those responsible for bids don't pad their estimates and that the estimates of others are not unrealistically high.

Padding the Estimate

Beware the *creeping pad* when more than one person contributes to an estimate. Example: You ask a staff member (Joe) to estimate the labor for part of the project. Joe asks a second staff member (Jane) to provide an estimate to him. Feeling that Jane may have estimated *light,* Joe pads it a bit. When the estimate comes to you, you feel that Jane may be *light* and pad her estimate—hence, the creeping pad. Before long, what was supposed to take seven working days is increased to twelve because everyone feels that Jane has not added in any slack.

There is nothing wrong with padding estimates to compensate for the underestimates of others. Only one person, however, should be charged with the responsibility of padding. If not, you may become the unwitting victim of the creeping pad, and you may grossly overprice your services. For a much more detailed discussion of estimating, see *The Contract and Fee-Setting Guide for Consultants and Professionals* by Howard L. Shenson (see the bibliography).

The Written Proposal

The written proposal is an important part of selling your services. It shows the client what is needed and how you can supply it, without giving away or underpricing your services. If the sale has already been closed, the proposal is an outline of the project and does not need to emphasize the qualities that would convince a client to sign.

This section will outline how to produce a proposal that will sell your services. A simple working proposal is similar and can be based on this outline. For an expanded, step-by-step guide to writing winning proposals, and samples/examples of proposals, see *The Consultant's Guide to Proposal Writing* by Howard L. Shenson (see the bibliography); for a quick sample see Figure 8.7.

The proposal should be developed only when you believe that a good opportunity for success justifies the expenditure of time and effort. The proposal must communicate your ideas so that the reader (the decision maker) is convinced that you can achieve what you propose within the budget estimate or fixed price you quote.

You must convince the client that the need for the consultation is important. This involves showing that not implementing the consultation will harm the client's interests and that your goals and objectives will correct the problem and take care of the need. The client must be convinced that the procedures you propose are the best and only alternative for taking care of the problem or need. And you must accomplish these objectives without giving your services away.

The proposal is divided into three sections: the front section, the main section and the conclusion.

The Front Section

The front section of the proposal communicates your understanding of the purposes of the consultation and the needs it is intended to fulfill. If your services have been sought by the client, you will show your understanding of those needs. If you are seeking to inform the client of the need for using your services, you need to show what undesirable consequences will develop for the client if you're not retained.

The front section establishes objectives and goals that will direct the services you will deliver. Goals are statements of broad direction or intent. Objectives are specific statements of outcome presented in a format that will enable the client and consultant to determine when they have been met. This section also establishes a mandate for action, such as compliance with existing or expected laws, cost effectiveness, warding off adverse publicity and increased profits.

The front section usually includes the following:

- A letter of transmittal
- The proposal cover
- The proposal title page

- An abstract
- A table of contents
- A statement of assurances
- A statement of objectives
- A statement of need

In addition to indicating that the proposal is being delivered to the client organization, the letter of transmittal also conveys your availability and high level of commitment to the proposed project.

The cover should be of professional quality. The title page may include limitations on distribution. The abstract is a one-page, single-spaced summary—brief and to the point. The table of contents is a road map through the document. It should make the reader want to go on by arousing interest in the same way newspaper headlines do.

The statement of assurances can communicate that:

- Your proposal is, in your estimation, the most cost effective possible consistent with needs.
- There are no lawsuits or judgments pending against you.
- You do not discriminate in hiring.
- You self-insure and hold your client blameless and will defend any lawsuits.

This statement should be signed by the highest official of your consulting practice and dated.

The statement of need and statement of objectives are the two most important parts of the front section. The statement of need enables the reader to independently assess the extent and validity of the needs that the proposal addresses and creates a sense of obligation to respond to the needs you have identified. Be sure to describe the problems in terms that are meaningful to the client. Avoid the use of soft terms such as *a substantial number*, *a high degree* and *a downward trend*. Use hard and quantifiable terms.

Each objective that you formulate in the statement of objectives must convey some specific information to the reader. Each objective should:

Describe the outcome you intend to produce.

Provide a means of *measuring the results*.

Set the level or quality of outcome necessary to carry out the project.

The Main Section

The main section of the proposal contains the functional flow diagram (FFD), a time-line communicating when the work should be/will be done and a written narrative explaining the results and benefits to be achieved by each activity outlined in the FFD.

We have already discussed how to formulate the FFD. The time-line gives dates or periods of time needed to complete each stage of the project. The time-line can be expressed as a line with the dates and project stages marked on it. Don't be too concerned about having exactly the right amount of time between events; just be sure that you have them in order and that you have left sufficient time for the necessary client reviews and approvals.

The written narrative communicates the outcomes, results and benefits of the consultation to the reader. It shows how the FFD will achieve the objectives and communicates the fact that the client will have the opportunity to manage you, the consultant. For each activity/box in your FFD diagram, write a one-paragraph or two-paragraph statement about the activity, and describe in general terms which procedures will be employed. Your written narrative should be specific enough to communicate to the reader the type of work you will be doing and general enough to prevent your client from taking your work and getting a free or lower cost consultation.

The Conclusion Section

The concluding section of the proposal may include:

- Evaluation plan and procedures
- Reporting and dissemination plan
- Consultation/project management and organization plan
- Consultation/project price/bid
- Consultation staff statement of capability

Not every proposal will require all these elements. The evaluation plan, when required, is important to the client in accepting or rejecting your proposal. It provides some type of measurement of the quality of your work and the viability of the specific plan you are proposing. The evaluation plan is the means by which the client can hold you accountable for the funds that have been spent.

The project management plan contains information that enables the reader to assess your qualifications to be awarded the contract. The plan must show that the consultation will be conducted by individuals who have an understanding of client needs and can work with the client's administrative structure. The management plan also demonstrates that the consultant has management and administrative skills as well as creative ideas. Many people are creative, but they have trouble getting results because they are poor managers.

The management plan should describe the administrative structure of the project, including:

- A detailed list of any key positions and associated responsibilities and duties.
- A description of the connective link between consultants working on the project and the client's organization.
- Estimates of the personnel that you anticipate will be needed to complete the project (a personnel loading analysis).
- A description of the background and qualifications of personnel who will be assigned to the project.

- A description of any outside individuals or organizations that will be needed to carry out the project, if necessary.

The personnel loading analysis gives the distribution of work hours or days for each element of the project. If you find that certain elements require too many personnel or hours, you may reorganize the time-line to spread out the functions more evenly over time.

The fee or bid is most often introduced in the proposal at this point. Depending on the distribution of your written proposal, you may wish to include the price/bid here or put it in a confidential letter that is delivered separately with your formal proposal.

The statement of staff capability usually includes a statement of the resources and talents of the organization and the specific resumes of key personnel who will contribute to the client's project. Staff resumes should be completed in a standard format. Have staff members prepare their own resumes within the confines of your standard format, and have them update at least every six months.

In packaging the proposal, consider using index tabs or dividers and keying the table of contents to the index tabs. If the client gives you a specific format, follow it as closely as possible. If you are sending examples of previous work that run more than five or six pages, put them in an appendix that can be detached from the main body of the proposal.

Don't be afraid to spend a few dollars on the package. Use good quality cover stock, color paper and comb binding to enhance the appearance of your proposal. You don't wish to appear lavish and wasteful, but you can produce a superior-looking document that is both cost effective and worthwhile.

The written final report has become commonplace for many client organizations. It may call for up to 100 or more copies to be disseminated.

Tips

This chapter has taken you from the initial stages of selling in a face-to-face situation to estimating the requirements of the project and drawing up a proposal. Part of the estimate is your daily billing rate. The next chapter will go into detail about setting your fees and determining your billing rates. When you go into a sales session with solid figures on your costs and fees as well as confidence in your worth and understanding of the needs of a particular project, you have a much better chance of making a close and getting a contract with which you can work.

Figure 8.7   Sample Proposal

Date

Name
Company
Address
City/State/Zip

Dear   :

I enjoyed our telephone conversation of _____. AAA has
an excellent marketing opportunity for its video seminars as public
seminar programs, and this letter is designed to serve as a proposal
to define the steps that I believe should be undertaken to evaluate
and capitalize on the marketing potential. When we spoke, I had
received only the video introduction, leader guide and participant
materials for _____. Following our conversation, I received
your letter of _____ and enclosures. The enclosures were
particularly beneficial in the preparation of this proposal, and I
apologize for taking your time on the telephone to answer questions
that were handled by the enclosures.

In my estimation the decision of how to distribute should be
based upon a recognition that AAA brings to the market for distributors a significant and very valuable asset. Accordingly, the analysis of options should carefully determine the market value of the
programs to ensure that the full profit potential be realized. Careful attention needs to be given to potential outside distributors
relative to such factors as:
   Market experience and capability;
   Financial viability and resources;
   Importance of the AAA opportunity to their business; and
   Credibility and capability to perform at a high level.
I believe that the following steps should be undertaken to evaluate and capitalize upon the marketing (as public seminars) of AAA
seminars in general and _____, specifically

1. **Determine the relative advantages and disadvantages of self-
   distribution in comparison to obtaining one or more established distributors.**

This step would include a competitive analysis of distributors, a
determination of their marketing capabilities and their financial
viability/future plans. It would also include an estimation of expenses and revenues (a pro forma) for self distribution and would

Figure 8.7 Sample Proposal (Continued)

Name
Company
Date
Page 2

evaluate various self-distribution models, such as licensing, fran-
chising and establishing an independent dealer network. Particular
attention would be paid to operating practices and distribution
models of successful and less-than-successful operating practices
and distribution systems of established seminar companies, including
such organizations as . . . . Further, the evaluation would concentrate on emerging learning methods that may, in time, prove more
efficient and effective that live seminars and the consequences than
such technological changes might have on AAA programs in general and
_____ in particular.

2. Identify and select potential outside distributors.

Step 2 would build on the work already accomplished in Step 1 and
would serve to identify those organizations that might serve as a
suitable distributor for AAA programs as public seminars in general
and _____ specifically. The result of this activity would
be to identify a list of candidate organizations that might be solicited by AAA for that purpose. It is anticipated that such candidates would include established seminar providers, as well as other
organizations not currently involved in the seminar business with
strong, related marketing capabilities who would be in a position to
serve as a viable distributor.

3. Establish requirements for performance by outside dis-tributors.

This step would establish minimum requirements that distributors
would have to meet to be acceptable to AAA and would be based on
marketing and financial information gained about providers in general and candidate distributors as a result of the analysis undertaken in Steps 1 and 2. It is anticipated that such requirements
would be quite specific about the nature and extent of marketing
effort to be provided by potential distributors to ensure that dis-
tributions proposals submitted in the future by such candidates
could be adequately evaluated relative to self-distribution options.

Figure 8.7   Sample Proposal (Continued)

Name
Company
Date
Page 3

4. Structure offering package to outside distributors.

On the basis of minimum requirements for distributors established as a result of the completion of Step 3 and the determination of the profit potential for self-distribution determined as a part of Step 1, the specific offer(s)/proposal(s) to be made to potential distributors would be developed.

5. Solicit outside distributors.

Offer(s)/proposal(s) developed in Step 4 would be forwarded to candidate distributors.

6. Review outside distributor responses.

Responses received from interested distributors would be reviewed, and acceptable respondents would be interviewed and evaluated.

7. Decide on method of distribution/select outside distributor(s).

Acceptable distributor offers/proposals (as modified as a result of Step 6) would be evaluated and compared to self-distribution options, and final decision would be made with respect to the distribution for _____, specifically and perhaps for other AAA programs as well.

I believe that the above activities can be accomplished as quickly as follows:

February 17 - March 6, 1992
1. **Determine the relative advantages and disadvantages of self-distribution in comparison to obtaining one or more established distributors.**

March 2 - March 13, 1992
2. **Identify and select potential outside distributors.**

March 9 - March 20, 1992
3. **Establish requirements for performance by outside distributors.**

Figure 8.7 Sample Proposal (Continued)

Name
Company
Date
Page 4

      March 9 - March 20, 1992
      4. Structure offering package to outside distributors.

      March 16 - March 27, 1992
      5. Solicit outside distributors.

      March 30 - April 17, 1992
      6. Review outside distributor responses.

      April 13 - April 24, 1992
      7. Decide upon method of distribution/select outside distributor(s).

I would be pleased to provide my services in connection with the above to AAA on either a per hour fee basis or on a fixed-fee plus expenses basis, as you determine to be in your best interest. Listed below is my estimate of the hours that I anticipate would be required on my part to complete the above activities. Also, please find the fixed fee that would be charged for the completion of each activity. If it is your preference to work on an hourly fee basis, the charge would be _____ dollars ($XXX) per hour.

    1. Determine the relative advantages and disadvantages of self-distribution in comparison to obtaining one or more established distributors.

        Estimated number of hours   30-40
        Fixed fee charge $_____

    2. Identify and select potential outside distributors.

        Estimated number of hours   12-20
        Fixed fee charge $_____

    3. Establish requirements for performance by outside distributors.

        Estimated number of hours   10-15
        Fixed-fee charge $_____

    4. Structure offering package to outside distributors.

        Estimated number of hours   14-19
        Fixed-fee charge $_____

Figure 8.7   Sample Proposal (Continued)

Name
Company
Date
Page 5

5. Solicit outside distributors.
　　Estimated number of hours　　　　01-04
　　Fixed-fee charge　　　　　　　　$_____
6. Review outside distributor responses.
　　Estimated number of hours　　　　10-30
　　Fixed-fee charge　　　　　　　　$_____
7. Decide on method of distribution/select outside distributor(s).
　　Estimated number of hours　　　　15-25
　　Fixed-fee charge　　　　　　　　$_____

In addition to the above, AAA would be charged for direct expenses incurred for travel and nonroutine communications, if any. The above estimates are based upon a total meeting time with you or others you might designate in amount equal to 15 hours. Should it become necessary to meet for a duration or frequency in excess of 15 hours, additional meeting time would be billed at $XXX per hour. There would be no charge for the first 25 hours of travel time, if any.

There is no requirement on my part for AAA to contract for all of the services indicated above. If you prefer, they can be taken one at a time, and you could reach a decision at each stage as to the wisdom of further retention of my services. In the event that you were to find it advisable to contract for all or several of the services outlined, please understand that AAA would be provided with the right to terminate my services at any time during the course of the consultation.

I hope that the above information is sufficient to meet your requirements. If I may provide further information, please don't hesitate to let me know.

I look forward to the prospect of working with you on this very challenging project.

Personal regards,

_____

9

Setting Your Fees

A successful marketing plan will bring in more calls than you can handle. After sifting through the many contacts, you have lined up a number of appointments with the most suitable prospects. You have driven to the client's place of business, you have been ushered into the office and made comfortable with a seat and a cup of coffee. Over the next hour you have discussed one or two very interesting and challenging assignments. The prospect seems all but ready to become your client. At this point she smiles and asks how much this will cost.

That moment is not the time to start thinking about fees. The time to set fees is at the very outset of your business. Your fee is based on your skills, the need for your talents and the assumption that you will give your clients *state-of-the-art* services. This chapter will introduce you to the basics and philosophy of setting fees. For a more detailed description of the process, see *The Contract and Fee-Setting Guide for Consultants and Professionals* by Howard L. Shenson (see the bibliography).

State of the Art

Businesspeople don't contract with consultants to get the same tired, old solutions and approaches. They want and deserve the benefit of the state of the art. If the client's work calls for computerized handling, you are not rendering a proper service by cranking out the data on a desk calculator over the weekend. Not only is cutting this kind of corner a disservice to the client; it can also reflect poorly on you in the long run. Asking clients to pay for cheap, shortcut methods is as unethical as overcharging them for top-notch processes.

For example, the compilation of field survey data is best done on a computer. The work may be done quickly on a tabletop personal computer or by a large-scale computer service. How much computerization you bring in depends on the amount of data and the processing requirements, as well as on the budget.

The same principle applies to human resources. Given an opportunity to use someone who is going to charge you a lower fee and enable you to make a greater profit, your concern must be whether you are shortchanging the client. If the same talent and ability can be purchased at lower cost, so be it. No one suffers, and you prosper. If your judgment indicates that the lower-priced talent does not meet the specifications of the contract or your own requirements, you are not giving your client the state of the art in human resources.

Name Your Price

Don't be afraid to lay your fee on the table. If you select one or more of the fee-setting methods in this chapter or as long as you arrive at your fee through a reasonable calculation, you should not allow that amount to be negotiated. Given a change in requirements or specifications, which in turn lowers the amount of time or the level of expertise required, the cost of a particular contract is certainly negotiable—but not your base rate and not your underlying calculations.

As a consultant you may find yourself about to lose a contract award to a competitor on the basis of price. In general *bidding lower* to keep the assignment is not good policy. Doing so gives the impression that your original bid was inflated in the first place. The logical and probably unasked question in the client's mind is: Why didn't I get this price the first time? From your point of view, if your fee contains a reasonable profit in the first place, you should not settle for a less-than-reasonable profit.

Competitors who underbid you dramatically tend to have short business lives. They *might* have a secret formula that enables them to survive, or perhaps even thrive, on lower fees. If so, they deserve the contract. More likely they are underpricing themselves just to get the work, which often turns out to be less than satisfactory to the client. Even if these low-ball competitors stay in business, they can become your best advertising. In such cases you will see that client again.

Don't be afraid to stick by your fee—as long as it is reasonable.

Determining the Dollar Value To Be Charged

If you feel you should be earning, say, $500 a day, you might have to bill out at $900 or $1,000. The difference accounts for something many consultants forget about—overhead and profit. You cannot price yourself as a laborer because you have an office to support.

The senior partner of a major CPA firm who charges $1,000 or more a day is not getting rich quickly. Large firms have a lot of overhead. A typical management consulting firm breaks down its fees into thirds. One-third covers the cost of the job, one-third covers the nonmarketing overhead and one-third covers the marketing overhead and profit. If such a firm is charging $750 a day, the consultant is earning $250. The other $500 is split between the two types of overhead and affords a reasonable profit.

As you know by now, going into business as a consultant means just that—going into business. Expenses must be controlled and accounted for, and profits must be calculated and monitored. As the owner/operator of a product-oriented business, you would be concerned with inventories, raw material costs, depreciation and other expenses related to manufacturing or shipping. In a service-oriented business, you must be just as concerned about expenses and profits, even though both take on a different form.

Setting fees, or a *price*, for your services involves several steps:

1. Establishing your *daily* labor rate, which is the expense of your time and the time of others.

2. Determining your *overhead*, which is the expense of being in business.

3. Fixing your *profit*, which is the value you place on the risk you take by being in business.

The Daily Labor Rate

Figuring the daily labor rate starts with deciding on the yearly amount that you are worth. That annual figure is then converted to a daily amount.

The median daily rate charged by consultants in some specialties is given in Figure 9.1. These figures represent the findings of a national survey conducted by *The Professional Consultant* to determine the overall economic status of the profession. Rates have been steadily rising, reflecting both inflation and the demand for consultant's services. For the six months ending March 31, 1991, consultants saw an increase in their daily billing rates of 5.1 percent. This raised the average daily billing rate to $1,102. Specialists in technical and scientific fields experienced the greatest increases. The survey was based on a sample size of 7,328. The data have been determined to be statistically significant at the .05 level.

Calculating the Daily Rate

Let's take an example. Jane Smith is resigning her position as a computer systems analyst with a major firm and becoming a consultant. Her position paid $52,000 a year, and she would like to earn at least that much as a consultant to start. She has determined her annual worth.

Figure 9.1 Median Daily Billing Rate & Income of Consultants by Specialty

The Professional Consultant ©199., HOWARD L SHENSON • 20750 VENTURA BOULEVARD
WOODLAND HILLS, CA 91364 • USA • TELEPHONE 818/703-1415

FEE MEDIANS BY GEOGRAPHIC MARKET LOCATION, MARKET POSITION, SIZE OF CLIENT

Field/Specialty	MajMkt	SmlMkt	Top10	Low10	BigCli	SmlCli
All Professionals	$1,218	$899	$1,994	$486	$1,173	$891
Accounting	$1,197	$915	$2,012	$495	$1,218	$604
Advertising	$1,280	$921	$2,513	$583	$1,224	$992
Agriculture	$815	$713	$1,187	$366	$823	$685
Aerospace	$1,095	$968	$1,490	$671	$1,222	$947
Arts & Cultural	$852	$633	$1,224	$319	$767	$645
Banking	$1,185	$967	$1,756	$601	$1,254	$898
Broadcast	$1,103	$851	$1,595	$660	$1,121	$873
Busn. Acquisition/Sales	$1,002	$832	$1,891	$456	$1,035	$840
Chemical	$1,256	$890	$1,955	$543	$1,156	$946
Communications	$914	$665	$1,312	$401	$838	$752
Construction	$1,049	$856	$1,744	$696	$1,059	$847
Data Processing Conslt	$1,159	$857	$1,715	$613	$1,190	$955
Data Processing Progrm	$861	$553	$1,098	$440	$913	$642
Dental/Medical	$1,338	$906	$1,993	$597	$1,231	$1,001
Design (Industrial)	$1,088	$762	$1,239	$556	$959	$848
Economics	$1,128	$899	$1,678	$639	$1,077	$972
Education	$836	$581	$1,306	$412	$855	$670
Engineering	$1,351	$992	$1,723	$667	$1,332	$1,044
Estate Planning	$1,001	$720	$1,777	$554	$1,014	$835
Executive Search	$1,087	$783	$1,780	$586	$1,101	$919
Export/Import	$1,199	$937	$1,678	$641	$1,075	$987
Fashion/Beauty	$635	$456	$983	$354	$569	$548
Finance	$1,267	$956	$2,231	$605	$1,179	$980
Franchise	$1,013	$937	$1,688	$546	$1,126	$929
Fund Raising	$910	$753	$1,456	$500	$888	$759
Grantsmanship	$812	$585	$1,190	$433	$759	$681
Graphics/Print Trades	$850	$649	$1,451	$522	$778	$662
Health Care	$1,378	$994	$2,142	$738	$1,312	$1,001
Hotel/Restaurant/Club	$975	$686	$1,415	$539	$872	$763
Insurance	$846	$723	$1,368	$511	$834	$680
International Business	$1,234	$967	$1,974	$686	$1,256	$997
Investment Advisory	$1,033	$792	$2,112	$451	$968	$853
Management	$1,195	$981	$2,210	$535	$1,113	$976
Marketing	$1,173	$915	$2,034	$513	$1,288	$966
Municipal Government	$914	$679	$1,201	$544	$859	$680
New Business Ventures	$919	$750	$1,387	$487	$944	$742
Packaging	$957	$901	$1,399	$581	$1,024	$757
Pension	$1,067	$816	$1,655	$641	$1,087	$747
Personnel/HRD	$935	$744	$1,986	$535	$1,146	$773
Production	$1,136	$855	$1,824	$533	$1,198	$731
Psychological Services	$809	$638	$1,446	$452	$1,010	$550
Public Relations	$970	$711	$1,552	$499	$998	$648
Publishing	$1,234	$783	$1,577	$636	$941	$736
Purchasing	$1,058	$812	$1,629	$539	$992	$824
Quality Control	$1,056	$963	$2,088	$590	$1,283	$899
Real Estate	$952	$686	$1,930	$542	$1,126	$659
Records Management	$733	$626	$1,391	$476	$924	$541
Recreation	$832	$677	$1,116	$450	$874	$584
Research & Development	$1,301	$1,065	$2,211	$805	$1,438	$967
Retail	$1,113	$799	$1,564	$613	$1,214	$770
Scientific	$1,301	$1,224	$2,256	$843	$1,395	$1,082
Security	$891	$734	$1,486	$644	$1,180	$657
Statistical	$880	$723	$1,392	$655	$888	$661
Telecommunications	$1,215	$910	$1,597	$671	$1,210	$791
Traffic/Transportation	$946	$781	$1,539	$547	$1,094	$672
Training	$959	$774	$1,652	$668	$996	$586
Travel	$675	$588	$1,244	$512	$854	$482

While there are 365 days in the year, there are only 261 working days (365 days less 104 Saturdays and Sundays). To arrive at her daily labor rate, she divides her desired annual salary by the number of working days:

$52,000 / 261 = $199.23

Her daily labor rate can be rounded off to $200.

How Many Hours in a Day?

How many hours constitute a work day? As an employee your work day is clearly defined. In our society eight hours constitute the commonly accepted workday. Yet even in a so-called "9 to 5" position, a conscientious professional often puts in more time than the prescribed eight hours.

Like other professionals, consultants sometimes have to put in more than eight hours a day but bill for just a day. You can expect to do that occasionally and chalk it up to goodwill. Very probably, you will work less than an eight-hour day for the same client and bill that as a day. In most cases the give washes out with the take.

In other cases clients may take advantage of you, either deliberately or inadvertently. You find yourself working 10 to 12 hours a day for a client on a steady basis. Regardless of the client's culpability for the overtime, you should take measures to account for your time. One measure is better planning of the daily work agenda. Perhaps you have not been realistic about how much you can accomplish in one day. If so, you need to reevaluate your daily agendas.

Another measure is to bill on an hourly basis. To calculate your hourly rate, simply divide your daily rate by eight hours. Jane's hourly labor rate would be $24.90 ($199.23 / 8 hours), which could be rounded to $25.

Overhead

Consultants incur two types of expenses. One group includes the expenses that you have regardless of how much work you do. These expenses are fixed at one level whether you are working on one project or fifty. This group includes such costs as the rent for the office, the lease payments on the photocopier, the office assistant's salary, your accountant's fee. These are your overhead expenses.

The other group of expenses, called direct expenses, varies with the work you do. They are related directly to and arise from the work on a particular project. Direct expenses might include the daily labor rates of associates, travel expenses on an assignment, long-distance phone charges, materials, supplies for mock-ups or presentations, and so on.

Between these two groups is a gray area of expenses that could be classified either way. Travel expenses can constitute a direct expense if they were incurred on a particular, contracted assignment. On the other hand, let's say that you traveled to meet with a prospect or two without the assurance that you would actually get a contract. In this case the travel expense would become part of your overhead. In general the nature of the expenditure does not determine how it is classified, but its purpose does. The discriminating question is: Can this expense be related directly to an assignment?

Each type of expense, overhead or direct, is handled differently. Overhead is best converted to a fixed percentage and added to your daily labor rate. It is not recalculated for each job. As a general rule-of-thumb, it usually falls between 65 and 150 percent. Direct expenses are calculated for each job and added to the amount reflecting the daily labor rate plus fixed overhead and profit.

Calculating Overhead

The percentage of overhead charged by consultants depends on costs or expenses incurred. Although amounts charged differ from one consultant to another, Figure 9.2 shows a realistic rather than contrived or theoretical example. The clerical expenses are billed partly as direct expenses and partly as overhead. About two-thirds of the clerical work is charged directly to the clients for such activities as typing reports and reducing survey data. The rest is spent on tasks, like answering the phone, that have to be done routinely and are part of overhead.

Office rental is a clear part of overhead. Even if a consultant avoids paying rent, the daily rate should include the amount of rent that normally would be paid for an office as part of the overhead budget. Otherwise, they will seriously underprice their services. The same holds true for any other overhead expenses for which the consultant does not actually expend money.

Telephone bills are divided into overhead and direct expenses like clerical expenses. The overhead part is for the telephone calls that resulted from just being in business. The rest is charged to clients directly.

The charge for automotive expenses covers the cost of leasing and maintaining an automobile for business purposes. When the automobile is used in behalf of clients, they are charged directly by the mile. Most bill the per-mile charge permitted by the IRS.

Personnel Benefits

Just because you go into business on your own, doesn't mean you aren't entitled to fringe benefits. Your overhead budget should therefore contain a charge for such expenses as:

- Paid vacation
- Health insurance
- Life insurance
- Paid sick leave
- Retirement plan

These expenses are normal and routine in American business. The cost of such items usually falls between 21 percent and 33 percent of direct salaries.

Figure 9.2   A Typical Overhead Calculation

Jane Smith, Full-Time Consultant
Daily Labor Rate = $200
Overhead (Monthly)

Clerical ($1,525)	$525
Office rent	700
Telephone	225
Postage and shipping	80
Automotive	350
Employment taxes	575
Personnel benefits	450
Insurance	200
Business licenses and taxes	95
Marketing	
Direct $275	
Personnel 800	1,075
Professional development	100
Dues and subscriptions	35
Printing and photocopying.	80
Stationery and supplies	85
Accounting and legal	150
Practice management	150
Other expenses	250
Total Overhead	**$5,125**

Marketing

In Figure 9.2 the consultant charges $1,075 to overhead every month for marketing expenses. The $800 amount is categorized as *Personnel,* and the balance of $275 is called *Direct.* The total amount represents what this consultant feels that she must spend to market her services.

The larger amount represents four days' worth of income to Smith. These four days she plans to spend on marketing projects of her choosing. Somehow, those days have to be

Figure 9.3   The Feast and Famine Cycle

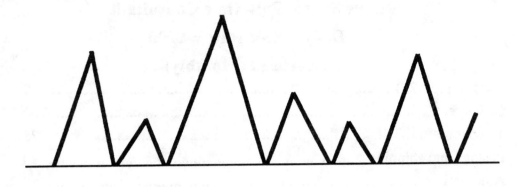

Figure 9.4   A Smoothed Business Cycle

included in her overhead as a cost of doing business. She must account for the days on which she is not billing clients.

In contrast some consultants charge each client for the actual marketing costs that they in-curred to get the client. They bill for some of the marketing money spent on prospects who did not become clients. Besides being very unfair to the clients billed, this practice is neither wise nor recommended. It is like the taxi driver who throws the meter before the passenger closes the door. This practice usually produces poor and rushed marketing.

You might regard allocating so much for marketing expense as a bit too much. It is not. You should give marketing the same time and care that you give your most important client. No matter how busy you become with client work, you must religiously set aside time each month for marketing. Failure to do so inevitably results in a kind of yo-yo cycle in which you go from feast to famine.

Figure 9.3 shows how this feast and famine cycle works. At the low points, you have no clients and no business. What do you do? You spend time marketing. You do so well that you become overloaded with work. Your schedule of client work becomes so heavy that you have no time to market. As a result you come back to a low point of no work. And so the cycle repeats itself.

This cycle is not only a poor business practice, it is also psychologically unsettling. Far better to discipline yourself to market in a consistent and regular fashion to create a business cycle that looks like the one in Figure 9.4. The latter type of cycle gives you a smoother cash flow and greater peace of mind.

Professional Development

To maintain and improve your professional standing, you normally have to spend money and time to pay for courses, seminars, books, audio cassette training programs, and the like. These expenses arise either from legal requirements or from the need of the professional to keep abreast of the state of the art. These expenses are almost always treated legitimately as overhead. Clients must expect to share the costs much as they would when visiting the family doctor.

The Overhead Rate

In the field of professional services, overhead is always expressed as a percentage of the labor rate. To determine the daily dollar value for overhead, divide the total overhead amount by the number of days that you expect to be billing clients. The resulting dollar amount must be added to the daily labor rate for each day the client is billed.

For example, Smith's overhead rate is calculated by taking the total dollar amount for her monthly overhead, $5,125, and dividing that by the number of days she expects to bill clients each month, 15 days. Dividing $5,125 by 15 days gives $342, which is her daily overhead.

To find the overhead rate as a percentage, simply divide the daily dollar value for overhead by the consultant's daily labor rate. In our example Smith's daily labor rate is $200. The calculation is $342 divided by $200 = 1.71 or 172 percent. An overhead percentage rate is then applied to the daily labor rate charge for each day. One day of Smith's time would be billed at her daily rate plus 172 percent for overhead plus whatever percentage of profit she charges, say 20 percent.

Daily Labor Rate	$200.00
Overhead (172%)	<u>342.00</u>
	542.00
Profit	<u>98.60</u>
	$640.60

The number is usually rounded up to the nearest $25. Thus, Smith's daily billing rate would be $650.

Adding Goodies

Goodies are the not-so-necessary items that are very appealing to you and that you feel can be paid for as part of your overhead. You may want a fancy office or additional vacation time. These are nice to have, but take care that you don't price yourself out of the market by living too well. Be reasonable before loading something onto your overhead rate.

Bureaucratic Growth

As your business ages, it tends to grow. With growth comes a higher overhead. Increased overhead is a reality of business life. As a practice becomes larger, it requires more labor to meet client demands.

On the surface this growth seems obvious and even more profitable. Lower-paid people may be used to handling less demanding tasks. Yet just the sheer addition of personnel requires more management, more supervision, more communication—and more risk. The larger practice has more of a reputation to protect, and the control of it is less direct than when its founder started it. Additional expenditures have to be studied, supervised and controlled. Many of these added expenses might well be judged as wasteful or as indicative of poor management to all but the most seasoned bureaucrat. With growth, organizations tend to accumulate flab in their overhead rates.

Watching Overhead

To keep your overhead at a level that is appropriate to your size, you should compare your current actual expenses to those in the past. Where did the money go? Where did expenses decrease? What new expenses appeared? Which ones dropped off the list? In your first year in business, the absolute longest you want to go without checking your actual expenses is six months. For better control you should do so each quarter.

After the first year, expenses should be checked once or twice annually. If sudden or radical changes take place in your practice, more frequent comparisons are warranted. If you are expanding your practice and taking on new partners and employees, you should have more frequent audits of expenses to keep overhead under control.

Profit

Over and above your daily labor rate and overhead, you should charge a profit. Many consultants overlook the need for profit. Their rationale is that since they are charging for their labor, charging a profit would be immoral or improper.

One reason profit is overlooked is that it has acquired a negative connotation in some quarters. Somehow it has become associated with the supposed evils of Big Business. Most people resent the profits of the oil, utility and phone companies. This resentment carries over into small business. The other reason is that most people don't really understand how the free enterprise system works. Profit is the whole purpose of running any kind of business.

Consultants who don't understand this point seem to think that all they have coming to them is their labor rate.

Profit is the reward for the risk of being in business. Even if consultants invest little or no capital in their businesses, they are still investing their time, which translates ultimately into money. They place their valuable time at risk, and they deserve to profit by that risk.

Consultants must distinguish between their labor rates and profits. They deserve their labor rates whether they work for someone else or for themselves. Their profits belong to them by reason of their being in business.

Typically, consultants charge between 16 percent and 24 percent of the combined sum of their daily labor rate and overhead charge. Some consultants charge more and some less. The rate depends on whatever the consultant judges to be fair and appropriate.

The Government Client

To get a government consulting contract, you have to be sensitive to the special requirements, policies and attitudes of different agencies. Often you find yourself dealing on two levels: the official level and the realistic level. Officially, you may be entitled by policy or law to only this much profit or that much labor rate. Realistically, the program managers for the government agency may recognize that you simply cannot adequately or profitably perform the services within the confines of the policy. They are caught between the rock-like policy and the hard place of getting the programs going.

We can describe only some of the practices that result from this dilemma. They are not recommended because, officially, they are improper. To be a well-informed consultant, however, you should know that a few consultants report that they do make use of such tactics even though they are unethical or illegal.

With a government agency as a client, unique rules often govern the disclosure of the fee by the consultant to the client. Given the legal and procedural considerations that govern procurement by government agencies, you sometimes have to make your responses strategic. Your chief considerations are:

1. The maximum on labor rates.
2. The client's understanding of overhead.
3. The acceptability of overhead charges.
4. The acceptability of profit.

Maximum Limitation on Labor Rates

Some government agencies have maximum acceptable labor rates. Whether established by executive decision or legislative mandate, these agencies can pay only so much per day. In such cases consultants should be sure that the labor rates they disclose to the client do not exceed the allowable maximum. If the agency is not permitted to pay any employee more than $175, consultants would not want even to hint that their daily labor rate is $250.

You might assume that the solution is to work on a fixed-fee contract. Unfortunately, working on a fixed-fee contract is not always possible. Most government agencies require full disclosure of all estimated price breakouts, even if the contract is fixed price. In the private sector those who hire a consultant on a fixed-price contract usually are not told anything other than the total dollar amount of the contract. But most government agencies work on line-item budgets. The entire pricing sheet must be shown to the governmental client. Suppose that you cannot work on a fixed-price contract and that your labor rates exceed the limits of acceptability. Some consultants rearrange the work responsibilities so that the lower-compensated personnel can do more of the work. If the professionals and associates are obliged to work at a lower rate, they need not do so for as many days. The total billed amount can then come out the same, but the distribution of the work load changes to meet the agency's requirements. This practice is illegal and should be avoided.

What of the propriety of accepting lower labor rates and rearranging the workload? Officially, these practices are neither recognized nor advocated, particularly by the fiscal personnel in the government agency client. Some program management people accept such adjustments *to get the project through.*

Client's Understanding of Overhead

Because consultants must reveal their pricing details to the governmental client, they must be sure that the client program personnel understand the nature of overhead and the process by which it is calculated.

In government agencies many personnel are not experienced in buying consultant services. They may regard your charges as excessive and unreasonable. You may have to instruct them on the nature of overhead and its method of calculation.

Acceptability of Overhead Charges

Some government agencies don't accept certain expense items as overhead charges. Expenses such as marketing, entertainment and interest are typical. If your contract is subject to certain audit provisions, these expenses will not be accepted. So inquire about the acceptability of such items before submitting a bid for services.

Acceptability of Profit

Some agencies have policies governing the acceptable rate of contractor profit. Others lack specific policies, but their employees have *attitudes* about such matters. You must ensure that the profit charged is acceptable to the client organization's policies or to the client's representatives.

To learn about policies on profits, you might use precise questioning or fact-finding. Or you might ask the client to provide you with a copy of one or more prior consulting contracts that the client has awarded in a similar situation.

However you get your information, suppose that profit rates of five or ten percent are required or expected. Should you work at such low rates of return? Technically, yes, but in reality no.

Do consultants really work for government clients for such low returns? Some do, some do not. Fortunately, the personnel working for many government agencies have realistic attitudes toward contracting out for services. They recognize the economic need for legitimate profitability. Some consultants engage in the practice, while the profit line may reflect a low percentage; some consultants often hide that extra profitability elsewhere in the budget. It may consist of a higher labor rate than actually paid, more labor days than actually expended, higher direct costs than are actually incurred, or the like.

Of course, if the contract is auditable, they take greater care to ensure that the expenses claimed are supported by evidence. If you anticipate substantial work on auditable government contracts, study the subject in detail.

Some consultants get the additional profit without showing it on the profit line by creating an additional category of expense, such as General and Administrative Expense (G&A), that government agencies are often used to paying but that small consulting practices rarely have. G&A is an expense that is handy for large businesses to account for things like corporate-wide auditing and communications.

While such a practice certainly won't be found in the policies and procedures manual of government procurement agencies, it is relatively widespread. Whether the fiscal personnel within government agencies recognize the practice is not really known. Most program personnel who seek out the consultant's services know about it, even if they do not generally admit it. Some government agencies make half-hearted attempts to police this situation.

Fee Collection

As in any business, consultants sometimes have trouble collecting their fees. A number of precautions can help you avoid this problem, and several tactics can solve difficulties when they occur.

A Good Contract

With an adequate, point-for-point contract in hand, you and your clients know just where you stand. A written contract is usually enough to make your obligations more *legal* in their minds. For small billings a wave of the contract is usually enough to shake the payment loose. Only the lawyers get rich as a result of litigation. For large fees litigation may become necessary. If so, a detailed contract is invaluable. A contract with an arbitration clause might get your money *and* keep you out of court.

Mutual Understanding

There is no substitute for having a good head-to-head understanding with clients. No contract and no agreement can substitute for it. If you and the client cannot see eye-to-eye up front, your contract is going to run into trouble at some time in the future. Make sure that you and the client both look at the written contract in the same way—a strong mutual understanding can be an important asset when collecting the fee.

Progress Payments

Most clients are quite willing to pay on a progress basis, either at prescribed intervals or after a percentage of the work is completed. Don't be afraid to ask for progress payments. If you can arrange accelerated progress payments, you can always be working on the client's money. The payments are larger up front and smaller at the end. The earlier payments cover the work already performed and part of the remaining work. That helps your cash flow and requires only a little ingenuity in dividing up the invoices.

Even if you do not a. k for progress payments, you should ask for cash disbursements of $100 or more in advance. Perhaps you have to get something printed, or maybe you have to lease a piece of equipment.

Withholding Output or Resources

Sometimes a client has held payment in the past or seems likely to do so. In this case you might consider withholding the results or product of your service. One accountant holds his client's books until he is paid. He even writes out the checks and has the clients sign them!

Factoring/Receivables Financing

Occasionally, you do business with large, solvent organizations that pay but pay slowly. The money is coming, but your cash flow needs an injection right away. Factoring is sometimes a handy solution. It won't work if you are working for relatively small or unknown clients. With clients like IBM or the New York Board of Education, a bank will usually advance you a percentage of your accounts receivable.

Once work is billed to the client, bring the invoice down to the bank you work with and ask the officer to advance a percentage of it. Typically, you can get up to two-thirds of the invoice amount right away and pay it back with interest when the check comes in. You might even ask the client to let you submit invoices early so that you can get it factored.

Collection Proceeding

Ultimately, you may have to resort to collection proceedings. Unfortunately, collection agents are not suitable for collection of consulting fees. They charge a lot, and all they can do is send out a series of letters, each one a little more threatening than the last. When they run out of letters, nothing happens.

Instead of a collection agency, you have to use your ingenuity. Somewhere in the organization is a spot that you can touch to embarrass or hurt the one holding up your money. Find that spot. Sit down, diagnose the organization and determine who can make life uncomfortable for the culprit client. Don't be vindictive. Being vengeful could cost you business in the future, not to mention referrals. But, if you can find that sensitive spot and raise a concern on the part of the client that it is better to pay, you can come out ahead.

Tips

Some consultants feel that by submitting a low-ball estimate on the first assignment from a client they can *buy some business*. Their rationale is that they will work their way into the good graces of the client and eventually make back their losses on the low estimate. The fact is that they don't buy any worthwhile business that way. Your client will be eager to tell everyone what great work you do for such low prices. Getting rid of that image may take a very long time.

On-the-Spot Estimates

Telling clients your hourly or daily rate is one thing. Quoting a whole job on the spot is quite another, even if you know right away. Ascertain the client's needs, think about the job, do an estimate of your own if necessary, then submit a reasoned estimate. Clients will be more impressed with a considered estimate than with a snap judgment.

Increasing Fees

Increasing fees is necessary and expected, since prices are always on the increase. Keep in mind that your increases should not occur too frequently. You don't want to create the impression that every time your client turns around your fees are up again. Limit your increases to once or twice a year at most. Your increases should be substantial enough to last six to twelve months. Informing regular clients by letter 90 days before a fee increase will serve ample notice for client planning and spur those considering your services to do so now rather than later. When informing clients that fees will be increased, provide a letter with a justification of why fees are being raised. Point out all factors that have given rise to increased costs: rent, utilities, secretarial assistance, increased self-employment taxes, and so on.

Now that you know how to make a sale, set your fees and get what you are worth, you are ready to handle the actual consulting work. The next chapter covers negotiating the job with the client, setting up a contract and handling client relations.

Contracts and Client-Consultant Relationships

The cornerstone of a good relationship with your clients is a solid contract. Although this document is an advisable absolute legal protection, it is nothing more than the reflection in black and white of the meeting of minds between two parties. The practical value of the contract depends on the quality of the relationship between you and your client. The contract becomes a tool that both parties can use for mutual benefit. If the contract is the product of mistrust, it becomes a two-edged sword. We will look at both the kinds of contracts and the underlying relationship they embody.

A complete treatment of the topic of contracts requires much more space than is available in this chapter. You can find a more detailed and extensive coverage of the topic, including examples and sample contracts, in *How To Strategically Negotiate the Consulting Contract* by Howard L. Shenson (see the bibliography).

The Form of the Contract

The contract can take the form of a simple letter of agreement, or it can be a formal contract with clauses, subclauses and all the legal trappings. A verbal contract is usually legally binding, but it is hard to enforce and suffers from the well-known vagaries of the human memory. You can always take a written contract out and look at it, but when two or more people are trying to remember what was said weeks or months ago, the result is nearly always conflict and confusion.

For most jobs a simple letter of agreement is sufficient. It outlines the project, sets the milestones and deadlines, and establishes a scale for paying the consultant. It can also deal with matters such as support the consultant will receive on the job, performance expectations, handling unexpected problems and other important items. A letter of agreement is actually a contract and is legally binding.

For large or complex projects you may need to draw up a contract, often with the help of a lawyer. If several consultants are involved in the execution of the project, a contract is essential. To avoid confusion and establish clear lines of authority on a major project, you probably will need a formal contract.

Whether you use a letter of agreement or a formal contract, there are a number of standard arrangements, which are listed and discussed below. You want to choose the kind of arrangement that is appropriate to the project and the client. When you begin work with a clear understanding of responsibilities and financial arrangements, the job will be done more smoothly and will almost always end with both parties feeling satisfied. See the appendix for sample contracts.

The relationship between consultant and client can take a number of forms:

- Fixed-price contract
- Fixed-fee-plus-expenses contract
- Daily rate contract
- Time and materials contract
- Cost reimbursement contract
- Retainer contract
- Performance contract

Each type of contract may be useful at one time or another, depending on the situation and the demands of a particular project.

Fixed-Price Contracts

The fixed-price contract is very simple. After ascertaining the client's precise needs, state that you can perform the services required for a flat dollar amount of your choosing. Once the fixed price is accepted and a contract is drawn, you are bound to deliver the services for that amount. If you handle the work efficiently and the services cost you less than you estimated, you make more profit than expected. If your expenses are higher than estimated, you lose some profit.

Payment is linked to your performance. At the conclusion of the work, if the contract has not been fulfilled by the consultant, not only could the final payment be withheld, but also the progress payment amounts might have to be returned. Clients run little or no risk with a fixed-price contract. The consultant assumes nearly all the risk. Why, then, would you undertake this type of agreement? The reason is that the fixed-price contract is usually more profitable than other types of contracts.

There are several types of fixed-price contracts:

- The firm fixed-price contract
- The escalating fixed-price contract
- The incentive fixed-price contract
- The performance fixed-price contract
- The fixed-price contract with redetermination

Firm Fixed-Price Contract   This contract offers a firm, fixed price for specified work and is not subject to change except when the scope or character of the work is changed. All risk is with the consultant, whose opportunity for profit in compensation is greatest for this risk.

Escalating Fixed-Price Contract   This agreement is similar to the firm fixed-price contract except that it has provisions for upward or downward adjustments of the fee on the basis of predetermined contingencies, such as the cost of living index.

Incentive Fixed-Price Contract   This contract has an *adjustment formula* designed to reward the consultant for additional efficiency and penalize inefficiency. If the consultant is below the ceiling price, he or she gets the extra profit. If the consultant exceeds the ceiling price, the costs are divided according to a predetermined schedule. Both parties might agree that additional expenses are to be borne by the client at a rate of 75 percent and by the consultant at a rate of 25 percent, reducing the consultant's profit by one-fourth.

Performance Fixed-Price Contract   This agreement is similar to the firm fixed-price contract except that it compensates the consultant for special performance. The consultant might get a bonus for bringing the contract in early or as a result of some other special achievement.

Fixed-Price Contract with Redetermination   This contract is the same as a firm fixed-price contract except that it has a provision that allows both the consultant and the client to redetermine or reset the price after the contract has been signed. This contract is best used when the nature of the task is so vague, uncertain or unknown that an accurate estimate cannot be made. At the time the contract is signed, both parties agree on a point in time for redetermination on the basis of their experience with actual costs and expenses. By agreement the parties determine whether the change in price will affect prior work, future work or both. This kind of contract is usually in the interest of the consultant who is working on some blind or unknown task for which the costs may be much higher than anyone would have conceived. Yet the redetermination may be downward, too. If actual costs are a great deal less than anticipated, this contract may be to the advantage of the client.

Fixed-Fee-Plus-Expenses Contracts

When the direct expenses are difficult or impossible to foresee, the consultant can submit the direct labor charge, overhead and profit as a fixed-fee, but the client is liable for the direct expenses.

Daily Rate Contracts

Working on a daily-rate basis may be safer than submitting a fixed price. Some consultations smack of hidden pitfalls. They are too speculative or too unpredictable for consultants to guarantee either services or expenses. The client's personality may even create an element of uncertainty. Sometimes a situation just *looks* as if it has surprises in it. You might pad the fixed-price contract you are going to submit. A little padding should not hurt; however, a lot not only can dull your competitive edge but can also border on being unethical.

In daily rate contracts consultants submit an estimate of time and expenses, but they are not responsible for overruns. The clients assume all risk for overruns in both cost areas, and they enjoy all the benefits of underruns.

Time and Materials Contracts

This contract works exactly like the daily labor contract with a couple of exceptions. One is that the consultant pays for expenses and adds a handling charge, normally at the same rate as the consultant's profit. The consultant then bills the client for the total. The client does not pay the expenses directly. Another exception is that the clerical support is not built into the daily rates. Instead, this work is usually charged as an expense. A time and materials contract is a kind of fixed-price contract in that the labor and overhead rates are fixed. What the client winds up paying, however, is far from fixed. Hence, this time and materials contract is an incentive for consultants to be anything but efficient—the longer the project takes, the more money they earn.

Cost Reimbursement Contracts

Cost reimbursement contracts focus on costs rather than on fees. In such contracts consultants are reimbursed for the costs that they incur. In the contracts that call for fees—some of them do not—the fees are emphasized less than the costs.

The underlying assumption for these types of contracts is that the clients pay all costs or the consultant ceases performance. Whereas consultants act as principals in a fixed-price contract, they act as agents of the client in a cost reimbursement contract. They run no risk of loss and do not earn the profit normally associated with fixed-price contracts.

Cost reimbursement contracts are used when the consultant cannot accurately estimate costs and when the consultant's cost accounting system enables clients to monitor the consultant's costs. Clients as a rule do not favor these contracts because they have to expend a lot of effort keeping track of the consultant's costs.

The success of these contracts depends on the definition of costs. At the outset, both consultant and client must agree on *allowable costs*. Perhaps the consultant considers the cost of capital an allowable cost, while the client does not. Other costs, such as automobile transportation, might also be disputable. If you enter into a cost-reimbursement contract, define what you mean by cost.

Several different types of cost reimbursement contracts are used by consultants, including:

- The cost contract;
- The cost-plus-fixed-fee (CPFF) contract;
- The cost-plus-incentive-fee (CPIF) contract; and
- The cost-plus-award-fee (CPAF) contract.

The Cost Contract   With this contract the client agrees to reimburse the consultant for all allowable costs but pays no fee. It is most widely used when a nonprofit consulting agency can learn technology that will benefit it in the future. Cost sharing, in which the client agrees to cover a part of the costs or to share the costs, is another alternative.

Cost-Plus-Fixed-Fee Contract (CPFF)   This contract is the most frequently used form of a cost reimbursement contract. Its popularity in general consulting developed as a result of its widespread use by the federal government. The client and the consultant agree on the total estimated cost of the consultation. They further agree on the allowable fee or profit to be earned by the consultant over and above these costs. If the actual costs are lower than those estimated, the consultant earns a higher percentage fee on the costs.

In theory the consultant is motivated to keep costs down and thus earn a higher percentage return. In actual practice this is not always the case. Consultants are largely assured of reimbursement for all *allowable* costs. They are normally not required to spend funds in excess of the agreed-upon amount, even though the project or consultation has yet to be completed.

Cost-Plus-Incentive-Fee Contract (CPIF)   Similar to the CPFF, the CPIF is designed to provide greater cost-saving motivation for the consultant. Rather than a fixed fee, this contract form has a minimum and maximum fee. The minimum fee may be negative or zero. Clients and consultants may also share costs in some contracts. If the actual costs turn out to be lower than estimated, the consultant gets a greater fee—up to the maximum. If costs run over the estimate, the fee is smaller, and it may even be reduced to zero if the cost overrun is great enough. In theory the risk for the client should be equal to that of the consultant. In practice each party tries to get as much advantage as possible during contract negotiations. Frequently CPIF contracts involve multiple incentives—one for early completion, another for cost efficiency, and so on.

Cost-Plus-Award-Fee Contract (CPAF)   A cross between the CPFF and the CPIF contracts, this contract was first used in federal procurements to handle technical items that were too difficult to estimate in contract negotiations. In the CPAF, unlike the CPIF, an external third party awards the minimum or maximum fee based on an objective evaluation of the consultant's cost efficiency and compliance.

There is no requirement that the evaluation take place at the end of the contract. Evaluations are often scheduled on a monthly or quarterly basis. One advantage of frequent evaluations is that they provide feedback that may enable consultants to perform more in line with the client's expectations and thus earn the higher fee.

Retainer Contracts

While the term *retainer* is used in many ways, it generally implies an open-ended agreement between client and consultant to make the consultant available to the client for a specified amount of time or scope of work. Usually, additional work is billed out at some pre-established hourly or daily rate. From the consultant's viewpoint, the retainer contract makes good sense only when the consultant is able to predict with strong accuracy the amount of time needed by the client. From the client's standpoint, a retainer agreement is of value because the client can tap quickly and easily the specialized talent of the consultant without extensive formal arrangements.

Availability Retainer Agreements   Availability retainer agreements have become more common in recent years. In these arrangements consultants make themselves available in the event that the client needs their services. The consultants agree to reserve a specified block of time for the client in the event of need. Since this reservation reduces the time flexibility of consultants, they are rewarded a portion of the value of the reserved time. Usually, this amounts to a sum of between 20 percent and 30 percent of the value of their time.

In a time retainer agreement, the consultant performs a specific activity on a periodic (usually monthly) basis. Occasionally, consultants find themselves spending more time with the client than the retainer is worth. Yet they put up with the *overwork* because the up-front money is a kind of insurance policy. After a while these arrangements tend to break down because the consultant starts to cut corners and the output suffers. The client becomes dissatisfied, and the relationship is no longer fruitful for the client or consultant.

Making Retainers Work for You   A retainer will work if it is for a specified scope of work or a specified number of clock hours or days for a specific fee. Suppose that the consultant is to train all new sales personnel about product competition. An analysis by the consultant suggests that such items as anticipated sales, production capacity, turnover rate, knowledge of new sales personnel will result in four days of work per month. If the consultant's daily billing rate is $400, the retainer could be set at $1,600 per month.

If the amount of time to be expended is variable, the retainer can be tied to the clock. Suppose the client's technical staff needs high-level engineering data and resources to meet the requirements of specific customer applications. Both you and the client don't know how much such help will be required. You figure your time at $50 per hour and agree to provide the client with 40 hours a month of such time for a fixed amount of $2,000. If the client needs only 30 hours, you still get your $2,000. If the client needs 50 hours in a given month, you will collect $2,500.

With everything clearly specified, clients are well aware of what they are getting, and consultants do not feel as though they are being taken advantage of. In this case the retainer is a smart idea.

If you decide that an up-front payment is best for you, obtaining it generally depends on how well you can exert your will on others. In American business most people expect to pay for services rendered, not for services to be rendered. If you ask for a retainer, you are cutting across the grain of that tendency, so you must be very firm about your practice. If you give the impression that you might make an exception, if you seem afraid to lose the client, you will not get your way. Be firm, be insistent. Your only risk is that you will encounter an equally strong-willed client or one whose employer policy forbids up-front payments.

Performance Contracts

In any contract when the payment of your fee depends on performance, make sure you and your client both agree on what performance means. A performance contract is not one with a clause that says: *If the client is happy, he or she will pay the consultant.* Performance has to be something measurable, such as a ten percent increase in sales volume, a four percent increase in gross volume, or a three percent decline in personnel turnover. That's the type of performance that you can prove in court, if need be. The performance-related contract is valuable when there is high-gain potential, and it can help overcome client resistance.

High-Gain Potential   In a situation with high-gain potential, you see that a client will reap substantial and perhaps ongoing financial benefits from the consultation. The performance con-tract enables you to participate in those benefits. Perhaps the most important point to remember about performance contracts is that you should not speculate with the client. Do not assume more risk than you have to.

Almost as important a rule is this: *Never share in profits.* At the flick of a pen, profits can be either created or turned into losses. A less-than-honest client could leave you with nothing. Even a perfectly honest client is put into an uncomfortable spot by sharing in profits. To reduce taxes, the client has to show reduced profits. Yet doing so also reduces your fees.

So negotiate for participation in gross sales, gross margin or some aspect of cost savings. Share in anything that is easily measurable and that is defined in one way by accounting standards.

Client Resistance   If your client simply doesn't believe that you can do what you say you can, you might offer to work on a performance contract. That way, the client regards you as someone who is sure enough of success to take a share in the risk. The offer is an effective way to overcome the uncertainty of a client who otherwise might hesitate to sign a contract.

Surprisingly, that contract is not likely to be a performance contract—even though you offered one. Client organizations are simply not disposed to deal on a performance basis. From a legal viewpoint, these organizations generally do not have standard performance contracts in the drawer. So either they have to confer with the legal department, which may mean a weeks-long delay, or they have to hire outside legal help, which means a fairly heavy cash outlay. Additionally, client organizations could have to make up special accounting procedures for handling your account. Finally, although the people you deal with may be able to approve a check for a flat payment, they may not have the authority to encumber their employers with a performance-related obligation. Getting that authorization may draw more attention to their consulting needs than they care to have. All in all, you're likely to get a contract if you offer to work on a performance basis, but that contract can still be one that entails less risk for you.

You are more likely to enter into performance contracts with small businesses. In most cases the owner will be handling the negotiations and can authorize such payments. Small businesses may not have the money available to pay for your services as you deliver work, so making part of the payment dependent on future events should facilitate payment. It may cost the business more in the long run, but the increased profits should offset the expense.

Enforcing a Performance Contract   Occasionally, clients may not follow through on the consultant's recommendations. Although the consultant may design and develop a system for improvement in performance, the client may fail to implement it. Or the client may implement the plan haphazardly or ineffectively. No savings are realized, no volume increases effected—and the consultant gets no performance fees.

The solution to this problem, which is all too common, lies mainly with foresight. A clause in the contract should stipulate that the client is to pay you a certain fee if the plan is not implemented fully and as mutually agreed. With such a clause you have some protection. Without it you may be out of luck.

Relations with the Client Organization

The contract embodies your relationship with the individual you call *client*. In a broader sense you have a contract with a *client organization*. Even though your contract sits well with the individual or small group that negotiated the deal, you often have to build a good relationship with other members of the organization—particularly the employees. The people in the rank and file can determine your success or downfall, so a close rapport with the company's personnel is also essential to the success of the consultation.

The Consultant as Hatchet Man

Perhaps the biggest threat to that success is the common perception among employees that consultants pose a threat to their jobs. You become *the efficiency expert* who is going to put in new equipment and cut jobs. A quick note from the boss to employees that you're going to be *coming around* on a given day usually only heightens those fears.

The key to keeping employees on your side is communication. More specifically, have the boss bring you to the site of your consultations for the day. Get introduced, get familiarized, answer questions and let people get to know you. Informally you can *brief* them on what you're doing and why. If too many people are involved in the consultation for you to work face-to-face in small groups, organize a briefing session. Send out a memo on your own letterhead that is copied and distributed by the client. At the briefing give a short presentation, leaving plenty of time for questions. After the meeting, as the consultation progresses, you can show up at the site unannounced anticipating much more cooperation than if you walked in cold.

Keep the employees as involved as possible. Usually, some information has to be kept confidential. Yet, to the extent possible, get employees to contribute to the consultation, and share the output with them. You not only make the project easier on yourself, but you may also receive some unexpectedly helpful input.

Disagreement within the Organization

Sometimes an employee of the organization will set out to torpedo your project. Some old-timers in the company can sabotage you simply by creating a lot of disagreement over what has to be done. In such situations you find yourself with clear orders from the signers of the contract but are up against endless confusion on the site.

You can deal with this deliberate confusion two ways—with a meeting or a memo. You can bring the employee and the client together in a meeting with you. Face-to-face you might be able to iron out the differences. In most cases, however, the client will not attend the meeting. The client usually knows what the employee is doing but doesn't want to confront it. Very likely, that confrontation is the underlying reason for retaining you. If a meeting does not work out, try a memo. Whether the organization is large or small, you protect yourself with a memo on record. More important, you can follow up with a polite insistence for a clarification.

"Free" Consultation

Whether negotiating a contract or executing it, consultants often realize suddenly that they are giving away services for no compensation. Most free consulting results from subconscious tendencies to provide additional services. You can avoid giving away your service by being aware of those tendencies and avoiding them. Aside from the proposal, you should be wary of the *free consulting* tendency in at least three situations:

1. The follow-up consultation.
2. Diagnostic work.
3. The add-on assignment.

The Follow-Up Consultation

The follow-up consultation consists of services or advice rendered to the client after a project is completed. Invariably this kind of freebie takes the form of a phone call from the client, just to ask questions. If the client does indeed need only a call to straighten out a wrinkle in the original consultation, courtesy and good business sense dictate that you consider the call a part of the fee. On the other hand, when one call leads to so many others that you find yourself giving away time and fresh advice, several options are open to you. You could put the client on a per-call basis. Bill a certain amount for phone consultations and another amount for on-site follow-ups.

Another possibility is to negotiate a retainer agreement. One of two kinds might be appropriate:

1. *The Time Retainer.* With this contract you complete a specified quantity of work or a discrete activity on a regular, periodic basis, perhaps monthly. You might agree to conduct a psychological screening of all new employees of the client organization. Given the client's size and rate of personnel turnover, you assume that you will need to spend two days each month to fulfill this obligation. Since your daily rate for consulting is $400 per day, you sign a retainer agreement with the client that pays you $800 a month, each and every month, for conducting this psychological screening.

2. *The Availability Retainer.* You contract to make yourself available to a client for a specific time each calendar period. For example, you agree to analyze a client's financial statements and interpret them for management. You calculate that performing this activity takes you three days. At a daily rate of $500, you are compensated $1,500 each month that you are requested to undertake this assignment.

The client does not desire that you perform this service each month but wishes you to be available for the three days when the need arises. Since making yourself available for three days a month reduces your flexibility and freedom, you collect a fee for making yourself available.

You may set this fee at whatever you wish, but most commonly it would run about 25 percent of the value of your time. If you follow the 25 percent guide, you would charge the client $375 a month simply to be available. What do you get paid if you actually do the work? Our research demonstrates that 44 percent of the consultants working on such a basis would credit the $375 against the $1,500, while the rest would charge a total of $1,875.

Diagnostic Work

Many clients know exactly what their problems are and have set expectations as to the precise accomplishments they are seeking from the consultant. Some clients, however, are not even aware of their problems, much less appropriate solutions. In this case consultants often decide that undertaking a diagnostic evaluation for the client is a profitable investment of marketing time. They develop a proposal that not only identifies the problems or needs but also specifies a particular action plan to be followed. The psychology of this approach is that the client is sufficiently impressed with your diagnostic powers that they end up awarding you a contract to implement your action plan.

At times, however, you feel that no matter how good your diagnosis is, the client will not retain your services to implement the action plan. Perhaps the client has a brother-in-law in the consulting business, or maybe the client won't be motivated to do anything about the problem even if identified. Whatever the reason, undertaking a diagnosis in such a situation probably will result in your giving away valuable time without compensation.

How do you handle such a situation? You could just walk away, telling the client that you have no interest. If the prospective business is too good to pass up, you could propose that the client award you a diagnostic contract. This contract would compensate you for your analysis and the action plan you propose. When complete, the client may either select you or another consultant or do nothing about your findings. In some cases you may inform the client that if you are selected to implement the action plan, the charge for the diagnostic work is deducted from the total charges incurred.

Add-On Assignment

In this situation the client, in effect, is saying: As long as you're doing X, why not do Y, too? Your contract covers X, but not a cent is available for Y. Although you are concerned that you won't be compensated for the extra work, you may not be sure just how serious the client is about really doing this extra work. You hate to make an issue of it.

How do you handle such a situation? Too frequently consultants ignore the client with the hope that the idea will go away. It doesn't go away. The best approach is to pick up on the client's suggestion. A very effective response to such a request is that you would be glad to take a look at that, and you're sure that the cost would not be unreasonable. You might even state a figure, if you are sure of your estimate. As a rule you should make yourself available for add-on assignments, as long as the client understands that there will be add-on charges.

Protecting Yourself When Using Other Consultants

From time to time you may have to call in other consultants to help you on a project. The steps required to guard your interests depend largely on the people with whom you are working. Some are so entrepreneurial that they draw clients away from you as soon as you turn around, while others are so scrupulous that they would never dream of approaching your clients for work.

One way of protecting yourself against your more aggressive colleagues is to maintain a high profile with the client. Although you have other people working on the assignment, let the client know that you alone are managing these people. Another way is to be the collector and disseminator of all information. Controlling the flow of information from the client to the other consultants, and vice versa, is vital to your interests. As long as you are monitoring and regulating the two-way flow, you can limit the free advice that might otherwise *leak* out of your organization. You can also detect any efforts by the other consultants to develop greater visibility with your client.

Personal Involvement

Self-protection brings up another common problem in consulting. When marketing themselves to prospects, consultants often use the word *I* more than they should. Clients come to expect a personal commitment from consultants and assume the consultant will do everything, when some of the tasks can just as well be handled by less trained and lower-paid staff. Even when the client is willing to pay for the consultant's time, the consultant may not want to tie up so much time on one client or on routine work. On the other hand, if the consultant allows others to become too involved with the client's work, they could become more prominent in the client's eyes than they should be.

One solution to the problem is to involve the staff or associates early on in the marketing phase, directing the focus from *I* to *we* or *you*. To solve the problem of losing business, always talk to clients in a way that convinces them that you are controlling a team of staff and associates. Build the impression that the team would be just so many individuals without your guidance. Also, do not give any staff member or associate complete control over the available information.

Tips

If you followed good marketing principles, you don't end a project only to find that you are out on the street looking for another. You have already set aside enough time and marketed yourself so that you are working on several projects at once and looking for more at the same time. This way, you will never suffer from a shortage of work.

Good consulting is simply good business. The good consultant delivers a quality product at a fair price and makes a respectable profit. In many ways the consultant is the last of the true entrepreneurs, carrying on the best traditions of the American free enterprise system.

Appendix

Sample Contracts

As with the Letter of Agreement, the formal written contract may be prepared by either the client or the consultant. Review of the general form of a specific contract by competent legal authority is recommended for both parties, as it is recommended for Letters of Agreement, too.

This form constitutes an agreement between consultants and their clients governing a complex business transaction to be undertaken by the client but with detailed advice and supervision to be provided by the consultants. The consultants not only advise the client on the proper method of carrying out the project involved but also are given specific management authority over most aspects of the project. This type of situation may be necessitated by the requirements of a third party, such as a lender or lessor, who believes the services of the consultant are necessary to the successful operation of the project involved.

Provision is made for compensation of the consultants based on the amount of work they perform for the client with a minimum and maximum dollar amount of compensation provided for each month. The consultants also agree to provide a minimum number of hours of service to the client and that the amount of time to be spent in addition to this shall be at the sole discretion of the consultants. If disputes arise under the agreement, provision is made for arbitration in accordance with the rules of the American Arbitration Association. To protect the reputation and good name of the consultants, the contract contains a provision declaring the uniqueness of the services to be provided by the consultants and the irreparable harm to them that would result if such services were not fully performed. It provides that equitable remedies, including injunction and specific performance, may be obtained by the consultants if the contract is breached by the client. In this situation, the main force of this provision is to ensure that the consultants will continue to manage the client's project so that the third-party investor may be fully protected.

Sample Business Consultant and Management Agreement

AGREEMENT made this ____ day of _____19XX, between [name of client], _____ (e.g., a Delaware corporation), hereinafter referred to as the "Corporation," and [name of consultant(s)], (both jointly and severally), hereinafter referred to as the "Consultants":

Recitals

The Corporation is presently in the process of negotiating [description of project, e.g. , to build or lease and to conduct and operate a general hospital at the following location]:

It is the desire of the Corporation to engage the services of the Consultants to perform for the Corporation certain functions in the management and operation of [e.g., the hospital] and to consult with the board of directors and the officers of the Corporation and with the administrative staff concerning problems arising in the fields of [e.g., hospital management; fiscal policies; personnel policies; purchases of equipment, supplies, and services]; and other problems that may arise from time to time, in the operation of [e.g., a general hospital].

AGREEMENT

Term

1. The respective duties and obligations of the parties hereto shall commence on the date [e.g., that the Corporation enters into said lease].

Consultations

2. The Consultants shall make themselves available to consult with the board of directors, the officers of the Corporation, and the department heads of the administrative staff, at reasonable times, concerning matters pertaining to the organization of the administrative staff, the fiscal policy of the Corporation, the relationship of the Corporation with its employees or with any organization representing its employees, and in general, concerning any problems of importance concerning the business affairs of the Corporation.

Management Authority of Consultants

3. In addition to the consultation provided for in Paragraph 2 above, the Consultants shall be in complete and sole charge of the administrative staff of [e.g., the hospital]. The administrative staff of the hospital shall include all the employees of the Corporation directly or indirectly engaged in the affairs of the hospital other than the board of directors of the Corporation, the president, vice president, secretary and treasurer of the Corporation, and the medical staff of the hospital. The medical staff of the hospital is defined as those persons who are licensed by the State of Delaware to perform, and are performing, services as physicians,

surgeons, nurses, physiotherapists, social workers, psychologists, psychiatrists, pharmacists and other services of a professional standing in the healing arts and sciences.

Management Power of Consultants

4. The business affairs of the Corporation that affect, directly or indirectly, the operation of [e.g., the hospital], and which arise in the ordinary course of business, shall be conducted by the administrative staff. All the members of the administrative staff shall be employees of the Corporation; however, the Consultants shall have the sole and complete charge of the administrative staff, and shall have the absolute and complete authority to employ (on such terms and for compensation as they deem proper), discharge, direct, supervise and control each and every member of the administrative staff. It is the intention of the Corporation to confer on the Consultants all the powers of direction, management, supervision and control of the administrative staff that the Consultants would have if the members of the administrative staff were direct employees of the Consultants.

Business Manager

5. The Consultants, in their sole discretion, may employ, in the name of the Corporation, a business manager. If such a business manager is employed, he shall act as administrative assistant to the Consultants and as the chief administrative officer of the administrative staff. The business manager shall be under the direct control and supervision of the Consultants. The Consultants may, from time to time, delegate to the business manager as much of the Consultants' authority as they deem proper with respect to the employment, discharge, direction, control and supervision of the administrative staff, and the Consultants may withdraw from said business manager, at any time the Consultants deem it expedient or proper to do so, any portion or all of the said authority theretofore conferred on the business manager.

Fiscal Policy

6. The Corporation recognizes the necessity for a sound fiscal policy in order to maintain and promote the solvency of the Corporation. To this end, it is hereby agreed by the parties hereto that the Corporation will establish reserve accounts for the following purposes:

a. A reserve account for the payment of any and all taxes that may be charged against the Corporation by any governmental jurisdiction.

b. A reserve account for the payment of all sums withheld from the salary or wages of the employees of the Corporation and for which the Corporation is chargeable under the laws of any and all governmental jurisdictions.

c. A reserve account for the payment of all obligations due [name of lessor] pursuant to the terms and conditions of the above referred-to lease.

d. A reserve account for the purchase of equipment necessitated by the wearing out or obsolescence of the equipment in use, or by the development of new equipment.

e. A reserve account for building maintenance and for the expansion of the physical facilities. The Consultants shall, from time to time, advise the Board of Directors of the amounts of corporate funds that should be deposited in each of said reserve accounts. This determination on the part of the Consultants shall be based on the principles of sound business management and the availability to the Corporation of said funds. The Corporation agrees to deposit corporate funds in said reserve accounts pursuant to the recommendations of the Consultants. The reserve accounts shall be deposited in one or more national banks, or branches thereof, located within [county and state]. All checks, drafts or other instruments by which funds are withdrawn from said reserve accounts, in addition to any other signature that may be required, shall bear the signature of one of the Consultants.

Consultants To Act as Agents

7. From time to time, the Corporation may deem it advisable to enter into agreements with [e.g., insurance companies, prepaid medical plans, and other firms and associations that pay all or part of the expenses incurred or to be incurred by the hospital patients for the care and treatment afforded them while patients in the Corporation's hospital]. With regard to said agreements, the Consultants shall be the exclusive agent of negotiating the terms and conditions of the said agreements. However, the Consultants shall not bind the Corporation to said agreement without first obtaining the approval of the terms of said agreements from the board of directors of the Corporation.

Authority To Contract

8. From time to time, the Corporation may wish to expand the physical facilities of [type of facility] or remodel or modify the same. If the costs to be incurred by the Corporation for such expansion, modification or remodeling are less than $_____, then the Consultants may contract for the performance of the same in the name of the Corporation under the authority given them in Paragraph 4 above; however, if such expansion, modification or remodeling is to be of such extent that the cost to be incurred by the Corporation for the performance thereof is $_____ or more, then the terms and conditions of said contracts for said expansion, modification or remodeling shall

be negotiated by the Consultants, and Consultants shall be the exclusive agents of the Corporation to said contracts without first obtaining the approval of the terms and conditions of said contracts from the Board of Directors of the Corporation. The provisions of this paragraph shall apply with equal effect to the purchase of equipment and supplies.

Employment of Certified Public Accountants

9. It is understood and agreed by the parties hereto that the services to be performed by the Consultants do not include the auditing of the books of the Corporation or of [name of project], the preparing of any financial statements, the preparing of any tax returns or other documents required to be prepared by any governmental body having jurisdiction to tax, or any other acts or services normally performed by public accountants. The Consultants may engage, hire, retain and employ, in the name and for the account of the Corporation, one or more, or a firm of, certified public accounts to perform for the Corporation the services denoted above in this paragraph. Said accountant or accountants may be employed, hired, engaged and retained on such terms and conditions and for such compensation as the Consultants deem reasonable. [E.g., it is understood by the Corporation that the Consultants are partners of a firm of certified public accountants known as (name of firm). It is specifically agreed that the Consultants may be, and the Consultants are, hereby authorized to employ said partnership, or its successors in interest, to perform for the Corporation the services denoted above in this paragraph, and the Consultants may obligate the Corporation to pay to said partnership, or its successors in interest, a reasonable amount for the performance of said services.]

Employment of Assistants

10. If it is reasonably necessary for the Consultants to have the aid of assistants or the services of other persons, companies or firms to properly perform the duties and obligations required of the Consultants under this agreement, the Consultants may, from time to time, employ, engage or retain the same. The cost to the Consultants for said services shall be chargeable to the Corporation, and the Corporation shall reimburse and pay over to the Consultants said costs on demand.

Limited Liability

11. With regard to the services to be performed by the Consultants pursuant to the terms of the agreement, the Consultants shall not be liable to the Corporation, or to anyone who may claim any right due to his relationship with the Corporation, for any acts or omissions in the performance of said services on the part of the Consultants or on the part of the agents or employees of the Consultants; except when

said acts or omissions of the Consultants are due to their willful misconduct. The Corporation shall hold the Consultants free and harmless from any obligations, costs, claims, judgements, attorneys' fees and attachments arising from or growing out of the services rendered to the Corporation pursuant to the terms of this agreement or in any way connected with the rendering of said services, except when the same shall arise due to the willful misconduct by a court of competent jurisdiction.

Compensation

12. The Consultants shall receive from the Corporation a reasonable monthly sum for the performance of the services to be rendered to the Corporation pursuant to the terms of this agreement; however, in no event shall the compensation paid to the Consultants by the Corporation be less than $_____ per month nor more than $ _____ per month. The Corporation and the Consultants, by mutual agreement, shall determine the compensation to be paid the Consultants for any particular month by the fifteenth (15th) day of the next succeeding month. The final determination of the monthly compensation shall be based on the reasonable value of the services rendered by the Consultants, and within the range prescribed above in this paragraph. If the Corporation and the Consultants fail to agree on said compensation within the said fifteen (15) days, the amount of monthly compensation due the Consultants shall be determined by arbitration pursuant to the provisions of Paragraph 14 below. Anything contained in this agreement to the contrary notwithstanding, the minimum monthly remuneration of $_____ shall be paid to the Consultants on the first of every month during the term of this agreement and the acceptance of said minimum amount by the Consultants shall not in any way diminish, affect or compromise their rights to additional compensation as provided for herein.

Minimum Amount of Service

13. The Consultants shall devote a minimum of _____ hours per month to the affair of the Corporation. Anything to the contrary notwithstanding, the Consultants shall devote only so much time , in excess of said _____ hours, to the affairs of the Corporation as they, in their sole judgment, deem necessary; and Consultants may represent, perform services for, and be employed by such additional clients, persons or companies as the Consultants, in their sole discretion, see fit.

Arbitration

14. Any controversy or claim arising out of or relating to the compensation to be paid by the Corporation or the Consultants for the services rendered by them pursuant to the terms of this agreement shall be settled by arbitration in accordance with the rules

of the American Arbitration Association and judgment on the award
rendered by the arbitrator or arbitrators may be entered in any
court having jurisdiction thereof. Any part to this agreement may
submit to arbitration any said controversy of claim.

[The following paragraph may be used where more than one Consultant is a party to the agreement.]

Failure To Act by One Consultant

15. It is understood and agreed that any direction or consultation given or service performed by either one of the Consultants,
pursuant to the provisions of this agreement, shall constitute the
direction or consultation or the performance of service of both of
the Consultants. If, for any reason, one or the other of the Consultants is unable or unwilling to act or perform pursuant to the
terms of this agreement, such event shall not void this agreement
or diminish its effect, and the performance on the part of the
other Consultant shall constitute full and complete performance of
this agreement on the part of the Consultants.

Legal and Equitable Remedies

16. Due to the uniqueness of the services to be performed by the
Consultants for the Corporation, and due to the fact that the Consultants' reputation in the community as business managers may be
affected by the financial success or failure of the Corporation in
the operation of the [project], in addition to the other rights and
remedies that the Consultants may have for a breach of this agreement, the Consultants shall have the right to enforce this contract, in all of its provisions, by injunction , specific performance or other relief in a court of equity. If any action at law or
in equity is necessary to enforce or interpret the terms of this
agreement, the prevailing party shall be entitled to reasonable
attorneys fees, costs and necessary disbursements in addition to
any other relief to which he may be entitled.

Right To Manage

17. Except as specifically provided to the contrary herein and
to the greatest degree allowable under the Corporation Code and
other laws of the State of Delaware, it is the intent of the Corporation to confer on the Consultants the exclusive and absolute
right to manage and direct all the business affairs of the Corporation that in any way concern the operation of [project] and that arise
in ordinary course of business of [project]. Should any one or more of
the provisions of this agreement be adjudged unlawful by any court
of competent jurisdiction, the remaining provisions of this agreement shall remain in full force and effect. Further, should one or
more of the provisions of this agreement be adjudged invalid by a

court of competent jurisdiction, such determination shall have no affect whatsoever on the amount or amounts of compensation to be paid to the Consultants pursuant to the terms of this agreement.

Governing Law

18. This agreement shall be binding on and shall be for the benefit of the parties hereto and their respective heirs, executors, administrators, successors and assigns, and shall be governed by the laws of the State of _____.

Executed at [name of State] on the day and year first mentioned above.

_____

CLIENT
[typed name of client]

_____

By [signature]
[typed name and designation of person signing]

_____

CONSULTANT
[typed name of consultant]

_____

[Signature]
[typed name and designation of person signing]

Sample Fixed-Price Service Contract

AGREEMENT

THIS AGREEMENT is made, this_____ day of _____, 19XX by and between _____, hereinafter referred to as the "University" and _____, a California Corporation, hereinafter referred to as the "Contractor."

WITNESSETH:

WHEREAS, the University desires to develop and conduct a training program for its personnel and the personnel of such other eligible education agencies as may become participants in this program; and

WHEREAS, the purposes of said training program are to:

Upgrade the managerial and technical skills of career counseling and placement personnel; and increase the professional stature of career counseling and placement personnel; and provide a cadre of trained professionals appropriate materials to continue further training as required with minimum funding support needed; and provide a vehicle for the ongoing assessment of in-service training needs of career counseling and placement personnel.

WHEREAS, the Contractor is particularly skilled and competent to conduct such a management training program; and

WHEREAS, funds for this contract are budgeted for and included in federal project plan approved under _____, and as described in the program prospectus identified as Grant _____, which is hereinafter referred to as the "Project"; and

WHEREAS, said Project was approved [date] and project expenditures approved on [date]

NOW, THEREFORE, it is mutually agreed as follows:

1. The term of this Agreement shall be for the period commencing [date], continuing to and until [date].

2. The Contractor agrees to develop and conduct a training program consisting in part of a series of three workshop session presentations. Each of said workshop presentations shall be of eight hours' duration and shall be conducted at [place]. The aforesaid training program shall be developed and conducted by the Contractor in accordance with the project prospectus submitted by the University for funding under _____and in a particular with the "attachment" to said program prospectus, which is marked Exhibit "A," attached hereto and by reference incorporated herein.

3. The aforesaid workshop presentations shall include three days of intensive training using an approach that has demonstrated

considerable success working with career counseling and placement personnel of this type. Specific workshop topic coverage shall include the following:

a.

b.

c.

4. The aforesaid training workshop will be conducted during the contract term in accordance with a schedule mutually agreed upon by the University and the Contractor.

5. In connection with the conducting and development of the aforesaid training program, the Contractor agrees as follows:

   a. The Contractor will plan for and prepare such necessary materials as are needed to conduct the various program sessions as described. Such material preparation and development will include the preparation of participant resource material, development of worksheets, orientation materials, participant guides and handbooks. All materials developed will reflect the highest standards of quality applicable to education material development state of the art.

   b. The contractor will provide expert session facilitation staff as follows:

      A minimum of one (1) expert staff for the first twelve (12) participants in attendance at each session; further the Contractor will provide one (1) additional expert staff for each additional twelve (12) participants in attendance at each session to a maximum of 48 total participants per session.

   c. The Contractor will regularly consult with designated personnel of the University for the purpose of monitoring program progress and planned activities so as to improve and strengthen the overall program.

6. The Contractor further agrees to:

   a. Furnish the University on or before [date] with a final report. This report will describe all relevant aspects of program activity and will be in such style and format as to comply with the requirements of the enabling grant.

   b. Prepare appropriate pre-session and post-session participant testing materials to enable the ongoing assessment of the overall program activities. The Contractor shall collect, analyze and interpret these findings as an integral part of the program development and conduct activity.

c. Conduct, within four to six months after the conclusion of the work-shop presentation, a post-test follow-up survey that will seek to discover what difficulties, if any, the participants in the program have encountered in applying the principles developed in the workshop training activity to career counseling and placement problems. A component of the follow-up survey will probe for participant attitude and individual assessment of the relevancy of the workshop training activity and the topic material in the context of program administration experience during the intervening period.

d. Furnish the University with copies of all written and visual materials produced for distribution to the workshop participants. The Contractor will retain no proprietary rights to such materials, said rights being vested to the University.

7. The University agrees as follows:

a. To designate one of its staff members as project director to represent the University in all technical matters pertaining to this program.

b. To arrange the necessary pre-program advertisement and participant notification so as to encourage participation.

c. To provide or otherwise arrange for facilities that are adequate to conduct the workshop sessions.

d. To limit session attendance, exclusive of Contractor staff, to the maximum eligible number of _____ participants plus up to three (3) additions nonparticipating persons.

e. To make the necessary arrangements with the participating educational agencies to make personnel available as participants in all specified training activities.

f. To arrange for the use on an as available basis of University instructional equipment, including 16mm slide projectors, tape recorders and/or related audio visual equipment, as requested by the Contractor in response to program requirements.

The University agrees to provide competent personnel to operate all such equipment. The University will provide adequate maintenance and care of such equipment and will provide operational assistance to the Contractor as requested.

g. To distribute to the program participants at the request of the Contractor, various project materials that are relevant to the program. Such materials may include training session handout material, descriptive information, questionnaires and announcements.

h. To provide or arrange for assistance to the Contractor at training session locations as mutually agreed in connection with facility arrangement, scheduling and other matters pertaining to the successful conduct of the program.

8. It is expressly understood and agreed by both parties hereto that the Contractor while engaging in carrying out and complying with any of the terms and conditions of this contract is an independent Contractor and is not an officer, agent or employee of the University.

9. The Contractor shall provide worker's compensation insurance or self-insure his services. He shall also hold and keep harmless the University and all officers, agents, and employees thereof from all damages, costs of expenses in law or equity that may at any time arise or be set up because of injury to or death of persons or damage to property, including University property, arising by reason of, or in the course of the performance of this contract; nor shall the University be liable or responsible for any accident, loss or damage, and the Contractor, at his own expense, cost and risk shall defend any and all actions, suits or other legal proceedings that may be brought or instituted against the University or officers or agents thereof on any claim or demand, and pay or satisfy any judgment that may be rendered against the University or officers or agents thereof in any such action, suit or legal proceeding.

10. In consideration of the satisfactory performance of the Contractor, the University agrees to reimburse the Contractor in the amount of Fifteen Thousand Dollars ($15,000) in accordance with the following schedule:

30 May 19XX	$ 4,000.00
30 June 19XX	$ 5,000.00
30 July 19XX	$ 4,000.00
30 August 19XX	$ 2,000.00
	$15,000.00

IN WITNESS WHEREOF, each party has caused this agreement to be executed by its duly authorized representative on the date first mentioned above.

CONTRACTOR   UNIVERSITY

_____   _____
Name   Name
Title   Title

Sample Product Development Agreement

Date

Name
Company
Address
City/State/Zip

Dear

1. This letter shall serve as an agreement between _____ (CLIENT) and _____ (CONSULTANT) governing the provision of professional consulting services by CONSULTANT for CLIENT relative to the development, marketing and licensing or similar distribution of CLIENT information and technology. CLIENT has developed and will continue to develop unique and highly regarded proprietary information and concepts on _____. CONSULTANT has developed and will continue to develop unique and highly regarded proprietary information and concepts on the marketing and licensing of such information. It is the mutual intent of the parties to combine their unique information and capabilities through a professional consulting relationship in which CONSULTANT shall receive professional fees and commission income in exchange for the synergy which is created by the combining of efforts and knowledge.

2. The purpose of this agreement is to spell out the working and financial relationship between CLIENT and CONSULTANT regarding the development and marketing of certain proprietary products and services of CLIENT designed to assist third parties (LICENSEES) with _____ on their own behalf or on the behalf of others, such as the LICENSEES clients employees of organizations in which the LICENSEES have management responsibility.

3. These proprietary products and services would be based on technology already developed by CLIENT as augmented by proprietary concepts developed by CONSULTANT relative to the marketing of this type of technology and new proprietary concepts that might be developed by CLIENT or CONSULTANT alone or in combination as they relate to the development and marketing of information on _____.

4. The intent of this working relationship is to provide the LICENSEES with a subscription and/or license service that would provide LICENSEES with a limited right to use such technology on terms and conditions to be determined by CLIENT.

5. It is the objective of the parties to this agreement to package and sell the above referenced technology to the LICENSEES and to profit, as described herein, in doing so.

6. While the specific nature and description of the offerings to be made to the LICENSEES is subject to broad change and interpretation based upon analysis and market research/response, it is intended that LICENSEES would be charged a subscription and/or license fee to use and be trained in the use of the technology so as to enable its use with and resale to parties who might become the clients or customers of the LICENSEES.

7. CLIENT shall undertake the development, modification, packaging and promotion of the technology and marketing strategies for this proprietary concept with the professional consulting assistance of CONSULTANT at such times and places as determined appropriate. Each party shall provide the highest and best state of the art known in the execution of this agreement and shall provide best efforts to insure the success of this venture. Both parties acknowledge that this agreement relates to a speculative venture and that no assurances of success, sales levels or profits can be assumed or predicted.

8. All direct expenses and investment capital required for this venture shall be contributed by CLIENT and all revenues and profits earned from the venture shall accrue to CLIENT, except as noted in paragraph 9. In this regard, all charges for licenses, training fees, license renewal fees, related rights and sales of services and products provided shall be paid to CLIENT under such names and business entities as CLIENT shall direct or establish.

9. CLIENT agrees to pay CONSULTANT for professional consulting services and efforts in connection with this venture as follows:

a. A sum equal to _____ dollars ($XXX) per hour, which is equal to one-third of CONSULTANT's customary hourly consulting fee, said sum to be provided on an advance retainer basis as required by progress made; plus

b. A sum equal to five (5) percent of gross sales to LICENSEES to include license fees, training fees, license renewal fees, subscription fees, related rights, products and services; to be paid monthly on the fifteenth (15th) day of the month for the prior month; for a period of five (5) years from the receipt of the first revenue from LICENSEES; plus

c. Reimbursement for direct expenses incurred by CONSULTANT in connection with the provision of services to include travel and communication expenses, but not routine overhead expenses that CONSULTANT would normally incur in the operation of his business. Travel expenses are taken to include automobile mileage at _____ (XX) cents per mile, standard coach air travel, ground transportation, rental car expense, and daily travel per diem of _____ ($XXX) per day or the cost of hotel lodging plus _____ ($XX) per day, whichever is greater, whenever responsibilities require that CONSULTANT travel in excess of one-hundred (100) miles from _____. Such sums to be paid within ten (10) days of the receipt of an invoice for such expenses.

d. CONSULTANT has estimated that the planned scope of work on the part of CONSULTANT shall not exceed one-hundred forty-six hours of CONSULTANT professional time during the first ninety days of this agreement. In the event that the activities included within the planned scope of work (as evidenced by a plan submitted to CLIENT on _____) should exceed this amount, additional hours expended by CONSULTANT shall be deducted from the commission payments due CONSULTANT under the terms of paragraph 9.b., above. Additional hours may be expended by CONSULTANT and not subject to such deduction from commission income due to an expansion in the scope of work requested by CLIENT or within the defined scope of work when expressly authorized or requested by CLIENT. CLIENT shall have the right to notify CONSULTANT in writing, at any time, that such authorization or request must be in writing from CLIENT to CONSULTANT.

10. This agreement shall remain in effect for a period of five (5) years from the date on which the first revenues are received from LICENSEES or six (6) years from its execution, whichever is greater, and may be terminated by either party upon thirty (30) days written notice at any time commencing with the sixth (6th) month following the provision of the first fifteen (15) hours of professional consulting services by CONSULTANT. In the event of termination of this agreement, CLIENT agrees to continue to pay CONSULTANT commission income due for a period of time equal to the number of months from the date of execution of this agreement until its termination or six (6) months following the receipt of the first five-thousand dollars of gross receipts from the LICENSEES, whichever is greater.

11. CONSULTANT shall have a reasonable right to inspect the books of account and records of CLIENT, at CONSULTANT expense, as they pertain to the payment of commissions due under the terms of paragraph 9.b., above. In the event that a discrepancy of one-thousand dollars or more is determined as a result of such inspection, if any, CLIENT agrees to pay for the costs incurred for such inspection of records.

12. This agreement pertains only to activities and revenues related to the licensing or subscription sales of licenses, training, license and subscription renewal fees, products and services to the LICENSEES, as herein defined. CONSULTANT shall not receive a percentage commission on sales of CLIENT that are obtained through the regular and ongoing activities of _____.

13. This agreement shall be binding upon and inure to the benefits of the parties hereto and their respective heirs, assigns, successors, executors, administrators and personal representatives.

14. This agreement shall be governed by the laws of the State of _____.

15. No waiver of any of the provisions herein shall be deemed or shall constitute a waiver of other provisions of this agreement.

16. In the event of a dispute between the parties hereto on any matter governed by this agreement, either party shall have the right to request that a resolution of the dispute and a determination of rights and remedies of the parties shall be determined by a process of binding arbitration under the rules and regulations of the American Arbitration Association.

17. Should CLIENT not sign and deliver a copy of the signed agreement to CONSULTANT on or before _____ this agreement shall become voidable at the option of CONSULTANT.

Sincerely,

Name of Consultant

Accepted for _____

_____

Date_____

Sample Marketing Agreement

Date

Name
Company
Address
City/State/Zip

Dear

    This letter shall serve as an agreement between _____ (CLIENT) and _____ (CONSULTANT) governing the provision of professional marketing consulting services for CLIENT by CONSULTANT relative to the promotion of _____.

    CONSULTANT shall prepare copy and rough mechanicals (suitable for use by professional typesetting and graphics arts personnel or clerical personnel, as appropriate, to develop camera-ready copy) for the following:

    1. A letter to _____ seeking their cosponsorship of the seminar;

    2. A direct mail brochure for _____ designed to obtain registrations for the seminar;

    3. Two (2) advertisements for use in _____ newspapers and/or magazines to advertise the seminars for the purpose of obtaining registrations; and

    CLIENT shall provide to CONSULTANT data, documents and information in verbal and written form, as required and appropriate, to enable CONSULTANT to successfully complete the above responsibilities.

    CONSULTANT shall complete the assigned tasks on a schedule consistent with the responsibilities involved and in accord with CLIENT requirements, as mutually agreed.

    CLIENT and CONSULTANT both understand that the promotion of a seminar is a speculative venture and that no assurances can be made as to the effectiveness of the promotional effort relative to number of cosponsors or participants obtained or attending or revenues obtained from such participants.

CONSULTANT shall provide the above described services for a fee of _____ ($X,XXX) plus direct expenses for travel and communication, if any, incurred by CONSULTANT. The provision of additional services above and beyond those specified above, if any, that may be requested shall be invoiced at the rate of _____ dollars ($XXX) per hour.

CONSULTANT shall provide services on an advance retainer arrangement. Under such an arrangement, CLIENT shall advance sums to CONSULTANT prior to the provision of services and CONSULTANT shall charge against such advance, providing a statement of account not less frequently than twice monthly. Upon conclusion of the consultation, funds advanced and not used shall be returned.

In the event that CLIENT elects to terminate this agreement, CLIENT shall provide at least thirty (30) days written notice to CONSULTANT and shall be responsible for any and all costs incurred to date and experienced in the winding down of the project, if any.

If the terms of this agreement meet with your acceptance, please indicate same by signing below in the space provided and return a signed copy of this agreement along with your initial advance retainer deposit.

Sincerely,

_____

Accepted for _____

By _____

Date _____

Sample Financial Consulting Agreement

Date

Name
Company
Address
City/State/Zip

Dear

This letter shall serve as a letter of agreement between _____ (CLIENT) and _____ (CONSULTANT) governing the provision of professional financial consulting services for CLIENT by CONSULTANT.

CONSULTANT shall provide such consulting services as determined appropriate and as specifically requested by CLIENT.

CLIENT agrees to compensate CONSULTANT on an advance base retainer arrangement. Under the terms of such an arrangement CLIENT will provide CONSULTANT with a check in the amount of _____ ($XXX) per month on or before the first day of each month (except for the first month, _____, when payment shall be due on or before the tenth day of the month). In exchange for this compensation, CONSULTANT shall provide up to six (6) hours per month consultation. Additional time expended by CONSULTANT shall be invoiced at the rate of _____ ($XXX) per hour and CLIENT shall provide payment to CONSULTANT within ten (10) days of the date of such invoices.

CLIENT agrees to reimburse CONSULTANT for direct expenses specifically incurred as a result of providing such services to CLIENT, to include travel and communications within ten (10) days of the date of an invoice for such expenditures. Travel expenses, if any, shall be invoiced as follows:

Air Travel: Standard Coach Rates

Per Diem: $XXX per day or $XX plus the cost of hotel lodging, whichever is greater, for any travel in excess of 50 miles from _____. Partial day per diem (where no hotel room is required) at $XX.

Ground Travel: Personal car mileage at $0.XX/mile and rental cars and public conveyance at actual charges incurred.

CLIENT may terminate this agreement upon thirty (30) days written notice and the agreement shall otherwise be terminated on _____.

If the terms of this agreement meet with your approval, please indicate same below by your signature and return a copy for my files.

Sincerely,   Accepted for _____

_____   Date _____

Sample Presentation Engagement Letter

Date

Name
Association
Address
City/State/Zip

Dear

　　Thank you for your letter of _____. I am looking forward to participating with you at the _____ Annual Meeting. This letter shall serve as an agreement between the Association (XXX) and _____ (YYY) governing the presentation.

　　YYY shall undertake the development and delivery of a presentation for XXX at the Annual Meeting on _____ evening, _____ at the _____ _____ Hotel of a duration and on a topic to be determined. If desired, YYY shall also make himself available to handle questions and answers on the presentation topic or related subjects. XXX agrees to inform YYY not later than _____ of the particulars concerning the duration and topic of the presentation as well as the number of individuals expected to attend the presentation.

　　In consideration of the above, XXX agrees to pay YYY a sum equal to _____ dollars ($XXX) plus round trip standard coach air fare at rates prevailing on _____ said sum due and payable not later than _____.

　　If the terms of this agreement meet with your acceptance, please signify same by signing below in the space provided and return a copy of this letter for my files.

　　I look forward to being with you on _____.

Sincerely,

_____

Accepted for _____

By_____

Date_____

There are certain situations where the engagement is of such limited duration and/or where the time between scheduling an appointment and providing the consulting service is so short that entering into a contract between the parties is impractical. Yet, the consultant may still desire to inform the client of the terms and conditions under which he or she is willing to provide services. In such cases, the engagement letter may be utilized.

It is a good idea to provide your client with a letter that acknowledges the engagement you and the client have agreed upon. Such a letter should contain several features. Chief among them are:

1. Acknowledgement of the time and place of the first formal/work meeting.

2. Specifications of the purpose of the first meeting and purpose of the consultation in general.

3. An indication of the time or duration that you expect will be involved in the consultation, or a statement as to why it is not possible to provide such an estimate.

4. A communication as to what the fee will be for the service to be provided, if possible. Or, an indication of the basis on which the fee will be charged.

5. Specification of the payment arrangements as well as the invoice schedule. In the past consultants have tended to be satisfied by just telling clients when the invoice will be sent, leaving so-called "trade custom" to govern when payments will be made. With trade custom increasingly turning into 60 to 90 days or more it is a good idea to inform the client, and obtain his or her approval, for a more reasonable period of time between invoice date and payment date.

Sample Engagement Letter

[letterhead]

[date]

John Q. Doe, President
Doe Industries
1234 Main Street
Anytown, Anystate   Zip

Dear Mr. Doe:

This letter will confirm our telephone conversation of this morning. It is my understanding that we will meet for a full day on May 19th at your office for the purpose of developing a proposal for the sale of your widgets to XYZ industries. I will plan to arrive at 8:30 A.M.

Please be advised that the fee for my services is [amount] a day. It is my policy to work on an advance retainer basis. Under such an arrangement, my clients deposit with me any sum they wish, and I invoice against the retainer that has been deposited. Funds deposited that are not utilized are returned.

Due to the short time between now and the time of our meeting, you may either forward your check for [amount] in advance of our meeting or plan to pay for the services provided at the time of the consultation.

I look forward to working with you next week on what should prove to be a most interesting project.

Sincerely,

Consultant

Sample Short-Term Consultation Letter

Date

Name
Company
Address
City/State/Zip

Dear

    I am writing to confirm our appointment for a consultation. It is my understanding that we will be meeting for a consultation at my office on Friday, _____ at 10:30 A.M.

    The fee for my services, on an initial consultation basis of this type, is _____ dollars ($XXX) per hour. It is my policy to work on an advance retainer basis. Under such an arrangement, my clients deposit funds in advance of the consultation and I invoice against such deposits. Funds deposited but not used are returned following the completion of the consultation. Due to the short time between this letter and our meeting and the limited duration of the consultation, an advance retainer will not be required; however, you may plan on providing me with a check in payment of the services at the time of our meeting.

    I am enclosing a copy of my _____ as well as some other information that I think may be useful for you.

    I look forward to working with you and if I may be of assistance prior to that time please don't hesitate to let me know.

Sincerely,

_____

Bibliography

This thoroughly revised and expanded bibliography contains six distinct sections, including:

Whenever possible, annotations have been provided to guide readers to material of particular relevance.

General Directories and Reference Works

It is well worth any consultant's time to become familiar with the following standard directories and reference works. They are available at most larger libraries. For publishers' addresses and telephone numbers, consult *Literary Market Place* or *Publishers Directory* available at most public libraries (see their listings below).

All-in-One Business Contactbook. Karen Hill, ed. Detroit: Gale Research Inc., 1990. Provides address, chief executive and sales volume for approximately 10,000 U.S. companies. Telephone and fax numbers are also included.

America's Corporate Families and International Affiliates. Bethlehem, PA: Dun & Bradstreet Information Services, 1992 and annually. Lists U.S. companies with foreign affiliates and foreign companies with U.S. affiliates.

Annual Register of Grant Support. Wilmette, IL: National Register Publishing Company, 1992 and annually. Includes information on more than 3,000 private and public grant-giving agencies.

Business Firms Master Index. Donna Wood, ed. Detroit, MI: Gale Research Inc., 1985. An index, including more than 110,000 entries, of business firm names found in directories.

Business Organizations, Agencies and Publications Directory. 5th ed. Sandra Anne MacRitchie, ed. Detroit, MI: Gale Research Inc., 1990. A guide to approximately 24,000 new and established organizations, agencies and publications concerned with international and U.S. business, trade and industry.

Business Periodicals Index. Bronx, NY: H.W. Wilson Co. Monthly, with quarterly and annual bound cumulations. Indexes more than 350 journals on business and economics. Can access the information by subject areas. Also available online as WILSONLINE.

Business Publications Rates and Data. Wilmette, IL: Standard Rate & Data Service, Inc. Monthly. Provides advertising rates and other information about trade journals.

Business Rankings Annual. Brooklyn Public Library. Detroit, MI: Gale Research Inc., 1992 and annually. Provides wage and salary rankings and a subject guide to business, industrial and financial rankings.

Catalog of Federal Domestic Assistance. 25th ed. Washington, D.C.: Government Printing Office, 1991 and annually. Provides key information on more than 1,200 programs administered by 50 federal agencies. In loose leaf format with regular updates.

City and State Directories in Print. Julie E. Towell and Charles B. Montney, eds. Detroit, MI: Gale Research Inc., 1989. Organized geographically with title, key word and subject indexes.

Corporate 500: The Directory of Corporate Philanthropy. 8th ed. Detroit, MI: Gale Research Inc., 1992. Provides information on corporate funding programs.

Daniells, Lorna M. *Business Information Sources.* Berkeley, CA: University of California Press, 1985. Provides descriptions of basic business sources.

Direct Mail List Rates and Data. Wilmette, IL: Standard Rate & Data Service, monthly. Lists all known direct mail lists. Provides information on list size, source, segmentation, price and more.

Directory of Companies Required To File Annual Reports with the Securities and Exchange Commission. Washington, D.C.: U.S. Government Printing Office, 1991. Lists 13,400 companies by name only with industry classification and federal identification numbers.

Directory of Corporate Affiliations. Wilmette, IL: National Register Publishing Company, 1992 and annually. Described as a "who owns whom" directory; lists major U.S. corporations and their divisions, all companies listed on the New York and American Stock Exchanges, Fortune 1000 and many privately owned companies.

Directory of Research Grants. Phoenix, AZ: Oryx Press, 1992 and annually. Provides information on more than 4,000 research grants from business, foundation, government and private sources.

Encyclopedia of Association Periodicals. Detroit, MI: Gale Research Inc., 1987. Volume 1: business, finance, industry and trade association periodicals; Volume 2: scientific, medical and technical periodicals; Volume 3: social sciences, education and humanities periodicals. Entries provide editor's name, description of the publication, mailing address and more.

Encyclopedia of Associations. Detroit, MI: Gale Research Inc., 1992 and annually. Published in three volumes. Provides information on more than 22,000 national and international organizations; considered the "bible" for accessing information on associations.

Encyclopedia of Business Information Sources. 8th ed. James B. Woy, ed. Detroit, MI: Gale Research Inc., 1990. Includes more than 21,000 entries of directories, encyclopedias, databases, newsletters, indexing services, almanacs and more of interest in the business field. Provides a good starting point to accessing business information.

F and S Index of Corporate Change. Cleveland, OH: Predicasts, Inc. Quarterly with annual cumulation. Indexes business literature related to corporate changes within U.S. public and private corporations.

The Fortune Directory. New York: Time, Inc., 1992 and annually. Provides information on the 500 largest U.S. industrial corporations and the 500 largest U.S. service corporations, including banks, financial and insurance companies, public utilities and more.

The Fortune World Business Directory. New York: Time, Inc., 1992 and annually. Provides information on the 500 largest industrial companies with headquarters outside the U.S., the 50 largest foreign banks and the 50 largest industrial firms in the world.

The Foundation Directory. New York: The Foundation Center, 1991 and biannually. Provides key information on approximately 5,100 of the largest foundations in the U.S.

Foundations Grants Index. New York: The Foundation Center, 1992 and annually. Provides information on grants of $5,000 or more awarded by approximately 470 major U.S. foundations.

International Organizations. Kenneth Estell, ed. Detroit, MI: Gale Research Inc., 1992 and annually. Provides information on more than 9,000 international nonprofit membership organizations.

Lavin, Michael R. *Business Information: How To Find It, How To Use It.* Phoenix, AZ: Oryx Press, 1992. An excellent primer and basic reference book on accessing business and statistical information.

Literary Market Place. New Providence, NJ: R.R. Bowker, 1992 and annually. Provides detailed information on 15,000 companies or organizations in the publishing arena, including publishers in the U.S. and Canada, advertising and public relations firms, book clubs, agents, book manufacturers and direct mail firms.

Manufacturing USA: Industry Analyses, Statistics, and Leading Companies. Arsen J. Darnay, ed. Detroit, MI: Gale Research Inc., 1989. Provides statistical profiles for 450 types of manufacturing; also lists the top 50 companies in each product category.

Million Dollar Directory/America's Leading Public & Private Companies. Dun's Parsippany, NJ: Marketing Services, 1992 and annually. Provides key information on more than 160,000 top businesses in the U.S.

Moody's Manuals. New York: Moody's Investors Service, 1992 and annually. Published in eight volumes organized by type of manufacturing company, providing profiles of more than 15,000 companies and thousands of municipalities.

National Business Telephone Directory. Stanley R. Greenfield, ed. Detroit, MI: Gale Research Inc., 1989. Provides addresses and telephone numbers for more than 429,000 businesses and organizations.

National Trade and Professional Associations of the United States and Canada and Labor Unions. New York: Columbia Books, Inc., 1992 and annually. Provides information on more than 7,000 national trade associations, labor unions, professional, scientific, and technical societies and other national organizations.

Newsletters in Print. 5th ed. Robert J. Huffman and John Krol, eds. Detroit, MI: Gale Research Inc., 1991-1992, and annually. A descriptive guide to more than 10,300 subscription, membership and free newsletters, bulletins and updates published in the U.S. and Canada and available in print or online. Describes the publication and provides audience, editorial policies, circulation and price information.

Oxbridge Directory of Newsletters. 9th ed. New York: Oxbridge Communications, Inc., 1991. Lists more than 21,000 newsletters, providing information on personnel, circulation and more.

Principal International Businesses: The World Marketing Directory. Parsippany, NJ: Dun's Marketing Services, 1992 and annually. Provides information on more than 50,000 businesses located in more than 140 countries.

Publishers Directory. 12th ed. Linda S. Hubbard, ed. Detroit, MI: Gale Research Inc., 1992 and annually. Includes information on 18,000 U.S. and Canadian publishers and 600 distributors.

Scientific and Technical Organizations and Agencies Directory. 2nd ed. Margaret Labash Young, ed. Detroit, MI: Gale Research Inc., 1987. Provides information on 15,000 organizations and agencies, including a description, address and publication names.

Standard & Poor's Register of Corporations, Directors and Executives. New York: Standard & Poor's Corporation, 1992 and annually. Provides information on 55,000 corporations and 500,000 officers and directors.

Standard Industrial Classification Manual. Springfield, VA: National Technical Information Service, 1987. Gives the SIC code number—the number used by most business references in their indexes—for any field or industry.

State and Local Statistics Sources. M. Balachandran and S. Balachandran, eds. Detroit, MI: Gale Research Inc., 1989. A subject guide to data on business, financial and other topics for cities and states.

Statistics Sources: A Subject Guide to Data on Industrial, Business, Social, Educational, Financial and Other Topics for the U.S. and Selected Foreign Countries. Jacqueline Wasserman O'Brien and Steven R. Wasserman, eds. Detroit, MI: Gale Research Inc., 1992 and annually. Provides statistical information on more than 20,000 topics.

Thomas Register of American Manufacturers and Thomas Register Catalogue File. New York: Thomas Publishing Co., 1992 and annually. A comprehensive and detailed guide to products manufactured in the U.S. Contains information on 148,000 manufacturers with cross-references to more than 110,000 brand names. Emphasis is on products, rather than manufacturers.

Ulrich's International Periodicals Directory. 30th ed. New Providence, NJ: R.R. Bowker. 1991-1992 and biennially. Provides information on more than 118,000 serials published throughout the world. Organized by subject headings with multiple indexes.

U.S. Industrial Outlook. Washington, D.C.: U.S. Government Printing Office, 1992 and annually. Covers 350 manufacturing and service industries, providing trends and outlooks for each.

Ward's Business Directory of U.S. Private & Public Companies. Detroit, MI: Gale Research Inc., 1992 and annually. Provides basic information on approximately 130,000 business firms.

Who's Who in America. Wilmette, IL: Marquis Who's Who. Biennially. Provides biographical profiles of more than 75,000 noteworthy individuals in the U.S.

Who's Who in Finance and Industry. Wilmette, IL: Marquis Who's Who. Biennially. Provides biographical profiles of more than 17,000 individuals in finance and industry in the U.S.

The Working Press of the Nation. Volume 1: Newspaper Directory. Volume 2: Magazine Directory. Chicago: National Research Bureau, 1991 and annually. Lists newspapers and magazines, providing addresses, deadlines, personnel and more.

Writer's Market: Where and How To Sell What You Write. Mark Kissling, ed. Cincinnati, OH: Writer's Digest Books, 1992 and annually. Provides lists of technical and professional journals as well as consumer journals and features a "how-to" approach to placing your work.

Consulting Directories and Reference Works

The following books list consultants or resources specifically for consultants. For publishers' addresses and telephone numbers, consult *Literary Market Place* or *Publishers Directory* (see General Directories and Reference Works section for full citations).

Bradford's Directory of Marketing Research Agencies and Management Consultants in the United States and the World. Centerville, VA: Bradford's Directory, 1991-1992 and biennially. Includes more than 2,400 listings.

Consultants and Consulting Organizations Directory. 12 ed. James McLean, ed. Detroit, MI: Gale Research Inc., 1992. A reference guide to more than 17,000 companies and individuals in the consulting field. Also available online.

Directory of Consultants & Management Training Programs Intended for Local Non-Profit Groups. Marvin L. Peebles, ed. Philadelphia, PA: MLP Enterprises, 1985.

Directory of Experts and Consultants in Biotechnology.

Directory of Experts and Consultants in Electronics.

Directory of Experts and Consultants in Energy Technologies.

Directory of Experts and Consultants in Environmental Science.

Directory of Experts and Consultants in Lasers and Physics.

Directory of Experts and Consultants in Plastics and Chemicals.

Directory of Experts and Consultants in Robotics and Mechanics.

All of the above-mentioned *Directories of . . .* are published by Research Publications, Woodbridge, CT. Most are published biennially and are organized geographically by state with key-word indexes.

Directory of Management Consultants. James H. Kennedy, ed. Fitzwilliam, NH: Consultants News, 1990. Provides information on more than 850 consulting firms and individuals in the field.

Dun's Consultants Directory. Parsippany, NJ: Dun's Marketing Services, 1992 and annually. Lists approximately 25,000 consulting firms in a wide range of fields.

Management Consulting: ACME Annotated Bibliography of Selected Resource Materials. New York: Association of Management Consulting, 1988.

Research Services Directory. 5th ed. Piccirelli, ed. Detroit, MI: Gale Research Inc., 1992. Includes information on research and development firms, contract laboratories and consulting organizations.

Online Databases

This section lists several major business databases of interest to consultants. Consult a good business library for information on the many business databases available online.

ABI/INFORM. Louisville, KY: UMI Data/Courier. Provides indexing to business-related material from more than 800 periodicals from 1971 to the present.

Consultants and Consulting Organizations Directory. Detroit, MI: Gale Research Inc. Provides information on more than 17,000 consulting organizations and individual consultants. Updated annually.

Disclosure Database. Bethesda, MD: Disclosure, Inc. Provides an index to records filed with the Securities and Exchange Commission by publicly owned companies from 1982 to the present.

Dow Jones News. Princeton, NJ: Dow Jones and Co. Provides business news and stock quotes from 1979 to the present. Updated continuously.

Grants. Phoenix, AZ: Oryx Press. Provides information on grants by federal, state and local governments as well as private organizations.

Thomas Register Online. New York: Thomas Publishing Co., Inc. Provides key information on approximately 150,000 U.S. companies. Updated semiannually.

Trade & Industry Index. Foster City, CA: Information Access Co. Provides comprehensive indexing of approximately 300 business periodicals, and selective indexing of approximately 1,200 other magazines and newspapers.

WILSONLINE: Business Periodicals Index. Bronx, NY: H.W. Wilson Co. Provides access to 300 business periodicals.

Consulting Newsletters and Journals

This section lists several commercially available publications of interest to consultants. The list by no means includes all of the newsletters or journals published in the field. Many of the associations serving the consulting profession (see Chapter 2) publish newsletters available only as a membership benefit. Whenever possible, these have been mentioned with the associations' listing in Chapter 2.

Consultants News. Monthly newsletter, 8 pp. James H. Kennedy, ed. Fitzwilliam, NH: Kennedy and Kennedy, (603) 585-6544. $144.00 per year. Oriented toward large firm and management consulting. Provides information on management consulting and personnel changes in larger firms. Oldest newsletter published for the management consulting profession.

Consulting Opportunities Journal. Bimonthly newsletter, 8 pp. J. Stephen Lanning, ed. Clear Spring, MD: Consultants National Resource Center. (301) 791-9332. $69.00 per year. Concentrates on marketing strategies and business opportunities for consultants, especially relevant for new consultants and those with limited professional experience.

The Professional Consultant. Monthly newsletter, 8 pp. Paul Franklin, ed. National Training Center. (503) 224-8834. $120/yr. Continuously published since 1978. Deals with strategies for marketing and managing the consulting practice. Includes surveys on consultant fees and incomes, and other data based on research.

Journal of Management Consulting. Quarterly journal. Gerald A. Simon, ed. North-Holland Publishers (PO Box 211, 1000 AE, Amsterdam, Netherlands).

Journal Articles

Articles on the topic of consulting appear frequently and in a wide range of professional and trade journals or magazines, from such publications as the *Economist* and *Canadian Banker* to others such as *Training and Development Journal* and *Personnel.* To get a feel for what's being written on the topic or to find the complete citation for a specific article, consult *Business Periodicals Index,* which is available at most good public libraries (see the reference in the General Directories and Reference Works section of this bibliography). You will need to check under the heading "business consultants" or as appropriate, under headings specific to a consulting specialty, such as "personnel consultants" or "quality consultants."

Several major newspapers such as *The Wall Street Journal* and *The New York Times* also publish their own indexes which list articles published in that newspaper on the topic of consulting. These indexes, the *Wall Street Journal Index* and the *New York Times Index* are also available at good public libraries.

If you have access to a good business library, *Business Index,* published by Information Access Company, and available in microfilm, CD-ROM and online, can also be helpful.

Books on Consulting

This section lists and, if possible, describes a wide variety of books on consulting. Some are aimed at the beginner and some at the experienced practitioner. There are probably at least several sources here that can be valuable to any consultant. For publishers' addresses and telephone numbers, consult *Literary Market Place* or *Publishers Directory* available at most public libraries (see Directories and Reference Works section in this bibliography for full citations).

Ahoy, Christopher K. *Manual for Selection of Consultants.* Berkeley, CA: Comprehensive Facilities Management, 248 pp.

Allesch, J. *Consulting in Innovation: Practice, Methods & Perspectives.* New York: Elsevier Science Publishing Company, Inc., 1991.

Alston, Frank M. *Contracting with the Federal Government.* New York: John Wiley & Sons, Inc., 1989.

Arnoudse, Donald M. *Consulting Skills for Professionals.* Homewood, IL: Business One Irwin, 1988.

Bell, Chip R. and Leonard Nadler, eds. *Clients & Consultants: Meeting and Exceeding Expectations.* Houston, TX: Gulf Publishing Company, 1985, 346 pp. Written for those who use or plan to use the services of an internal or external consultant.

Bellman, Geoffrey M. *The Consultant's Calling: Bringing Who You Are to What You Do.* San Francisco: Jossey-Bass, Inc., 1990, 264 pp.

Bennett, Roger. *Choosing & Using Management Consultants.* Woodstock, NY: Beekman Publishers, Inc., 1990, 320 pp.

Bermont, Hubert. *The Consultant's Malpractice Avoidance Manual.* Sarasota, FL: The American Consultants League, 1981. A basic introduction to the issue of malpractice in consulting. Useful background reading, but not sufficiently authoritative to be comprehensive on the subject, 35 pp.

———. *How To Become a Successful Consultant in Your Own Field.* Rocklin, CA: Prima Publishing, 1991, 156 pp. A well-written and interesting autobiography on how the author began his own consulting practice. A bestseller and good philosophical background reading for the new consultant.

———. *Profitable Book Publishing for the Consultant.* Sarasota, FL: The American Consultants League, 60 pp. A complete how-to guide to publishing, from manuscript preparation through production, advertising and distribution.

Block, Peter. *Flawless Consulting: A Guide to Getting Your Expertise Used.* San Diego, CA: Pfeiffer & Co., 1981, 215 pp. A how-to-do book, providing tips on what to do and say in different consulting situations.

Cannon, J. Thomas. *No Miracles for Hire: How To Get Real Value from Your Consultant.* New York: AMACOM, 1990, 288. Provides guidance to managers on how to select and manage consultants.

Carmichael, Douglas R. *Guide to Small Business Consulting Engagements.* Fort Worth, TX: Practitioners Publishing Company, 1991.

Cohen, William A. *How To Make It Big as a Consultant.* New York: AMACOM, 1991, 320 pp. A practical guide to setting up a successful consulting business.

Connor, Dick. *Increasing Revenue from Your Clients.* New York: John Wiley & Sons, Inc., 1989, 259 pp. A self-teaching guide for professionals, providing strategies, skills and techniques to establish profitable, long-term partnerships with clients.

Connor, Richard A. *Marketing Your Consulting & Professional Services*. New York: John Wiley & Sons, Inc., 1990.

Franklin, Paul. *49 Proven Strategies for Selling Repeat Consulting Business*. Portland, OR: NTC Press, 1991. A practical how-to monograph.

Gray, Douglas. *Start & Run a Profitable Consulting Business*. Bellingham, WA: International Self-Counsel Press, 1990, 232 pp.

Greenbaum, Thomas L. *The Consultant's Manual: A Complete Guide to Building a Successful Consulting Practice*. New York: John Wiley & Sons, Inc., 1990, 228 pp.

Greenfield, Wendy M. *Successful Management Consulting*. Englewood Cliffs, NJ: Prentice-Hall, 1987, 192 pp. Provides guidance on consulting to newer and/or smaller, owner-operated companies.

Greiner, Larry E., and Robert O. Metzger. *Consulting to Management*. Englewood Cliffs, NJ: Prentice-Hall, 1983, 368 pp. An excellent book, well-written, of particular value to management consultants.

Guttman, H. Peter. *The International Consultant*. New York: John Wiley & Sons, Inc., 1987, 180 pp. Provides a region-by-region survey of international consulting opportunities and an overview of issues faced while consulting in foreign countries.

Hameroff, Eugene, and Sandra Nichols. *The Successful Consultant's Publicity & Public Relations Handbook*. Sarasota, FL: The American Consultants League, 1982, 100 pp. Provides techniques on marketing of consulting services.

Hand, D. J., ed. *The Statistical Consultant in Action*. New York: Cambridge University Press, 1987, 200 pp.

Harper, Malcolm. *Consultancy for Small Businesses: The Concept and Training the Consultants*. New York: Intermediate Technology Development Group of North America, 1986, 254 pp.

Harvard Business School Career Guide Staff. *Management Consulting: 1991-1992*. Boston, MA: Harvard Business School Press, 1990, 125 pp.

Hills, Curtis. *How To Save Your Clients from Themselves and Yourself from Them*. Phoenix, AZ: Olde & Oppenheim Publishers, 1988, 125 pp.

Holtz, Herman. *Choosing & Using a Consultant: A Manager's Guide to Consulting Services*. New York: John Wiley & Sons, Inc., 1989.

———. *The Consultant's Guide to Proposal Writing: How To Satisfy Your Clients & Double Your Income*. New York: John Wiley & Sons, Inc., 1990.

———. *The Consultant's Guide to Seminar Presentations: An Insider's Guide to Developing and Marketing Seminars as a Marketing Tool & Independent Profit Center*. New York: John Wiley & Sons, Inc., 1987, 240 pp.

————. *The Consultant's Guide to Winning Clients.* New York: John Wiley & Sons, Inc., 1988.

————. *How To Succeed as an Independent Consultant.* New York: John Wiley & Sons, Inc., 1988, 395 pp. Comprehensive and well-written, containing useful information on how to establish and maintain a consulting business.

————. *Utilizing Consultants Successfully: A Guide for Management in Business, Government, the Arts and Professions.* Westport, CT: Greenwood Publishing Group, Inc., 1985, 221 pp. A guide to finding, negotiating, contracting and working with consultants and service contractors.

Joseph, Richard A., Anna M. Nekoranec, and Carl H. Steffens. *How To Buy a Business: Entrepreneurship Through Acquisition.* Chicago: Enterprise • Dearborn, 1993.

Karlson, David. *Consulting for Success: A Guide for Prospective Consultants.* Los Altos, CA: Crisp Publications, Inc., 1991. A good primer for those interested in consulting.

————. *Marketing Your Consulting or Professional Services.* Los Altos, CA: Crisp Publications, Inc., 1988.

Kaye, Harvey. *Inside the Technical Consulting Business: Launching & Building Your Independent Practice.* New York: John Wiley & Sons, Inc., 1986, 183 pp.

Kelley, Robert E. *Consulting: The Complete Guide to a Profitable Career.* New York: Macmillan Publishing Co., 1986, 272 pp. A comprehensive book for the beginning consultant.

Kemppainen, Rudolph. *Power Consulting: Using the Media To Expand Your Business.* New York: John Wiley & Sons, 1988.

Kennedy, James H., ed. *An Analysis of Management Consulting Business in the U.S. Today.* Fitzwilliam, NH: Consultants News, 1989.

————. *An Analysis of the Outplacement Consulting Business in the U.S. Today.* Fitzwilliam, NH: Consultants News, 1986.

————. *Fee & Expense Policies: Statement of 24 Management Consulting Firms.* Fitzwilliam, NH: Consultants News, 1985.

————. *How To Break One Hundred in the Consulting Game.* Fitzwilliam, NH: Consultants News, 1982.

————. *How Much Is a Consulting Firm Worth.* Fitzwilliam, NH: Consultants News, 1987.

————. *Twenty-Five Best Proposals by Management Consulting Firms.* Fitzwilliam, NH: Consultants News, 1984, 510 pp. Includes actual proposals from the *Consultants News* list of 100 leading management consulting firms in the U.S.

————. *What Clients Really Think about Consultants: 169 Turn-Ons in 4 Phases of the Engagement.* Fitzwilliam, NH: Consultants News, 1985.

Kirby, Jonell H. *Consultation: Practice & Practitioner.* Muncie, IN: Accelerated Development, Inc., 1985.

Kleiman, Carol. *The 100 Best Jobs for the 1990s and Beyond.* Chicago: Dearborn Financial Publishing, Inc., 1992.

Kubr, Milan, ed. *Management Consulting: A Guide to the Profession.* Washington, D.C.: International Labour Office, 1988, 611 pp. Well written; large firm and European orientation.

Lant, Jeffrey L. *The Consultant's Kit: Establishing & Operating Your Successful Consulting Business.* Arlington, VA: VTNC, 1981, 203 pp. Well-written and interesting reading for the beginner.

———. *How To Make at Least One Hundred Thousand Dollars Every Year.* Cambridge, MA: JLA Publications, 1992.

Lee, Robert J., ed. *Consultation Skills Readings.* Alexandria, VA: NTL Institute, 1984.

Lippitt, Gordon L. *The Consulting Process in Action.* San Diego, CA: Pfeiffer & Co., 1986, 213 pp.

Messina, James J., ed. *The Handbook of Readings for the Training of Consultants & Trainers.* Tampa, FL: Advanced Development Systems, Inc., 1982, 127 pp.

Metzger, Robert O. *Profitable Consulting: Guiding America's Managers into the Next Century.* Reading, MA: Addison-Wesley Publishing Company, Inc., 1989, 191 pp. Covers a broad range of topics—from building a practice to protecting your client relations, from working with international firms to working with family-owned local firms.

Moore, Gerald L. *The Politics of Management Consulting.* Westport, CT: Greenwood Publishing Group, Inc., 1984, 176 pp.

Nicholas, Ted. *The Complete Book of Corporate Forms.* Chicago: Enterprise • Dearborn, a division of Dearborn Publishing Group, Inc., 1992, 264 pp.

———. *The Complete Guide to Business Agreements.* Chicago: Enterprise • Dearborn, a division of Dearborn Publishing Group, Inc., 1993, 344 pp.

———. *The Complete Guide to Nonprofit Corporations.* Chicago: Enterprise • Dearborn, a division of Dearborn Publishing Group, Inc., 1993.

———. *The Complete Guide to "S" Corporations.* Chicago: Enterprise • Dearborn, a division of Dearborn Publishing Group, Inc., 1993, 192 pp.

———. *The Executive's Business Letter Book.* Chicago: Enterprise • Dearborn, a division of Dearborn Publishing Group, Inc., 1992, 368 pp.

———. *43 Proven Ways To Raise Capital for Your Small Business.* Chicago: Enterprise • Dearborn, a division of Dearborn Publishing Group, Inc., 1993, 198 pp.

————. *The Golden Mailbox: How To Get Rich Direct Marketing Your Product.* Chicago: Enterprise • Dearborn, a division of Dearborn Publishing Group, Inc., 1993, 240 pp.

————. *How To Form Your Own Corporation Without a Lawyer for Under $75* . Chicago: Enterprise • Dearborn, a division of Dearborn Publishing Group, Inc., 1992, 128 pp.

————. *How To Get Your Own Trademark.* Chicago: Enterprise • Dearborn, a division of Dearborn Publishing Group, Inc., 1993, 192 pp.

————. *How To Publish a Book and Sell a Million Copies.* Chicago: Enterprise • Dearborn, a division of Dearborn Publishing Group, Inc., 1993, 256 pp.

————. *Secrets of Entrepreneurial Leadership: Building Top Performance Through Trust and Teamwork.* Chicago: Enterprise • Dearborn, a division of Dearborn Publishing Group, Inc., 1992, 168 pp.

Pyeatt, Nancy. *The Consultant's Legal Guide & Forms.* Sarasota, FL: The American Consultants League, 1980, approx. 100 pp. A basic but useful introduction to the legal environment in which consultants operate. Appropriate for the novice consultant in particular.

Radin, William G. *Billing Power!: The Recruiter's Guide to Peak Performance.* Cincinnati, OH: Innovative Consulting, Inc., 1990, 216 pp.

Rudman, Jack. *Business Consultant.* Syosset, NY: National Learning Corporation, 1991.

————. *Senior Business Consultant.* Syosset, NY: National Learning Corporation, 1991.

Schiffman, Stephan. *The Consultant's Handbook: How To Start & Develop Your Own Practice.* Holbrook, MA: Bob Adams, Inc., 1988, 252 pp. An overview for the beginning consultant on finding clients, making presentations, pricing services and organizing a consulting business.

Seiden, R. Matthew. *Breaking Away: The Engineer's Guide to Successful Consulting.* Englewood Cliffs, NJ: Prentice-Hall, 1987.

Shenson, Howard L. *The Consultant's Guide to Proposal Writing.* Portland, OR: NTC Press, 1992, 210 pp.

————. *The Contract & Fee-Setting Guide for Consultants & Professionals.* New York: Wiley, 1990, 263 pp. Covers the business of consulting—from fee-setting, through proposal writing, to drawing up the contract and issuing reports.

————. *How To Develop and Promote Successful Seminars and Workshops: A Definitive Guide to Creating and Marketing Seminars, Workshops, Classes and Conferences.* New York: Wiley, 1990.

————. *How To Strategically Negotiate the Consulting Contract.* Portland, OR: NTC Press, 1991, 120 pp.

————. *Shenson on Consulting.* New York: Wiley, 1990.

————. *The Successful Consultant's Guide to Fee Setting.* Sarasota, FL: The American Consultants League, 1986, 167 pp. Written for both the experienced and new consultant, the book contains complete information on calculating overhead rates, determining fees, alternative methods of disclosing the fee to the client and reimbursement for direct expenses.

Silver, A. David. *The Turnaround Survival Guide: Strategies for the Company in Crisis.* Chicago: Dearborn Financial Publishing, 1992, 352 pp.

Smith, Brian R. *The Country Consultant.* Fitzwilliam, NH: Consultants News, 1982, 300 pp. Useful book for the solo consultant who will practice in a rural environment.

Steele, Fritz. *The Role of the Internal Consultant: Effective Role-Shaping for Staff Positions.* Melbourne, FL: Krieger Publishing Company, 1990, 168 pp.

Tepper, Ron. *Become a Top Consultant: How the Experts Do It.* New York: Wiley, 1987, 264 pp.

————. *The Consultant's Problem-Solving Workbook.* New York: Wiley, 1987, 323 pp. A practical, how-to guide with sample forms, letters, contracts, sales-building pitches and checklists.

Thomsett, Michael C. *The Consultant's Money Book.* Sarasota, FL: The American Consultants League, 1980, approx. 100 pp. Provides guidance on establishing a simple accounting system, proper record-keeping, and accessible documentation.

Tyson, Kirk W. *Business Intelligence: Putting It All Together.* Oak Brook, IL: Leading Edge Publishing, 1986, 288 pp.

Ucko, Thomas. *Selecting a Consultant.* Los Altos, CA: Crisp Publications, Inc., 1990, 100 pp.

Weiss, Allen. *Million Dollar Consulting: The Professional's Guide to Growing a Practice.* New York: McGraw-Hill, 1992.

Index